D0065073

THE EUROPEAN COMMUNITY AND THE UNITED STATES

THE EUROPEAN COMMUNITY AND THE UNITED STATES

Economic Relations

Nicholas V. Gianaris

New York
Westport, Connecticut
London

Library of Congress Cataloging-in-Publication Data

Gianaris, Nicholas V.
    The European Community and the United States : economic relations
/ Nicholas V. Gianaris.
        p.   cm.
    Includes bibliographical references (p.   ).
    ISBN 0-275-93481-0
    1. European Economic Community countries—Foreign economic
relations—United States.   2. United States—Foreign economic
relations—European Economic Community countries.   I. Title.
HF1532.935.U6G53   1991
337.4073—dc20   90-7566

British Library Cataloguing-in-Publication Data is available.

Library of Congress Catalog Card Number: 90-7566
ISBN: 0-275-93481-0

First published in 1991

Praeger Publishers, One Madison Avenue, New York, NY 10010
An imprint of Greenwood Publishing Group, Inc.

Printed in the United States of America

∞

The paper used in this book complies with the Permanent
Paper Standard issued by the National Information Standards
Organization (Z39.48-1984).

10 9 8 7 6 5 4 3 2 1

6352

2.11.92

To my students

Contents

Tables and Figures

TABLES

FIGURES

Preface

Aging Europe and young America have had strong historical, economic, and sociocultural ties. From colonial times to its independence and gradual expansion and growth, the United States maintained strong links with mother Europe, through immigration, trade, and investment. Such links became stronger after World War II and continue to be tight today, especially on matters of capital formation, technological dissemination, and financial transactions.

Regarding the structure and the organization of the economies of Western Europe and the United States, there are great similarities in the relationship of the private and the public sectors, the new trend toward privatization and employee ownership, the degree of industrialization, and the related fiscal and monetary policies. Such similarities, particularly in business regulations and taxation and market competition, make mutual trade and investment, as well as joint ventures and acquisitions, attractive and profitable on both sides of the Atlantic.

Present trends for the creation of a unified Europe and an expected stronger economic cooperation of the United States, Canada and perhaps Mexico are presenting new problems of worldwide dimensions. The immediate problem for the United States is the impact of the continental-size market of the European Community (EC) on the United States economy. The expansion of markets for goods and capital and greater liberalization of the economies of Eastern European countries will create challenges and opportunities from the standpoint of capital investment, international trade, and economic growth. However, as the EC eliminates internal barriers and moves toward closer economic and political integration, the question is whether this bloc will turn to an inward looking group or a more open market to the United States and the rest of the world.

The removal of physical, technical, and fiscal barriers, as well as the elimination of restrictions on trade, services, and capital movements within the EC, would increase competition among European industries and between them and the United States and other outside firms. From that standpoint, the internal market program of the EC may be viewed as a potential opportunity for United States firms as long as it produces a more open market and liberalized business environment. However, in spite of possible broad trade benefits, certain United States industries may be adversely affected if the EC eliminates internal barriers only to create one larger barrier around the entire Community. There are concerns that EC regulations and directives may create quantitative and qualitative restrictions, reciprocity requirements for third countries and other provisions that may limit the benefits of liberalization to internal producers and traders, while United States-owned firms and merchants may be at a disadvantage.

Europe and the United States are regions whose markets are fairly easy to enter compared to the tough Japanese and other markets. They have more or less the same business environment and similar market conditions. Therefore, the feeling is that Western Europe and the United States are becoming more fertile markets for mutual trade and investment. Already the "big boys" (large American companies), well positioned for individual and joint ventures as well as for transfer of technology in Europe, are soliciting the advice of their European "grandparents" on matters of trade and business establishments while their European counterparts continue their investment operations in the United States economy.

The purpose of this book is to examine trade and investment relations and related economic policies that affect developmental trends in the European Community and the United States, particularly as a result of the economic integration of Western Europe in the largest single market in the world. After an overview in chapter 1, a brief review of the past economic relations and historical trends is presented in chapters 2 and 3. Particular emphasis is given to intensive postwar efforts of European integration, following, to some extent, the successful example of the United States. Chapters 4 and 5 deal with the similarities in economic organizations and related fiscal and monetary policies as they affect trade and other financial transactions between the EC and the United States. Chapters 6, 7, and 8 examine in more detail trade and investment relations as well as the phenomenon of growing joint ventures and acquisitions across the Atlantic; and chapter 9 briefly reviews economic relations with the dramatically changing Eastern European countries and the expected results of the unification of Germany.

I wish to acknowledge my indebtedness to Professors Ernest Block, Laurence Krause, Victoria Litson, James Martin, Bill Murphy, Gus Papoulia, Adamandia Polis, John Roche, and Paul Voura, as well as to Anver Suleiman, international management consultant, and to tax and exchange rates experts George Alikakos, William Gianaris, and Christos Tzelios for their stimulating comments during the preparation of this book. Mia Bagaybagayan, James Castiglione, Michael Gianaris, Harry Giannoulis, Liza Gurley, Mario Karonis, Ted Kasapis, and Frances Yu provided valuable services in reviewing, typing, copying, and other technical support.

THE EUROPEAN COMMUNITY AND THE UNITED STATES

1 Overview

A BRIEF RETROSPECT OF EUROPEAN TRENDS FOR INTEGRATION

Western Europe and the United States are located on two continents which historically have played a vital role in the formation and development of economic and sociocultural world events. From the dawn of history to present days, changes in economic and sociopolitical conditions in these two regions influenced and shaped western civilization as we understand it today.

From the ancient times of the Greco-Roman period on to the Middle Ages, the industrial revolution, and later, efforts for a united Europe were promulgated on many occasions. Writers and rulers in ancient Greece and Rome supported or enforced, from time to time, unions of city-states for parts or the whole of Europe. For centuries, emperors, kings, feudal lords, theologians, artists, and many common people vainly yearned for unity among the divided and, in many cases, belligerent nations of Europe. Writers and philosophers, such as Victor Hugo during the 1850s, and Voltaire and Goethe before him, as well as Edward Kine and Andreas Rigopoulous, dreamed about a united Europe. Michelangelo and Rembrandt in painting contemplated a peaceful and prosperous united continent. Handel, Beethoven, Mozart, Wagner, and other composers advocated a harmonious and unified Europe, while Dante Alighieri, centuries before them (1300), supported the creation of a peaceful nation to engulf the whole of Europe. Although centuries have passed and a unified Europe remains largely a dream, the near future may prove that the dream of yesterday will become the reality of tomorrow. In the words of Victor Hugo: "A day will come when . . . all nations of the Continent will merge . . . into some higher society and form a European fraternity."[1]

Eurocrats or "Euroenthusiasts," such as Aristide Briand, the French Foreign Minister, even before the Great Depression proposed to the then League of Nations the creation of a United States of Europe. His effort to unify Europe by peaceful means was interrupted by the Second World War, a war that can be characterized as a European civil war, as was the First World War as well. After the bombing raids were over, and animosity and hatred were buried in the rubble, the centuries-old dream of the peaceful unity of Europe started slowly but surely to come to reality. The hope is to create a multinational democratic community with a free flow of goods, people, and information as well as a mutual free exchange of ideas and cultures.

The variety of European peoples with their different cultures and habits presents problems for a rapid movement of integration. Italians are considered to have a great respect for obscurity, while the French seem to be brittle and afraid of the future with some degree of xenophobia and civilizing hypocrisy. On the other hand, the British are regarded as being preoccupied with a sense of economic and spiritual decline, while the Germans think about unification and economic expansion.[2] Spain, Greece, and Portugal, as less developed members of the European Community, and the East Bloc countries, which have come out of long and painful dictatorships only recently, try to catch up economically and politically with the rest of the community. In all these countries there is a strong spirit of a united Europe, a "Euromania," pushing for rapid economic and political development.

After World War I and particularly at the beginning of the Great Depression, new totalitarian fascist governments came into power all over Europe. The end of depression of the 1930s came finally with World War II in 1940–45. Thereafter, mostly labor parties came to power in Western Europe. They introduced reforms regarding distribution of income, extension of welfare services by the state, and nationalizations particularly in railroads, power, coal and other heavy industries.

The vision of a community of prosperous and unified Western European democracies, formed some four decades ago, has been realized. The devastation of World War II and the American economic and defense assistance thereafter helped extensively in the formation and growth of the European Community (EC). On the other hand, the liquidation of the cold war and the new spirit of cooperation between the Soviet Union and the Western countries are important elements of peaceful coexistence under which economic and political cooperation can flourish.

An important issue considered by the EC presently is the growing need for further political cooperation. Such cooperation may speed up and stabilize the long-run unification of Europe and prove the saying that "politics may turn influence into affluence." Although politicians, in their effort to improve society, are known as going "one step forward, two steps backward, and one step to the side," the expected economic benefits from a European partnership are forcing them to support a closer political cooperation among the European nations.

Moreover, improved East-West relations are renewing the hope of overcoming divisions in the European continent and deepening transatlantic relations with the United States and Canada as the European Council reaffirms.

From a practical standpoint, intergovernmental cooperation to combat terrorism, drug trafficking, and international crime has been gradually promoted. Also, the EC suggested the establishment of a European audiovisual area, known as "Audiovisual Eureka," with a conclave of private and public sector broadcasters, writers, producers, film makers, directors, advertisers and the like. In implementing the provisions of the Single European Act on the completion of the internal market, environmental problems are also to be considered. They include such issues as soil depletion, water resources, toxic wastes, acid rain and other forms of air pollution, depletion of the ozone layer, the "greenhouse effect," and nuclear contamination.

The EC integration program presents challenges and opportunities to United States companies not only for European markets but for domestic and indeed world markets. The challenges and opportunities would be not only in the field of exports but in direct and financial investment as well. However, the Europeans are expected to honor bilateral and multilateral agreements. They should not discriminate against non-EC companies, particularly those of the United States; that is, other non-EC firms should have the same opportunities to compete in the trade of goods and services as well as to invest into the community.

From an investment point of view, many American firms are expected to enter the European markets in the foreseeable future, establishing new enterprises and expanding old ones. At the same time international competition requires preeminence in business and world class quality in product trading. Also, familiarity with the legal aspects of trade and the EC directives and regulations is necessary. The bottom line in our growing global economy is more exports and investment for an improvement in the welfare of the countries involved. From a competitive standpoint, the United States annual budget deficits and growing debts are depriving the country of its economic leadership in the twentieth century. Within a few years, West Germany, united with East Germany, is expected to be the richest nation on earth and Japan the strongest economic power.

National interests, in the context of a rapidly changing European system, are gradually subordinated to a common regional and eventually global system in which narrow national goals must defer to the optimization of common goals. The growing interdependence of trading nations requires a shift from hierarchical decision making to negotiation among partners and from sanctions and subsidies to persuasion. From that standpoint, the United States should be constructively involved and stimulate the growth of interdependence of the European nations for financial stability and economic progress. It should strengthen multilateral arrangements by solving trade disputes and try to harmonize domestic policies that facilitate international competition.

On the other hand, the economic and political reforms and the new trade initiatives of the Soviet Union and the other Eastern European countries create new challenges and opportunities for both the EC and the United States. Such structural economic reforms and political openness or democratization in the Eastern Bloc may lead to further cooperation and eventual integration of the EC and Comecon (the Eastern European economic bloc). From that standpoint, the United States policy makers must be alert to tap potential resources and exploit investment and trade opportunities in both blocs for the foreseeable future and provide needed facilities and available information to American entrepreneurs and business adventurers.

ECONOMIC AND MILITARY COOPERATION OF EUROPE AND THE UNITED STATES

Since the discovery of the New World by Christopher Columbus (1492), many Europeans from Spain, Portugal, France, the Netherlands, Ireland, Germany, and England settled along the Atlantic coast from Maine to Florida. Religious and political freedom and the hope of making a better living were the main reasons of immigration from all the countries of Europe. The custom of giving the newcomer fifty or one hundred acres of land and the achievement of independence attracted the poor people and the peasants of Europe to the new land of opportunity.

The first colony was established in 1607 by the London Company at Jamestown, Virginia, which was changed into a royal colony because of mismanagement, starvation, and fighting with the Indians. English colonies sprang up to the north and south of Virginia, started by commercial companies or by friends of the king. The expansion of the frontier, by pushing the Indian natives westward, and the use of indentured servants and imported Negro slaves, mainly during the seventeenth century and afterwards, increased agricultural and handicraft production in the farms and the cities. The business of a town, such as tax collections, spending for roads and other public projects, was decided by "town meetings," a kind of direct democracy similar to that of ancient Greece. Although trade among the colonies increased rapidly until the American Revolution against the British (1776) and later, socio-cultural relations and trade cooperation with mother Europe continued, especially during the late nineteenth and early twentieth centuries with the influx of capital and the new wave of immigration from Southern and Eastern Europe. The painful events of World War I, the Great Depression, and World War II brought Western Europe and the United States closer together, economically and militarily.

For a joint defense of the United States and Western Europe, the North Atlantic Treaty Organization (NATO) was established in 1949. This treaty made the United States a military ally of Britain, France, Italy, Belgium, the Netherlands, Denmark, Portugal, and Luxembourg, along with Canada, Norway, and Iceland. Other western nations later joined this mutual defense pact. In May 1952, five NATO countries (France, Italy, Belgium, the Netherlands, and Luxembourg), together with West Germany, signed a treaty to organize the European Defense

Community (EDC) and agreed to establish a six-nation army and outlined plans to unite under a single constitution. In July 1952, the United States Senate ratified a "peace contract" with West Germany and indicated that it would approve a mutual defense treaty with the six countries of the EDC. Although France decided in 1954 not to ratify the treaty creating the EDC, the six nations did succeed in establishing Euratom and made plans for a common European market.

Strategic and military cooperation between the United States and Western Europe for common defense, during the post-World War II period, overshadowed trade relations and economic policies. More or less, the same relations prevailed between the United States and Japan. To avoid confrontations that could erode alliance relations, economic differences in steel and chickens, beef and the use of hormones, and monetary disputes were settled by national leaders and policy makers as secondary problems and byproducts of mutual defense protection, with the United States usually having the upper hand. However, the United States umbrella of defense and its initial economic support stimulated trends toward the integration of the Western European nations.

The postwar rehabilitation of Europe with American support, as well as technological dissemination and improvement, led to economic stabilization and growth to the extent that Western European countries, along with Japan, became serious competitors of the United States. Moreover, the formation of the EC and the gradual economic integration of Western Europe made it a large economic group with a huge market with trends toward political unification.

On the other hand, the new economic and political reforms of the Soviet Union and other Eastern Bloc nations, through economic restructuring, democratization, and openness, have reduced threats of conflict and thawed the ice of the cold war between East and West. As a result, trade relations and economic policies acquire more importance than defense considerations while economic competition across the Atlantic is growing. Therefore, a new system of Western economic cooperation, independent of defense and strategic military considerations, that can stand on its own merits may be considered. Policy makers on both sides of the Atlantic should devise new harmonious ways to coordinate trade and defense relations and avoid open ended threats for retaliation.

Making the United States economy more stable and competitive requires the Spartan way of development, that is, frugality and hard work. Such an approach, used successfully by Spartans in ancient Greece and present-day Japanese and Germans, would increase saving for financing productive investment and competitiveness in international markets. It would reduce the need to borrow heavily from abroad and place more emphasis on new investment in technology-intensive plant and equipment.

For the United States this Spartan approach would mean further reduction or elimination of budget deficits as well as trade deficits, reduction in consumption, and an increase in saving and investment. Reduction in budget deficits can be achieved through increases in taxes and/or decreases in expenditures or through a combination of a "flexible freeze" in spending and in economic growth. The last method, which is the least painful and objectionable, assumes a satisfactory rate of economic growth and zero real spending growth; that is, increases in spending for government projects no more than the rate of inflation; or raising real expenditures more in some programs and balancing them out with equal reductions in other programs. On the contrary, a substantial decline in the budget deficit would reduce the fiscal stimulus and cause a downturn in the economy, requiring a new round of deficits to stop the economy from moving into a severe recession or even depression. In connection with that scenario, the fact that the American economy continued to be in an upswing stage for the years 1982– 1990 brought forward arguments to keep deficits for economic stimulation and prosperity.

The opportunities that are luring European and other foreign capital inflow and investment into the United States may reverse themselves and make United States investment abroad more attractive than it may domestically. Already, American pension funds put more and more money into foreign investment, primarily in stocks in West Germany, Britain, France, Italy, and Spain, as well as in Japan, Hong Kong, and Singapore. Such pension funds, placed in foreign stocks, increased from $1.8 billion in 1979 to about $45 billion in 1985 and $80 billion in 1988.

As a result of the creation of a single European market, the economic stakes of American investors are significant. Substantial economies would emerge in production, marketing, and distribution for United States companies operating in a uniform EC market of more than $4 billion GNP with 324 million people and even more with the eventual association or integration of other European nations.

The harmonization of the EC product standards, its new testing and verification procedures, and the common technical and regulatory standards introduced to all member nations would make trade and investment by American firms easier and less costly, as they do not have to modify their products according to the regulations and specifications of each EC nation.

However, the EC may try to shield some of its enterprises from competition for a transitional period of adjustment, especially in the auto, textiles, and electronics industries. Some reciprocity measures may restrict trade in goods and services, as well as direct and portfolio investment, by granting the same opportunities into the EC offered by other nations to EC companies operating in their countries. These measures are of great importance for foreign banks and other firms expecting to expand operations in the European countries.

The boom times of the 1980s pushed aside the unsolved problems left over from the turbulent times of the 1970s. Rapid growth of military and other government expenditures and insufficient tax revenue generated large budget deficits and a huge national debt in the United States. This domestic debt, together with the growing foreign debt, may be considered as the economic time bomb for the American economy. In case a recession begins, a real probability in the near future, the twin debts and their servicing may lead to high interest rates and ignite the bomb, generating waves of financial and economic problems affecting Europe and the rest of the world.[3]

Failure to recognize the new conditions created by the EC and the growing world interdependence may create an economic crisis not only in the United States but in many other developed and developing countries. By delaying to discipline its domestic economy and continuing to finance its debts by drawing on foreign savings from the EC, Japan, and other countries, the United States undermines the soundness of its economy and creates a dark cloud over its own prosperity. In light of current conditions, United States policy makers should re-examine national economic objectives and take needed painful actions to correct the twin imbalances of budget and foreign trade accounts. Although there is the will to right such imbalances, it becomes increasingly difficult to find the way to do that. In any case, the next few years may turn to be the most challenging and traumatic years in recent American economic and military history, especially in light of the dramatic changes in Eastern Europe.

ECONOMIC INTERDEPENDENCE

Stabilization Policies

During the postwar years the American and the European economies became slowly but surely interdependent. From time to time destabilizing factors led to turbulence in the form of inflation, exchange rates disturbances, and financial instability. On both sides of the Atlantic, the dilemma is how to achieve economic stability with high employment and no chronic inflation. Current economic theories, including the dominant monetarism and orthodox Keynesianism, as well as countercyclical fiscal and monetary policies, seem to be unable to mitigate or eliminate inherent instability, especially in financial markets. From that point of view, one of the main problems of the economies of the United States and the EC is how to avoid stagnation and inflation.

Western Europe together with Japan and the newly industrializing nations are formidable economic competitors of the United States. They sell products to the relatively open American economy and accumulate trade surpluses that force the dollar down and undermine the dominance of the United States as the world's largest economy. However, the fact that these competitors need the American market gives the United States leverage to pursue a policy of making them accept greater responsibility on defense and to make their markets more accessible to American products.

Presently, it is difficult for any nation to grow alone. Without international cooperation and competitive adjustment, economic growth on a national and global level will stagnate. At the same time, some of the unfair trade practices by United States competitors, such as export subsidies, import restrictions, and unfavorable government policies, should be considered. Also, adjustments of wages to labor productivity should be made so that competitive costs and fair factor price payments among trade partners prevail.

The costs of a fragmented European market in the past were high, and the benefits from a unified European market in the future are expected to be significant. Healthier competition, business and professional mobility, economies of scale, job creation, improved productivity and better consumer choices are the European challenges. The political and economic future of the EC and Eastern Europe would be of great importance to foreign trade, investment, and international finance. It is a historical challenge which will change the global economy forever: it will enhance Europe's role in the world and effect the redistribution of power in the twenty-first century.

As the Old World of Europe is struggling to renew itself, the United States is confused and somewhat skeptical that Europe may become a fortress. Moreover, as the nations of Eastern Europe struggle to free themselves from Soviet domination, those of Western Europe are pursuing greater unity, and the United States' policy seems unprepared to deal with these events. These events have not only economic but military and geopolitical importance that involve problems of international influence and direct or indirect world dominance.

The United States, along with other nations, awaits the outcome of a gestating Europe with different sociopolitical traditions and economic institutions. The eventual European monetary union, with a common currency and a central bank, and the formation of a European parliament, with perhaps a European government in Brussels, present new and complex problems for United States economic and foreign policies.

Brussels, where the EC has its headquarters, is gradually growing in importance, like Washington, D.C., in the United States, in dealing with individual states. It is expected that it will achieve interventional powers over national budget deficits, monetary cooperation, and trade transactions. The role of Brussels seems to be particularly important at a time when Eastern Europe is in the midst of economic reforms and political upheaval. From that standpoint, West Germany is expected to play a major role, especially after its unification with East Germany, regarding developments on both sides, Western and Eastern Europe. Anti-Brussels arguments of Mrs. Margaret Thatcher, the Prime Minister of Britain, and some other conservatives that the EC tends to be bureaucratic and socialist rather exist in their imagination than in reality. Otherwise, there appears to be a split even within the British Conservative Party, in addition to the pro-EC policy of the Labor Party which overtook the Conservatives in recent elections of the European Parliament. However, the formation of a federal EC government in Brussels is expected to be beneficial to the United States as it would have to deal with one economic and political unit rather than twelve different governments.

For the United States and the world economy, it is a promising moment in history as Western Europe moves toward integration and Eastern Europe attempts to implement drastic economic and political reforms. The EC countries are in a better position now to share responsibility for providing resources and leadership to rebuild the global economy. Although they are the main rivals of the United States, they are at the same time its closest allies. The main United States strategic goals in the postwar years, that is, the economic reconstruction of Western Europe and its political cooperation, seem to have largely been achieved and a further genuine partnership may develop.

Through bilateral and multilateral arrangements, risks of protectionism can be avoided and the economic pooling of the EC member states may be considered an opportunity rather than a threat. Although Europe tries to be on its own, taking care of itself, this does not mean rejection of the United States. It means some degree of independence, some distancing from United States interests, particularly on economic and financial management and self-defense issues, because, for Europe, defense security (continental insecurity) seems to help the dollar more than the European currencies. However, there are calls for burden-shifting, leadership-sharing, and aggressive trade and investment policies towards more international competition and economic growth. Some politicians and economists, seeing the American chronic trade deficits and the growing foreign debt, unwisely ask for protection and a return to neo-isolationism.

To raise the rate of productivity, increase competitiveness, and improve the living standards of their population, both the United States and the EC must collaborate closely to achieve external trade and payment equilibrium, and foster greater stability on monetary and exchange rate matters. The formation and development of regional economic groups, such as the EC and perhaps the North American Community (NAC), with the United States, Canada, and eventually Mexico should be supported, as long as they do not raise new barriers to trade with the outside world.

To avoid trade wars and to further liberalize world trade, the United States and the EC are moving toward successful compromises on such disputes as sales of United States hormone-injected beef and refusals of the EC to gradually scale back and finally eliminate trade distorting subsidies in agriculture. The EC became America's largest trading partner, with a total trade of more than $165 billion annually, and further economic cooperation is necessary for the improvement of the welfare of peoples on both sides of the Atlantic. The spirit of accommodation and compromise in trade relations should also aim to end barriers in financial, tourist, accounting, and other services, and to protect trademarks, patents, copyrights, and other intellectual property.

There seem to be two main trends moving into the community concerning a more or less open market for the United States and other nations. France and Italy, where nationalistic and protectionist elements are strong, present pressures for less openness to trade with countries outside the Community. Article 115 of the EC treaty allows individual members to limit trade with non-EC countries as the French and Italians have already done for their auto industries. However, EC countries with advanced industries competing effectively in international markets, such as West Germany and Britain, reject protectionism and support an open EC market to the rest of the world in accordance with the rules of the General Agreement on Tariffs and Trade (GATT), and especially the Uruguay Round. In any case, many American and other foreign companies are locating operations into the EC in order to avoid possible protectionist measures in the future, such as those of Italy limiting Japanese auto imports. Already there is skepticism that national quotas may be used as EC quotas, and the trend toward establishing protectionist regional trade blocs may intensify at the detriment of free trade.

The immediate problem for the United States is the impact of the continental-size market of the European Community on United States firms doing business in Europe. More specifically, examination of the business options available is critical regarding country-by-country or pan-European entry, joint ventures, and acquisitions. Furthermore, competitive assessment of various business sectors is needed for strengthening a strategic foothold in Europe in such industries as electronics, chemicals, telecommunications, computers and software, consumer products, and financial and other services.

International Position

As a result of the growing external debt, the volume of foreign assets in the United States exceeds that of American assets abroad by more than half a trillion dollars. However, American assets were acquired primarily in Europe in the 1950s and 1960s with relatively low prices, whereas foreign assets in America were mostly acquired in recent years with high nominal prices. The evaluation of such assets in their purchasing prices is, therefore, partially responsible for the large net debt of the United States to the EC and other countries. Hence, the difference in the United States debt position may be less than it appears. This can be seen from the difference in the inflow and outflow of earnings every year, which is not as significant as statistical data indicate.

Nevertheless, continuation of trade deficits and growing external debt would result in a loss in the United States competitive position and reduction in living standards for years to come. Regardless of the accounting gimmicks, the United States can rejuvenate its economy by better exploiting its vast resources and markets as well as its leverage throughout the world. At the same time, United States allies, particularly Japan, West Germany, and other strong EC economies with trade surpluses should share partially with the defense responsibilities, so that the American rambo-style policies and the massive global burden of military expenditures can be reduced. Meanwhile, the United States foreign economic policy should be redefined and change unrealistic expectations to enable EC policies to gear to American steadiness and economic relevance. It seems that the main economic problem of the United States is not so much the trade deficit or the unwillingness of the foreigners to treat it fairly. It is rather the failure to invest in collective productivity and add value to the national and international economies instead of borrowing for consumption. The United States borrowed heavily from Europe in the nineteenth century also, but the loans were invested in railroads, factories, oil wells, inventions, and other productive assets. Now, America is consuming its way into economic oblivion.[4]

Europe is taking a historic step and it deserves support from other nations, especially the United States. Eventually, the European Common Market will become the largest integrated economy. The EC countries are recovering from the symptoms of nationalistic superiorities and the sickness of Eurosclerosis, and are moving gradually toward closer cooperation and eventual unification. They are trying to revive the unifying aspirations that emerged from World War II. The success lesson of the United States of America may lead them to the formation of the United States of Europe. The community of twelve European democracies is winning a fine victory over national egoism and prejudice without much cost. It is moving from a bitter past to a better future and the United States is expected to play a vital role in this movement, as it did in the past. Likewise, the Eastern European socialist countries recently introduced drastic reforms toward a freer market and are preparing their economies for a closer cooperation and, why not, a possible integration with the EC.

There seems to be a technological war among the Asian group (Japan, Taiwan, South Korea, Hong Kong), the European group (the EC and probably the East Bloc countries), and the North American group (the United States, Canada). Each group is preparing its own economic bloc to face competition from the other groups. The key areas to improve technology are research, industrial innovations, and advancement in education to increase productivity. From that standpoint there is an outcry that the United States is becoming a nation of highly intelligent machines but ignorant people.

The following chapters focus primarily on the comparative issues common to the industrial societies on both sides of the Atlantic, as well as the main differences regarding economic policies, joint ventures, trade, and development trends between the common market of Western Europe and the United States, as well as the effects of the significant changes in Eastern Europe.

2 The European Community

ORIGINS AND EXPANSION

Brief Historical Review

In Paleolithic times, the Neanderthal race was common to the continent of Europe. It was replaced by the Cro-Magnon race in the late Paleolithic period. The vast majority of Europeans were grouped by anthropologists into the Caucasian race, one of the great divisions of mankind that first appeared in Eastern Europe during the Neolithic period of the Stone Age. Almost all of the varieties of speech used in Europe belong to the family of Indo-European languages, which include the Balto-Slavic (Russian, Polish, Czechoslovakian, Serbian, Bulgarian), the Teutonic (English, German, Dutch, Scandinavian), the Italic (French, Catalan, Spanish, Portuguese, Italian, Romanian), the Hellenic (Greek), and the Celtic (Gaelic, Welsh, Breton) linguistic sub-families.

According to archaeologists, the island of Crete was the place of European man's emergence from the Stone Age into the age of metals (bronze, iron). The Cretans (Minoans) were distinguished by their maritime and commercial activities along the Mediterranean shores (third millennium B.C.). The Hellenes or Greeks (mainly Achaeans or Mycenaens, Ionians, Dorians or Spartans, and later Athenians) were the first to leave a record of themselves and their neighbors. They were descendants of a branch of the Indo-European race (living in the Alps and central Europe) to which Romans, Germans, Slavs, and other Europeans belong.

Although the concept of European union gained significant attention and started being implemented in the post-World War II years, previous attempts were made throughout history toward a European economic and political integration. On a small scale, federations or unions of city-states, which operated as independent economic and political units, can be observed in ancient Greece and Italy (in the fifth century B.C. and afterwards).

The first economic and political unions or confederacies in history were the Achaean League and the Delian League developed in ancient Greece during the sixth to the third centuries B.C. They were established to formulate common economic and foreign policies on trade, coinage and other matters. In the Achaean League, which resembled modern federal systems and economic unions similar to the present European communities (EC, EFTA, Comecon), each member retained its independence but all members participated in a council that met twice a year to formulate legislation and enact common economic policies. Moreover, a monetary union was formed between the city-states of Phocaea, close to Lydia (where the first coins appeared in 640 B.C.), and Mytilene on the island of Lesbos (Greece), in the early years of the fourth century B.C.

The Delian League or the Confederation of Delos, with headquarters on the island of Delos in the Aegean Sea, founded in 478 B.C., was mainly a military and foreign policy confederation to prepare its member states against possible aggression, mainly from Persia. Each of the member states, which at one time numbered over two hundred, made a contribution in proportion to its capacity, initially in men and ships and later in money. After the Peace of Callias ended the war against Persia (449 B.C.), the treasury moved to Athens, which exercised significant economic and political influence until its defeat by Sparta in the Peloponnesian War (404 B.C.). The league was reconstituted in 377 B.C., under imperialistic Athens, until Philip II, emperor of Macedonia, defeated the Athenians (338 B.C.). This organization of a federal alliance of sovereign states, that was maintained over a long period, resembles the present North Atlantic Treaty Organization (NATO), which includes the Western European countries and the United States among some sixteen member-nations, and the Warsaw Pact of the Eastern European Bloc.

Philip II and his son Alexander the Great, a student of Aristotle, unified the Greek city-states (338 B.C.) and other people as far as the Danube River, primarily to oppose Persia, the main enemy of the Greeks at that time. During the Hellenistic Age, trade was greatly improved among the coast cities of the Mediterranean Sea by the seafaring Greeks who reached as far as Spain and Italy (Syracuse, Torrent, Crouton) in their search for economic expansion. For many centuries after the division of Alexander's empire (323 B.C.), Greek culture had a profound influence on Europe in the final phase of antiquity and the following medieval era.[1]

In the meantime, the northern part of the Italian peninsula and the surrounding areas were colonized by the Etruscans (ninth century B.C.), a people who probably had originated in Asia Minor. The west central region, called Latium, belonged to an Indo-European tribe known as the Latins. This tribe, together with the related Umbrians, Samnites, Ligurians, and Itali, had moved from the north and settled in the entire region of present-day Italy.

After a century of Etruscan domination, a new power, Rome, originally a city-state of Latium, had developed (508 B.C.). The Romans dominated all of Latium and conquered Etruria (309 B.C.). Gradually they expanded their sphere of influence in the Mediterranean basin, conquering the Samnites, the Carthaginians in North Africa, the Iberian peninsula, and the Greek states (mainly between 264 and 146 B.C.). Also, they repelled repeated barbarian raids across the north and east frontiers. By 14 A.D., the Roman Empire embraced all of the continental mainland south of the Rhine and the Danube, Britain, Dacia, Parthia, Greece, Asia Minor, and most of the northern costal region of Africa.[2]

During the period of the Roman Empire (31 B.C. to 476 A.D.) agriculture was given high priority compared to other sectors. Small landholders and free laborers left the countryside and crowded into the towns to increase the number of plebeians. The possession of large estates by the wealthy class and the nobles created the *latifundia*, which, together with the inefficiency of slave labor and the introduction of heavy taxation, accelerated the decline of the Roman Empire.[3] The creation of a new commercial class, the patricians, and the new landowners necessitated a body of laws which later had a profound influence on legal and economic institutions.

The recognition of juristic or artificial persons (legal entities) by the Roman laws was the most important development from the standpoint of invention and expansion of the corporate form of modern enterprises. The laws of contract and of private property, as well as our maritime laws and the systems of jurisprudence and jury duties, originated in ancient Rome. The importance of Roman law to the development of economic thought and institutions has been significant, particularly for Europe and the United States. Many of its principles influenced the legal systems of most of the western countries, including those that are under the English common law. The corporation form of enterprise and the Roman laws are valuable contributions to long-term stability and growth of modern economies. Natural persons die and their enterprises are mostly dismantled, but legal or juristic (artificial) persons, such as private corporations and public enterprises, normally survive for many years and in some cases for centuries.

After the separation of the eastern section of the Roman Empire, cultural and commercial activities moved largely to New Rome (Constantinople), which became the capital of the so-called East Rome or Byzantium (326 A.D.). The Emperors of Byzantium introduced a common language (Hellenic) and religion (Christian), and stimulated trade by reducing taxes and making administrative reforms in their dominions. Jewelry, pottery, silk production, and shipping were the main industries that flourished at that time and Constantinople remained an international trade and intellectual center for about ten centuries until Byzantium was occupied by the Ottoman Turks in 1453. With the increase in imperial expenses, the weight of taxation became greater, economic mismanagement increased and, after the eleventh century, the Byzantine Empire and its capital city began a slow process of decline. However, a number of scholars fled or were summoned to Western Europe, carrying with them Greek philosophy and culture, "the seeds" of which "grew into some of the finest flowers of the Renaissance."[4]

Venice, an Italian city situated on some 120 islands in a lagoon at the northern part of the Adriatic Sea, was founded in the fifth century by refugees from northern Italy in order to escape the Teutonic invaders. Although nominally part of the Eastern Roman Empire (Byzantium), Venice became an autonomous republic in 697 A.D. and, thereafter, a great commercial center for trade mainly between Europe and the Middle East. Rich Venice used mercenaries and local people to occupy important islands and ports in the Adriatic Sea and the Eastern Mediterranean in order to facilitate its shipping and trade operations. In 1204, when Constantinople fell to the Crusaders, Venice occupied Crete (for over four centuries) and later, in 1488, Cyprus as well. In addition, there were many other islands and coastlands occupied by Venice at this time, where many old Venetian fortresses can still be seen today. In competition with the Genoese and the Greeks for the lucrative Mediterranean markets, Venice developed a prosperous commerce. In 1797 the Venetian republic was ended by Napoleon the Great and many of its possessions were transferred to Austria, which finally ceded Venice to Italy in 1866.

During the Middle Ages (476 A.D. to about 1350 A.D) and the Renaissance period (1350 A.D. to 1500 A.D.), trade among the European cities was limited. Agriculture, which was the main sector of the economy, declined and educational and technological advancement was at a standstill. It was thought that the Greco-Roman writers, particularly Aristotle, had provided complete scientific explanations for all subjects and no further improvement was possible. All over Europe ever greater administrative powers were placed with the owners of large estates (the largest owner being the Church), which became new political and economic units with their own laws and courts. There were the landlords acting as independent rulers, and the serfs who worked for them. The merchants formed crafts and guilds in the towns for protection—from which the capitalistic system emerged. Young serfs moved into the cities and new markets were further stimulated by trade as a result of the Crusades; this led to a new economic climate favorable to trade and handicrafts. Late in the Middle Ages the Fuggers and other banking houses provided financial services to merchants and handicraft guilds as well as to the Church of Rome.

In Western Europe and particularly in Germany the Protestant Reformation (initiated in 1517) contributed to the rise of capitalism, which first manifested itself in Italy in the thirteenth century. In contrast to the papal practice of indulgences, Protestantism supported individualism and considered worldly success to be a divine blessing, inspiring a work ethic that stimulated efficiency and economic development, not only in Europe but also in the United States and other regions. This speeded the rise of the merchant class and mercantilism in general.

The capitalistic system in the sixteenth and seventeenth centuries and its spread to Europe and the United States was further developed especially by Calvinism, a Protestant denomination that justified the pursuit of wealth, the payment of interest, and profit-making. Yet today these teachings are criticized in that they do not lead to the high economic growth that other religious creeds do, such as those of Japan. As the critics argue, the lagging growth of Scotland and the southern section of the United States, with their Calvinist and other Protestant religions, testifies to that.

Mercantilistic Colonialism

Under mercantilism (1550–1776) emphasis was placed on foreign trade as a means of accumulating precious metals as the most desirable form of national wealth, and the supremacy of the state over the individual. The state, being the locus of power, should support exports, create state monopolies, and establish colonies to increase national wealth. Commercial expansion by monopolies such as the Merchant Adventurers, the Eastland Company, the Muscovy Company, and the East India Company had initially as main objectives the search for and the accumulation of precious metals, mainly gold and silver, which could be used to finance trade, pay large armies for foreign wars, or be retained as luxuries. As Columbus said (1503), "With gold one can get everything he desires, even to get souls into paradise." This trade expansion led to colonialism. The mother countries, England, Spain, France, and other European nations, expanded not only trade with the colonies, including the future United States, but also their political and military domination for purposes of exploiting natural resources, including the mining of gold. The search for minerals and other productive resources and the expansion of markets were the main reasons for establishing colonies. Navigation acts increased mercantile profits by confining the carrying trade to the mother countries' own ships.

State and church financial facilities during the sixteenth and seventeenth centuries stimulated wealthy families, such as the Bardi, Medici, and Fuggers, to undertake commercial and financial adventures and thus displace the medieval feudal lords. This new system of commercial capitalism was characterized by economic freedom, technical progress, and profit-seeking, regardless of the social consequences and communal relationships.

The quest for material wealth, self-interest, and liberalism by the rising merchant and industrial classes during the mercantilist period, broke up the medieval controls and replaced religious, non-economic values with worldly material ones. The gradual development of maritime commerce in most of the Mediterranean and other European ports and the economic and other reforms introduced by the Renaissance, especially in Protestant countries, provided the necessary incentives for material success, technical advancement, and scientific progress. The discovery of new lands and the expansion of trade with the colonies led to the improvement of internal and external transportation, an increase in food production, the accumulation of profits, and a gradual shift of power from the land-owning nobility to the new merchant class. Low cost and high profits, to be used for further industrial expansion, were the economic objectives of the Mercantilists. Low wages and the consequent suffering of the enlarged urban laboring class, as well as the exploitation of the less developed colonial areas were the outcomes. All these factors were conducive to the development of the capitalistic system that was spread to the United States and other colonies.

Inventions and new technological methods of production in iron, textiles, and particularly the use of the steam engine (invented by James Watt in 1776) in England increased industrial production and created a new capitalist or entrepreneurial class. Similar movements of industrialization and urbanization occurred in France, Germany, and other European nations. Specialization in production, competition, and the search for new resources and markets caused the spread of industrial development to the United States and other countries. As a result living standards improved dramatically in Europe and the United States in the late 1800s and the beginning of the 1900s.

The doctrine of mercantilism in England, or cameralism in Germany and Colbertism in France (from Jean Colbert, the French Finance Minister), supported promotion of exports, protection of manufacturing and foreign trade by active government intervention. This intensified the policy of colonialism by the European nations, particularly England, Spain, France, Holland and Portugal.

With the approaching end of colonialism, the European nations turned against each other. The result was terrible destruction and crashing economic setbacks in the First and the Second World Wars during the 1910s and the 1940s. Subsequently, aging Europe, having learned a harsh lesson from previous belligerence and destruction, turned toward cooperation and eventual economic and political integration by forming the successful European Community, a dream that had been unrealized for centuries.

Efforts of European Unity

Europe, which stands at a momentous crossroads, has a history that radically changed its face and that of the world. To understand current events, a review of related historical trends in the Continent is needed. The road to European unity goes far back into history.

The Greco-Roman dream of a united Europe, mainly through conquests, had permeated the Continent for centuries. It prevailed during the Roman period (31 B.C. to 476 A.D.) and the Byzantine period (326–1453 A.D.), especially at the time of Justinian's rule (554 A.D.). Similar efforts were made during the years of the Frankish Kingdom of Charlemagne, "King Father of Europe" (800 A.D.); Otto the Great in 962 and later (during the first German Reich); the Austro-Hungarian Hapsburg Dynasty (mainly in the sixteenth century); and the period of the Austrian chancellor Metternich (toward the end of the eighteenth and the beginning of the nineteenth century). Also, forceful attempts to unify Europe were made during Napoleon Bonaparte's period (1799–1815); the new German

Empire or the Second Reich (1871–1918) under the Kaiser and Otto von Bismarck; and recently by the alliance of Benito Mussolini of Italy and Adolf Hitler of Germany. However, Winston Churchill, the British Prime Minister, pointed out that "We must build a kind of United States of Europe," as the Hapsburgs also suggested centuries ago.

Probably the lack of success in unifying Europe through so many centuries was due to the reliance on forcible conquests by the European rulers. However, the Renaissance (rebirth) movement, which had begun in fourteenth century Italy and had spread all over Europe during the late Middle Ages, incorporated a spirit of innovation and unity, a great reawakening of common interest in the literature, culture and philosophy of ancient Greece and Rome.

The Christian religion, under its main denominations (Catholic, Orthodox, Protestant, Anglican), played a significant role in stimulating efforts towards European unity. However, in many cases, nationalistic, economic, and political forces proved to be more powerful in leading the European nations into conflicts and destructive wars throughout history. And this in spite of the fact that a number of Patriarchs, Popes and other theologians appealed for unity and for a reawakening of the European religious soul as a root of unity.

From an economic point of view, the establishment of a German customs union (Zollverein, 1834), under Prussian leadership, may be considered as the closest attempt of a union similar to the present European Community (EC). It created a free-trade zone throughout much of Germany, removed commerce restrictions, and demonstrated the importance of cooperation and unity on economic and political matters.

EVOLUTION OF THE EUROPEAN COMMUNITY

For several years, six European countries, that is, France, West Germany, Italy, and the three Benelux nations (Belgium, the Netherlands, and Luxembourg) tried to strengthen their economic and political bonds. Actually Belgium and Luxembourg had had an economic union since 1921. This union was joined by the Netherlands in 1944 in order to form the regional economic group known as the Benelux countries. Negotiations among the three Benelux nations had begun even from 1943 when they were under Nazi occupation.

After the Second World War ravaged Europe, it slowly set out on the path toward its final and crucial revival and eventual unification. The destruction of the war raised the question of how to avoid the European pattern of historical catastrophes followed by revivals followed by catastrophes, ad infinitum. The consensus was that Europe should not be doomed to oscillations between order and chaos. Instead, a new way of peace, stability, and prosperity should be found. A European supranationalism or a European family of nations was needed to submerge individual nationalism and historic enmities.

One of the first Europeanists was Jean Monnet, a stocky French peasant figure, who wanted to promote Europe's recovery in the post-World War II years and eventually its economic and political union. He pointed out that people taking risks and offering innovative ideas for European integration deserve the laurels. However, emphasis should be placed on institutions, such as the EC, because they can transmit things to successor generations. Monnet wanted not so much to be somebody, but to do something, especially to contribute in liberty and diversity to the union of the European peoples. He persuaded the United States, through Franklin D. Roosevelt, to support the defense of Europe as "the arsenal of democracy." Also, he prepared the Schuman Plan, named for Robert Schuman, the French Foreign Minister (1950), for the creation of the European Coal and Steel Community (ECSC) in 1952, the forerunner of the EC.

The Schuman Plan was designed to effect Franco-German reconciliation and to make it impossible for the European nations to fight each other. Italy and the three Benelux countries (Belgium, Luxembourg, and the Netherlands), together with France and West Germany, signed the treaty which established the ECSC. The idea was to provide a practical basis for gradual concrete economic and political achievements. Europe, after all, is essentially compact and indivisible. From above (from a plane) the jigsaw frontiers make little sense. One wonders how the advanced people of Europe have rejected union and have stayed apart for so long.

The European Economic Community (EEC) was established by the Treaty of Rome in 1957 with six members: Belgium, Luxembourg, the Netherlands, France, West Germany, and Italy, commonly known as the "Inner Six." It was formed to gradually reduce internal tariffs. Because the group was successful, the United Kingdom and Denmark, as well as Ireland, joined the EEC in 1973. Greece and Turkey became associate members of the EEC in 1962 and 1964, respectively, and were allowed to export many of their products to the community free from duty, while retaining tariffs during a transition period. Special arrangements and association agreements have been negotiated or signed with a number of countries in Africa, Middle East, Asia, and Latin America, as well as Spain and Portugal. Greece became the tenth member of the EEC in 1981 and Spain and Portugal the eleventh and twelfth members, respectively, in 1986.[5] Because of political and other non-economic integration movements, the EEC is currently named the European Community (EC).

For Spain and Portugal a ten-year transitional period (1986–1995) was provided for agricultural products and a seven-year period for fish, for which tariffs would be gradually reduced by the EC. A similar five-year period was provided between the EC and Denmark, Ireland, and Britain. For industrial products the transitional period was three years for Spain and seven years for Portugal. No time interval was provided for the introduction of value-added tax for Spain and only three years for Portugal, compared to five years for Greece (extended for another two years later). Also, a seven-year period was provided for the free movement of the Spanish and Portuguese workers in the EC, as was initially provided for Greece. Now, trade policy is basically dictated by Articles 110–116 of the Treaty of Rome.

There are four major institutions in the European Community for the formulation and implementation of economic and other related policies: the Commission, the Council, the European Parliament, and the Court of Justice.

The Commission formulates and proposes related legislation and provides for the implementation of the Community's policies. There are seventeen commission members (two each from Britain, France, West Germany, Italy, and Spain and one from each of the other member-states) chosen for four-year terms by the twelve EC member-state governments. Jacques Delors, an energetic Frenchman, is the president of the Commission; Frans Andriessen, a former minister of the Netherlands, is the vice president responsible for external relations and trade positions with the United States and other countries. Martin Bangemann, former Minister of Economics of West Germany, is responsible for internal market and industrial affairs; Christiane Scrivener of France is in charge of customs and tax issues; Vasso Papandreau of Greece is responsible for employment, industrial relations and social affairs; Manuel Marin of Spain for development and cooperation; Fillipo Maria Pandolfi of Italy for telecommunications and research; and Leon Brittain of Britain for competition policy.

The rest of the Commissioners have other assignments such as agricultural production and subsidy, financial affairs, budgetary problems, regional policies, transportation, cultural affairs, and environmental protection. The members of the Commission act not in the interest of their individual home-states but as representatives of the European Community as a whole.

The Council approves the legislation of the Community and is its decision-making institution. In contrast to the Commission, its members act as representatives of the particular member-state governments. For certain problems, the council must consult with the Economic and Social Committee and the European Parliament. Under the revised procedures, a qualified majority is sufficient for the council's decisions, not unanimous approval as before. Individual member-states cannot exercise a veto any more. This is a change that allows quick passage of EC proposals for further economic and political integration.

The European Parliament elected by the voters of the individual member-states has 518 members seated in nine political party groupings. These groups are not national but Community groups, such as the Socialist Group, the European People's Party, and so on. The Parliament advises the Commission and the Council on legislative matters and exercises democratic control over their actions through amendments and delays on related legislation.

The Court of Justice acts as the Supreme Court of the Community regarding the validity and the correct interpretation of its legislation. It is comprised of thirteen judges and six advocates-general appointed for six years in agreement with the national governments. Through its decisions, the Court helped rapid integration by eliminating barriers to free trade and other restrictions within the community. Together with other EC bodies, it has been a driving force behind the introduction of the Single European Act, which became effective in 1987, and the gradual unification of Western Europe.

Of the total 518 Europarlamentarians, Liberal or Free Democrats, the environmentalist Greens and the Socialists were the main winners in the recent elections. The Conservatives and the Christian Democrats were the main losers. However, they both held strong positions with 100 and 48 seats, respectively in 1989, compared to 181 seats for the Socialists, forty-one for Communists, and thirty-six for the Green Party. In Britain, the labor party ended up with forty-five seats in the European Parliament to thirty-two for the Conservative Party under Prime Minister Thatcher.

Depending on the population of each EC member nation, the distribution of seats in the Europarliament is as follows: Britain, France, West Germany, and Italy eighty-one each; Spain sixty; the Netherlands twenty-five; Belgium, Greece, and Portugal twenty-four each; Denmark sixteen; Ireland fifteen; and Luxembourg six. Although EC budget approval is usually a nightmare, for the first time in five years the Community's budget for 1989 of 46.2 billion ECUs, or $52.7 billion, was approved unanimously by the European Parliament and the Commission. The total credits for structural funds (regional, social, and agricultural programs) were 9,485 million ECUs in 1989, an increase of 22 percent from 1988; for the Integrated Mediterranean Programmes 255 million ECUs, an increase of 29 percent; and for research 1,180 million ECUs, or 43 percent over 1988. Favorable international economic conditions, particularly for agricultural prices, are expected to reduce the burden of member contributions to the Community's budget in the foreseeable future.

Some 116 directives, related to the completion of the Single Internal Market, were introduced until December 15, 1988, while 142 more directives have been proposed by the EC for that purpose. In accordance with the Community's Single Act, the EC reaffirms that it will not be a fortress region but a partner with outside nations, particularly the United States. Moreover, more progress on the social aspects of the internal market is the intention of the EC Commission and the Community as a whole. Thus two key directives, which will significantly affect United States companies in Europe, are expected to provide for worker consultation and for standard employment contracts. These directives will introduce new rules requiring firms to provide corporate information to workers and labor participation on matters of workplace health and safety, training, and even transnational mergers.

TRENDS OF EUROPEAN UNIFICATION

The dismantling of Western European trade and other barriers and the economic and political reforms of Eastern Europe are gradually becoming a reality. A unified market of Europe is expected to benefit business, workers, and consumers alike. In spite of some opposition (mainly from left wing parties), politicians, economists, and the citizens in general support a unified Europe and talk about the creation of the United States of Europe (USE), with prospects of advancing it to the level of the United States of America (USA). Already campaigns to alert citizens and businesses in the European countries have been begun by almost all governments. They include conferences and seminars and even the creation of special ministries (Belgium) and other institutions to deal with the implications of a "border-free Europe." It seems that what once was regarded as a dream, a utopian concept, is becoming a reality.

The European Community of twelve nations, with a population of 324 million and a total GNP of more than $4 trillion, is almost equivalent in economic power to the Unites States, with a population of 244 million and a GNP of about $5 trillion. All the EC nations should prepare for the competitive race among themselves and together for the race with the United States. The gradual approach to a single market may be accompanied by a further political unification and in some years the European Parliament may become more influential and powerful than national parliaments.

However, it should not be disregarded that there are overall objections to the economic unification of the European Community and eventually the whole of Europe, especially by the left, as well as specific objections on agricultural policy, monetary unification, environmental considerations, and social interests.

British Prime Minister Margaret Thatcher is the main opponent of the Common Agricultural Policy (CAP) and the establishment of the European Monetary System with a stronger alliance of the community's currencies and a common central bank. Also, the Green Party in West Germany predicts environmental harm and deterioration of the weak, while labor unions are asking for protection and guarantees for the working classes. However, all see that there are no better alternatives and realize they must slowly change their attitudes or become gradually isolated. In the meantime, the community's economies are being tightly interwoven and other nations such as Norway, Sweden, Austria, Yugoslavia, and all the East Bloc countries want closer ties with the EC and eventual membership.

To reinforce Community cohesion, efforts are made toward the harmonization of the economic and social levels of the weaker and stronger member-states of the EC, by palliating economic asymmetries and social imbalances, reducing unemployment, improving training and education, and promoting health and social security. In addition to economic unification, and the possibility of political integration, their goal is to improve sociocultural conditions and to create a "community with a human face."

In the process of strengthening integration and reinforcing the European identity, relations with the Comecon (East European economic bloc) countries are rapidly improving and more trade agreements are being concluded. Also, negotiations with other nations, such as the United States and Japan, for trade improvement are regularly conducted, stronger linkages with the developing nations are created, and closer ties are pursued, through the Association/Cooperation Councils, with Cyprus, Turkey, Yugoslavia, and Algeria.

It seems that the EC influence is growing not only on economic but on sociopolitical matters as well. It has become more than the Europe of Charlemagne's conception. With its twelve member nations, it stretches from the Hebrides of Britain to Crete and it becomes more independent and powerful, instead of a mere collection of clients and allies of one group or another with different cultures. The drastic reforms in Eastern Europe and the reunification of a powerful Germany act as a spur in the movement toward rapid EC integration, as the related conferences in Dublin (June 1990) and in Rome (December 1990) indicated.

Although the French have always argued that they were superior, the Germans and the British could never be ignored. Their powerful cultures right on the borders of France frequently challenged her socioeconomic and military setting. On the contrary, the United States has never had powerful neighboring countercultures to force frequent cultural and socioeconomic re-examination. Mexico is poor and Canada is almost empty. However, modern communication and transportation technologies, as well as a growing world trade, have changed many things and made other economies such as those of Japan and perhaps China serious challengers.

The pressure of competition and the economic challenges from the United States and Japan, as well as the prospects of raising the rate of economic growth and reducing unemployment, made the idea of a single European market attractive to the Western and Eastern European politicians and citizens. However, after the initial enthusiasm and excitement, skepticism appeared regarding the surrender of large chunks of national sovereignty and difficult, real problems were expected. Such problems refer to the abolition of all frontiers and the consequent illegal immigration and subsequent crime; the inflationary expectations from a common currency and the creation of a European central bank; the leveling of tax rates; and the "social dimension" of workers' rights.[6]

While big business firms favor the single market for their rapid expansion, labor unionists worry about the institutional rights they have achieved via difficult struggles throughout the years. Even politicians of different persuasions are cautious and express their skepticism as they realize that their countries are going through a long tunnel before they come on the other side. Although there is no danger that the European integration project will be derailed, difficult testings lie ahead and tough decisions are expected to be made in the years to come. Nevertheless, Europeans remember their bitter history of wars. They know that "those who don't learn from history are doomed to repeat it." Looking back, they see that when Europe was divided catastrophic wars and massive destructions occurred, while in periods of peace and cooperation economic advancement and sociocultural development occurred.

The elimination of national frontiers of the EC will favor business, particularly big corporations. Labor unions, however, complain that this will be accomplished over the rights of the workers. The idea of a single market with free circulation of goods, services, and people may not mean a better living for everyone. Some workers argue that the free domestic market of Western Europe may be considered a paradise for corporations and capitalists but a nightmare for the working class.

Objections are raised mainly by French and German labor unions which expect a movement of business firms to southern Europe, where labor unions are not strong, and eventually to Eastern Europe with its cheap labor. British labor unions, on the other hand, seem to accept reality and now do not raise as much opposition as before.

Among the workers' guarantees demanded are the establishment of uniform policies regarding a 35-hour work week and related industrial guidelines. Safety standards, health measures, worker training, the right to collective bargaining, and the workers' participation in corporation decision-making are additional demands of the trade unions of the EC. Companies which choose to be "European," instead of remaining national, are expected, voluntarily, to introduce their employees' participation in management, which has prevailed for decades in West Germany. This is a measure needed to compensate for the weakness of trade unionism, to preserve diversity, and avoid conflicts that may stagnate Europe's economy.

Cooperation with the European Free Trade Association

Three years after the formation of the EC, that is, in 1960, the European Free Trade Association (EFTA) was created in Stockholm. It included Austria, Britain, Denmark, Norway, Portugal, Sweden, and Switzerland. Both groups, the EC of the "Inner Six" at that time and the EFTA of the "Outer Seven," were formed to gradually reduce their international tariffs, but the EFTA permitted the retention of individual external tariffs, including tariff preferences which Britain had given to Commonwealth nations.

In the process of closer cooperation, the EFTA group was not as successful as the EC. Furthermore, the British had fears that tariff discrimination by the EC would make things worse in the future. For these reasons, Britain applied again and again for EC membership and in spite of France's reaction, mainly on the suspicion that it would be used as the Trojan horse of the United States to destroy the EC, Britain became a member of the European Community in 1973. In the same year, Denmark, along with Ireland, joined the EC. Greece became the tenth member in 1981 and Portugal, together with Spain, joined the EC in 1986.

At present, the EFTA is in jeopardy as another two of its key members, Austria and Norway, contemplate dropping out to join the EC membership. On the other hand, Sweden, Switzerland, Finland, and Iceland face the dilemma of maintaining individual neutrality or joining the EC for more trade and economic betterment. It seems that the remaining members of the EFTA will soon join the EC as their preferential trade relations are approaching the end.

The remaining EFTA members, through bilateral agreements with the EC, export their industrial products duty free to the European Community (and vice versa) without contributing to regional or agricultural support programs and EC budget expenditures and policies. From that point of view, they may be considered not free traders but freeloaders. To avoid exclusion from the single EC market and to keep their current privileges, the EFTA members are considering replacing their present status with a customs union. In this case, they would have to adopt common import duties set by the EC for outside countries. Also, they might not be able to get cheap subsidized food products from the EC. Overall, the clearest option for the remaining EFTA nations is to join the EC as full members—and the sooner the better. The same thing can be said for the East Bloc or Comecon nations, especially Poland, Czechoslovakia, and Hungary.

Specifically, for Austria and Switzerland, the dilemma is how to link into the EC market benefits without being full members and losing their long-run neutrality on military and other matters. They are both close to the heartbeats of the EC center in Brussels, and it is difficult to escape joining it. Moreover, about two-thirds or more of their exports go to the EC (mainly to Germany) and about the same percentage of imports come from it. From that standpoint, both countries are in the process of adopting new rules concerning transit traffic and industrial norms according to the EC directives. Furthermore, closer cooperation between the EC and Comecon or the East Bloc countries diminishes the importance of neutrality of these two bridge countries.

Encouraged by the dramatic political and economic reforms in the East Bloc nations, the EC agreed with the remaining EFTA nations (Austria, Finland, Iceland, Norway, Sweden, and Switzerland) in December 1989 to create a "European Economic Space" and abolish remaining tariffs and quotas. Also, industrial and product standards would be harmonized and cooperation in education, the environment, and research and development would be increased. Moreover, democratization in the East European countries, notably Poland, Hungary, Czechoslovakia, Rumania, Bulgaria, and even Russia, removes the obstacle of neutrality and opens the road for eventual EC membership of such associated neutral members as Austria, Sweden, Switzerland, and Finland, as well as for the East Bloc countries.

In the case of full membership of these six EFTA countries to the EC, the group would have eighteen members and a total population of some 360 million. Out of a total trade of $880 billion of the EC in 1988, $220 was with the EFTA countries, compared to $164 billion with the United States, $70 billion with Japan, and $54 billion with Eastern Europe. The EC absorbs about 55 percent of the association's exports and the association absorbs 27 percent of the EC exports. As a result of their closer relationship, trade and investment between them would increase as entrepreneurs from both sides would move to each other's territory. This accord may be a model for future deals with the East Bloc countries. It seems that there is no danger of this larger group being protectionist against the United States and other countries. Rather it would create a larger market with more opportunities for trade and investment.

As mentioned previously, Austria, Sweden, Switzerland, and other neighboring nations are considering closer relations with the EC and possible membership. Also, Turkey, an associated member for about three decades, is trying to achieve EC membership.

In addition to Turkey, which had already applied for membership, Norway and Finland are serious candidates for EC membership. Although in a past referendum, 53 percent of the Norwegians voted against membership, the success of the EC and the introduction of a barrier-free market are attracting them and other outsiders to join the club. For Turkey, though, EC membership may be further delayed because of reports of human rights violations, illegal occupation of about 40 percent of Cyprus, and the shift of the EC attention to Eastern Europe. Also, Cyprus and Malta are expected to join the EC.

Business executives, who would be mostly affected by future economic conditions, lead the campaigns for membership, while polls indicate that more and more people of the neighboring outside countries favor joining the EC. Many of them are even willing to sacrifice their long-standing neutrality. Moreover, there are some sixty-six African, Caribbean and Pacific (ACP) countries with which the EC maintains cooperative agreements. Among other things, financial aid is provided by the EC to the ACP countries under such agreements.

Relations with Eastern European Countries

It is expected that trade between the twelve members of the EC and the seven neighboring members of Comecon or CMEA (the Council of Mutual Economic Assistance)—Bulgaria, Czechoslovakia, the German Democratic Republic, Hungary, Poland, Rumania, and the Soviet Union—will increase drastically in the foreseeable future. The recent dramatic economic and political reforms in Eastern European countries, individually or collectively, present serious challenges and opportunities to the EC and the United States. Already a rapid process of democratization and decentralization in these countries permits individual enterprises to seek trade, investment ventures, and new supply sources in the West. New incentive schemes permit exporting enterprises to use hard currency earnings to pay for their imports. However, tradition-bound bureaucrats are unlikely to proceed fast in implementing foreign trade reforms, and transactions with the EC and the West in general may be slow.

Hard currency shortages in the Eastern European countries result in less imported technology and modern know-how. This leads to the production of low quality obsolescent products and all kinds of difficulties in selling them in foreign markets. Certain Comecon or East Bloc countries, such as Hungary and Poland, tried to acquire hard currency and Western technology with foreign loans and accumulated debts, but with limited success. Nevertheless, legal reforms, introduced years ago by Hungary (1970), Rumania (1971), and more recently in all East Bloc nations, encouraged joint ventures with the EC, the United States, and other Western firms. In general, there seems to be some flexibility in negotiations for foreign investment and joint ventures, as well as in the opening up of the Comecon markets. This is expected to lead to improvement in productivity and better quality of domestically used and exported Eastern European goods and services.

Relations between the EC and the Eastern European countries other than the Soviet Union are steadily progressing. The signing of the agreement with Hungary on September 26, 1988, as well as the recent negotiations for further cooperation with Poland, Czechoslovakia, Rumania, and Bulgaria implemented the joint declaration of Luxembourg (June 1988) in which the EC and Comecon formally recognized each other after ignoring one another for more than thirty years. West Germany is particularly interested in improving relations with Comecon countries, mainly for expanding the market for its industrial products and for joint investment ventures. However, the French, the Soviets, and others fear that with the two Germanies united Germany would dominate central and perhaps the whole of Europe not only economically but politically and militarily as well.

As Moscow is loosening its economic grip on the other East Bloc countries, the EC and the United States move in with trade and investment. Thus, trade and investment agreements were made recently between the EC and United States firms with Hungary, and to a lesser extent with Poland and Czechoslovakia, while Bulgaria, Rumania, and the Soviet Union are seeking similar agreements. On the other hand, the German unification would transform Germany into a financial and industrial center for all of Europe.

These profound Soviet and Comecon changes and unsatisfactory results have led powerful Communist parties in France, Italy, and other EC countries to change their attitudes on ideological and economic matters, as they look elsewhere, perhaps to the West or China, for reliance and effective guidance.

Although trade between the EC and the Comecon represents only 7 percent of the total foreign trade of the EC, closer cooperation between the two groups is rapidly growing. However, it was realized in the related negotiations from the time of mutual recognition that Comecon countries are in a backward position economically and that the debt of Eastern Europe to the West is more than $150 billion and growing. From that point of view, the northern EC-rich countries should have to help the poor Comecon countries to narrow the gap of development, in addition to the help they provide to the poor southern EC countries. It is expected that Hungary and Poland, and perhaps other East Bloc countries, will apply for membership to the EFTA (European Free Trade Association) in the near future, as a first step toward eventual EC membership.

The opening of the Berlin Wall gates on November 9, 1989, which had kept West and East Germany apart for twenty-eight years, will speed up trade and investment in the region. As a result, economic benefits would spread across Eastern and Western Europe, particularly if Eastern European countries are accorded special status, such as associated membership, by the EC. Low paid, skilled workers of the East are needed in the West, while Western capital and advanced technology are needed by the East. However, low paid workers in Italy, Spain, Greece, and Turkey may face problems of no wage improvement and even higher unemployment from an eventual influx of competitive workers from Eastern Europe. Therefore, they may well push for more protectionism that may hurt EC-United States trade relations in the years to come. Under such conditions the economic convergence of Western and Eastern Europe may lead to the creation of a "Fortress Europe" with more trade barriers for outsiders.

The EC countries, principally Germany, and the United States, are rapidly taking advantage of the economic and political opportunities presented by the Eastern European reforms and encourage investment and trade into Comecon economies. Investment guarantees for joint ventures, tax advantages, and loans are offered to EC and other entrepreneurs. Also other forms of economic aid are presented to Eastern European countries as long as they follow a policy of decentralization, privatization, and democratization of their societies.

After 40 years of division and isolation, the Old Continent follows its new fate. The Soviet leaders realized that economic and political freedoms bring better results than oppression and confrontation. They realized that the crash of the Hungarian and Czechoslovakian revolts in 1956 and 1968, respectively, made things worse in the long run and that Eastern European nations should decide their own destinies. On the other side, the EC integration movement appears as a success lesson and as a magnet of interdependence with freedom and human dignity. As in the United States some 200 years ago, diversity and unity with liberty was achieved although with difficulties, likewise in Europe there can be integration with economic progress and political freedom.

The United States is supportive of pan-European unity for economic and strategic reasons. A reduction of United States troops from 300,000 to 190,000 (and less later) in West Germany would reduce defense expenditures, which can be used to reduce budget deficits and be allocated for domestic projects such as improvement in health, education, city renewal, highways, and other infrastructural facilities. Likewise, a reduction of Soviet troops (some 500,000) in Eastern Europe would help increase production and improve the standard of living in Russia.

At the Yalta Conference of 1945, United States President Franklin Roosevelt, Soviet leader Joseph Stalin, and British Prime Minister Winston Churchill agreed to divide Europe into two regions, East and West. In December 1989, George Bush, the United States President, and Mikhail Gorbachev, the Soviet President, met on a boat near Malta and agreed to let Europe unite. From that standpoint, Malta seems to be the opposite of Yalta. More details regarding the dramatic changes in the East Bloc countries and the unification of Germany are presented in chapter 9 of this book.

3   The United States: Relations with Europe

EMERGENCE AND ECONOMIC EXPANSION

Colonial Times

Since America was discovered by Columbus in 1492, the region has gone through many turbulent periods. However, through hard work and development, the United States of America has reached the status of being the first economy in the world. Parochialism and economic groupings were prevalent during the Colonial period. Sectionalism and cleavage could be observed not only between individual colonies but also between the coastline and the interior, as well as between the North and the South, primarily up to the American Revolution (1776). There were the mainly British colonial aristocrats (landlords, merchants, and slave owners backed by Anglican church officials) with economic and political power, and the small farmers and poor people in the back country who paid relatively more taxes and other fees. They were the debtors compared to the creditor Eastern seaboard commercial establishment. Taxation was levied primarily on persons, not on property.

For years American patriots were engaged in a difficult war of independence against the British colonists, especially after the Declaration of Independence on July 4, 1776. Help came from France with a 1778 alliance. The war climaxed in 1781 when over 5,000 French soldiers and George Washington with 9,000 patriots besieged Yorktown, Virginia, and forced the surrender of the British troops and the Loyalists under the command of General Charles Cornwallis. As a result, England acknowledged (Treaty of Paris, 1783) the independence of the thirteen states, with the Great Lakes as a northern boundary and the Mississippi River as the western boundary, while Florida, on the southern boundary, was returned by England to Spain. The rest of the present-day United States, with the exception of an unexplored northwestern part, belonged to Spain at that time, as did Mexico and other Central and South American countries.

With the termination of the Anglo-American war in 1783, the estates of the loyalists were confiscated and land was redistributed. Recent research, however, indicates only slight effects on the economy from redistributed loyalist estates. More important were the vast lands the new nation obtained from the peace treaty of 1783. This national domain played a major role in American economic and political developments (notably in the Homestead Act of 1862) regarding religious freedom, the separation of Church and State, and commercial expansion. Wages were determined primarily by the supply of and demand for labor, while the constant flow of immigration delayed the growth of labor movements for many decades.[1]

In 1803, the United States, under Thomas Jefferson's presidency, purchased the vast area of Louisiana west of the Mississippi from France for $11.25 million, an area which Spain gave to France under the pressure of the powerful Napoleon Bonaparte in 1801.[2] In 1819, Spain sold Florida to the United States, and Mexico won independence from Spain in 1821. Texas, which had revolted from Mexico in 1836, was annexed by the United States in 1845, Oregon was divided with England in 1846, and a large area west of Texas and south of Oregon (California) was ceded by Mexico to the United States in 1848. In 1867, the United States purchased Alaska from Russia, got possession of the Samoan Islands in 1867, and annexed the Hawaiian Islands in 1898. At present, the United States is composed of 50 states and the District of Columbia.

Immigration from Europe

From the time of its discovery to the present day, the New World (America) has been populated mainly by immigration from Europe. The total number of foreign-born persons who came to the United States from 1790 to 1950 amounted to 106.4 million. The United States population increased from 3.9 million in 1790 to 5.3 million in 1800, around 76 million in 1900, to 150.7 million in 1950. At present the United States population is 244 million. Every time a census was conducted, it was found that some 7 to 15 percent of the population was foreign born with 13 percent in 1790, about 15 percent in 1910, and 7 percent in 1950. The largest number of immigrants came in the decade of 1901–1910 (8.8 million), followed by that of 1911–1920 (5.7 million).[3]

The main source of immigrants up to 1890 was from Northern and Western Europe, particularly from England, Ireland, and Germany. After 1890, Southern and Eastern Europe became the predominant source of the new wave of immigration, mainly from Italy, Russia, Poland, Austria, Czechoslovakia, Hungary, and Greece. Overpopulation, political or religious persecution and, at times, the avoidance of oppressive military service, as well as other depressive factors in Europe, were the main reasons for immigration across the Atlantic. American railway and shipping companies sent agents to Europe and subsidized fares to attract immigrants primarily for the construction of railways, mining operations, and factory work in the rapidly growing cities. Also, slave labor from Africa was used mainly on the plantations of the South, particularly before the Civil War (1861–1865). Mexico and Canada became additional sources of immigration after 1900. Mexico and other Central and South American countries are expected to continue to be the main source of immigration in the United States in the near future.

American workers, under pressure of cheap labor from the flood of immigrants, opposed unrestricted immigration. As a result, Congress enacted legislation prohibiting advertising by employers that stimulated immigration and made it selective on grounds of nationality with other restrictions against undesirable aliens, including criminals, prostitutes and polygamists. Thus, the Chinese Exclusion Act was enacted in 1882. The Emergency Quota Act, passed in 1921, permitted only a 3 percent immigration increase for each nationality. The quota system, as altered in a number of cases, prevailed till 1968. The main reasons for such restrictions were nativism, labor pressure, and the decline in the railroad industry due to shipping competition and particularly to rapidly growing motor vehicle transportation of freight and passengers.

The influx of European capital, together with European workers and investors, helped the development of a large railroad industry and the corporation form of business, which increased economic growth in the United States. During the period between the Civil War and up to the end of the First World War, railroad building was booming with a total mileage exceeding that of all of Europe. Afterwards, because of unwise rail construction and overspeculation as well as new alternative means of transportation, many United States railways reached dismal conditions. Even today a number of lines are near insolvency and depend mainly on government subsidies.[4]

Tariffs and Trade

Because competition from Europe was strong and American industries were at an experimental stage, protection was needed until the infant industries matured enough and were able to compete with their European counterparts. Alexander Hamilton, using the infant industry argument, proposed tariffs and Congress approved them in 1789. Native and borrowed foreign capital plus labor and entrepreneurial skills were available, but foreign competition on a laissez-faire basis was severe. Then customs duties were required for industry and labor protection and for federal revenue for the newly established American government. However, Hamilton's tariff was primarily a revenue one and only mildly protective (average rate 8.5 percent).

The average annual revenue from tariffs was about $9 million in 1791–1811. It was the largest single source of federal revenue. Internal revenue receipts were less than $700,000 a year. During the period 1791–1815 customs receipts were $229 million, while internal revenue was $13 million. Sale of public land accounted for $10 million and direct taxes accounted for $6 million.[5] For additional revenue to service the debt of the nation, higher duties were imposed and excise taxes were introduced later.

During the years of colonialism and thereafter, United States trade relations with Europe and other countries in general continued to be important. Internal trade was largely governed by external trade. England and France, with strong economies at that time, were the main trade partners. However, after 1783 the United States was beyond the jurisdiction of the British Navigation Acts and foreign trade with England conducted by American vessels drastically declined. American merchants then turned to other countries for trade, mainly to China.

Before and after independence, American native investment was primarily directed toward domestic transportation (canals and trains), agriculture and manufacturing, rather than shipping and foreign trade. European merchants and shippers were the main competitors. By 1913, British ships carried about one-half and German ships about one-sixth of United States foreign trade, while American ships carried only about one-tenth. It was after World War II (1946) that the American merchant marine represented over 60 percent of the world's total, compared to only 15 percent in 1936.

For governmental revenue and, to some extent, for industry and labor protection, 8.5 percent tariffs were imposed on imports in 1789. In 1792, the average rate of tariffs increased to 13.5 percent. Tariffs were increased on a number of occasions, and the average level was over 47 percent in 1864 and 49.5 percent in 1890 (McKinley Tariff). The highest tariffs in American history were established in 1922 (Fordney-McCumber Tariff), allowing, however, the President to lower or raise duties by 50 percent to equalize cost differences with competing Europe and other nations. Pig-iron, chemicals, cheese, butter, and other dairy and agricultural commodities were among the high-duty products at that time. With the changes of the Hawley-Smoot Act (1930) tariffs were 33.6 percent for agricultural products, 35 percent for metals, and 59.8 percent for wool and woolens.[6] This protectionist policy of the 1920s stimulated monopoly at home and retaliations abroad, especially by Britain and France, and made it impossible for the European countries to pay their debts to America. This may be considered as an important reason for the world's economic depression of the 1930s.

Gradually, the United States became an exporter of primarily manufactured foods and a net creditor nation. Exports increased more than 20 percent (from $400 million to $8,600 million) from 1860 to 1920, while imports increased by 16 times (from $360 million to $5,730 million) during the same period. America then stopped serving mainly as a source of raw materials to European nations. Between 1911–1915, United States exports were composed of 46 percent manufactured products, 31 percent raw materials, and 23 percent foodstuffs, while imports were 40 percent manufactured products, 35 percent raw materials, and 25 percent foodstuffs. More or less, the same composition of imports can be observed in 1946, when exports of manufactured goods increased to 62.2 percent compared to a decline in foodstuffs to 23 percent, and only 15 percent in raw material exports.[7] Compared to the European nations, the United States remained for decades and still is a nation much less dependent on foreign trade. There will be more details on foreign trade in chapter 6.

Western Europe has been and still is an important customer of the United States, although there were some setbacks. During the Napoleonic Wars and World War I, United States trade boomed with Europe. Likewise, the United States has been and continues to be Europe's best customer. Up to the 1920s foodstuffs and raw materials were mainly exported from the new land to support the growing population and the expanding industrial plants of Europe. Manufactured and semi-manufactured products were exported primarily from Britain and Germany in exchange for the imported raw materials.

With the use of the first transatlantic cable in 1866 and refrigeration on vessels after the 1870s, communications and shipments of products were increased and trade was promoted on both sides. Increases in prices, particularly in 1896–1920, reduced mutual trade somewhat, but the volume of commodities continued to be satisfactory. Cotton and grain exports played a major role in trade with Europe. United States imports exceeded the value of exports until 1875, but after that year United States exports were higher than imports for almost every year until the 1970s.[8] Currently, the value of United States exports of goods are lower than that of imports and the resulting foreign trade deficit is a major problem for the economy of the country.

Money and Banking

Regarding early banking and monetary activities in the thirteen colonies, coins that European immigrants brought from their countries were used for transactions, along with wampum (beads made from certain shells strung together in belts or sashes), which was used as an ornament and for trade by the American Indians. Because such coins and wampum were limited and not well accepted, corn was made legal tender (1631) in Massachusetts, tobacco in Virginia, and rice in Carolina. In addition, wheat, rye, dried fish, and other commodities were used for barter exchanges. However, because much of colonial trade was conducted with Spanish colonies, Spanish coins and half or quarter pieces of such coins were extensively used.

Paper money (bills of credit) was used by the governments of the colonies and property as collateral for meeting expenses, because coins were in short supply. After 1775, the Continental Congress issued bills of credit to help pay for the War of Independence. By 1787, the severe depreciation of bills made them almost worthless and for seventy years after the inauguration of George Washington as the first American President (1789), gold and silver coins were the major means of exchange.

Alexander Hamilton (1757–1804), son of a Scottish father and a French mother, became the first Secretary of the Treasury in 1789. He encouraged shipping, introduced tariffs and excise taxes, and implemented measures to protect American industry. He also persuaded Congress to charter the Bank of the United States (modeled on the Bank of England) in 1791. Although the Bank was opposed by state banks and small capitalists as a centralized institution favoring the rich, it survived (with a gap from 1811 to 1816) till 1836 and played a vital role in the United States banking system. Moreover, Thomas Jefferson (1743–1826), the United States President from 1801 to 1809, and his followers came into conflict with Hamilton's economic policy, especially regarding the Bank of the United States. Jefferson was influenced by the physiocrats in France (where he served as an ambassador from 1785 to 1789) and favored decentralization and the laissez-faire economic system.

In 1862, under the presidency of Abraham Lincoln, Congress authorized the issue of $150 million United States notes or "greenbacks" and another $300 million in 1863 making them legal tender. In 1863, gold certificates with 100 percent gold backing and in 1878 silver certificates backed 100 percent by silver were placed in circulation. Also, in 1890 treasury notes (a temporary currency also backed by silver) were introduced and both greenbacks and notes of private banks constituted the major monetary units. To charter and supervise national banks, the post of Comptroller of the Currency in the Treasury Department was established by the National Bank Act of 1863. National banks could also be established by transfer from state charters.[9]

With the Gold Standard Act of 1900, gold and silver certificates were backed 100 percent by metal and were limited in supply, as were gold and silver coins and United States notes (after 1878). The amount of national bank notes was equal to the amount of government notes held by the banks. The inelasticity or arteriosclerosis of currency and credit to meet seasonal and cyclical changes ignited the crisis of 1907, the "rich man's panic." This led to the creation of the Federal Reserve Bank (Fed) in 1913, which controls the economy's supply of money and credit and supervises the commercial banks. There are twelve Feds with twenty-four branches in different regions of the United States. The main decision-making body is the Board of Governors (seven members appointed for fourteen years). Contrary to the central banks of Europe, the Fed is independent of the government. In addition to the currency already in circulation, the Fed added the Federal Reserve notes backed by 40 percent in gold reserve and 100 percent commercial paper as collateral. During World War II, Congress reduced the gold reserve requirement from 40 to 25 percent.

European and other countries more or less followed the United States. However, Winston Churchill, then British Chancellor of the Exchequer, put England back on the gold standard at a wrong price level, leading the country to stagnation thereafter.

In the United States, the unit-banking system prevails compared to the branch system in Europe. That is why there are many independent commercial banks (14,700) in the United States, about one-third of which are national banks, while the rest, primarily small banks, are under state supervision. All national banks are members of the Fed, as are most of the larger state-chartered banks.

INTERWAR PERIOD

The outbreak of World War I in Europe in 1914 helped the United States economy to grow mainly because of the heavy demand for American raw materials and war supplies for the belligerent European nations. By 1917 United States exports ($6.2 billion) exceeded imports ($3.3 billion) by about $3 billion. Gold poured into the United States and the value of European currencies, primarily the British pound, fell. Loans were extended to Europe (about $2 billion by 1917), and for reasons of economic interest, among others, the United States declared war on the German Empire on April 6, 1917. The United States became a strong economic power and the arsenal of democracy. United States trade with Europe increased significantly. United States imports from Europe increased from $896 million in 1914 to $1,128 in 1920, and exports rose from $1,486 to $4,466 million, respectively.[10]

The United States financial cost of World War I (April 1917 to July 1919) was about $33 billion, 31 percent of which was covered by taxation and the rest by loans, compared to over $360 billion for World War II. Although extensive government regulations, a mass of public agencies, and price controls were introduced to manage the war economy and to avoid inflation, the price index climbed to 187 in July 1917 (July 1914 = 100) and 206 in November 1918. Such control agencies, some of which proved useful later during World War II, dealt with fuel, transportation, finance, manpower, shipping, and other industries. Grain, raw materials, and other foodstuffs were bought from producers at minimum guaranteed prices, while termination of immigration and demand for labor led to an increase in the membership of the American Federation of Labor (A.F. of L) from two million in 1915 to more than four million in 1920. The eight-hour day and half-day on Saturday were introduced and an improvement in wages occurred.

As a result of World War I, the United States was transformed from a debtor to a creditor nation, while the European nations became debtors. Total private and governmental debts to the United States amounted to about $12.6 billion. Germany, with heavy reparation obligations, was in a dismal economic condition. The Europeans lost the income they had received from United States assets, and their economies turned still lower when the United States pressed them for loans and interest payments. Immigration from Europe was reduced by the United States quotas introduced in 1921, and European exports to the United States were substantially reduced due to very high protective tariffs (introduced by the Fordney-McCumber Act of 1922).

Moreover, gold payments drained reserves and crippled the European economies. Although in some cases interest payments were reduced (from 5 to 3 percent) and the installment period extended (from twenty-five to sixty-two years), mainly for Britain, things did not improve much. Britain, which had lent more to the allies than she had borrowed from the United States, advocated cancellation of all war debts with the hope of avoiding a worldwide financial crisis. Nevertheless, prices of United States farm products were reduced by about 50 percent, primarily because of the elimination of protective prices and the reduction in European demand. This significantly helped the consumers to buy cheap agricultural products on both sides of the Atlantic. However, the dollar shortage and the growing American investment in Europe intensified the dependence of Europe on the condition of the United States economy.[11]

To mitigate somewhat the severe economic problems of Germany from reparation payments, mainly to France and Britain, and the ongoing high inflation, the United States gave a gold loan to Germany. Also, American investments were flowing into Europe, mainly as the result of the Dawes Plan of 1924. By 1930, the United States net international economic position improved from $3.7 billion in 1919 to $15.2 billion. With a short setback during the recession of 1920–1921, the United States' prosperity during the First World War continued through the 1920s. However, textiles, coal, mining, shipbuilding, and some other industries had not improved as much as the auto, electrical, and construction industries. On the other hand, foreign trade had not expanded significantly. The ratio of United States imports to national income was only 5 percent compared to 6 percent for exports.

After a minor recession in 1927 in which wages in construction, mining, and some other industries declined, demand for durables and other goods declined and technological innovations continued to replace labor in the production process. Nevertheless, prices in the stock market continued to rise (from a total value of $27 billion in January 1925 to $87 billion on October 1, 1929) until the crash of October 29, 1929 (Black Tuesday), when stock prices declined by about 13 percent on the average and continued to fall thereafter. By 1932 average stock prices were only one-fourth their 1929 level. The stock market panic spread to other sectors of the economy. Investment and other spending declined; the wholesale price index gradually fell by one-third (from 95.3 in 1929 to 64.8 in 1932, 1926 = 100); unemployment increased to about 25 percent and the gross national product declined from $103.8 billion in 1929 to $55.8 billion in 1931.[12] The banking system neared collapse and borrowing was drastically reduced in spite of very low interest rates.

The wrong policy of reducing imports and trying to export some of the joblessness to other trade partners made things worse. High United States tariffs that were imposed in 1930 (Hawley-Smoot Act) made loan payments by Western European nations difficult as export revenues severely declined. Total United States imports fell from $4.4 billion in 1929 to $1.3 billion in 1932, as did exports from $5.2 billion to $1.6 billion, respectively. England and other European countries were losing gold and, under the prevailing gold standard system, they had to devalue their currencies or face bankruptcies. By 1931, England went off the gold standard, devalued its pound and encouraged internal expansion. Unlike France and Belgium, which abandoned the gold parity system later, England managed to recover from the Depression, while Germany, the United States, and other Western nations severely suffered from it. These dismal economic conditions contributed to Hitler's rise to power in Germany.

United States President Franklin Delano Roosevelt introduced the New Deal, a program of spending in public works through the Public Works Administration and other agencies and industrial self-regulation under the National Recovery Act of 1933. Also, a number of regulations were introduced to stimulate demand and to improve the economy through deficit spending, according to the Keynesian prescription. The United States came off the gold standard in April 1933, but gold could be used for international transactions, while the dollar was devalued by 50 to 60 percent. Federal Reserve member banks were not permitted to engage in stock market speculation, and insurance on deposits was provided. Also, a personal Social Security System was introduced in 1935, much later than similar programs in Germany (1880s), England, and other European nations. Furthermore, the Congress of Industrial Organizations (CIO, 1938) helped improve the position of labor unions.

Even before the Japanese surprise attack on Pearl Harbor (December 7, 1941), United States industries were partially transformed to the production of war material due to Lend-Lease and the defense commitments to European nations in 1940 and later. Wartime production contracts from European nations went to large United States corporations, primarily General Motors and other auto companies. Total industrial production almost doubled during the war. American industry produced enough to equip the allied armies and built harbors and airports in Britain and other countries.

Huge government spending and swelling total demand created inflationary spirals not only in Europe but in the United States as well where prices had risen about 25 percent from April 1941 to January 1942. Price regulations and even rationing of some products were used to curb inflation. Heavy taxation on personal and corporate incomes, excise and inheritance taxes, and the sale of war bonds were used in the United States to finance the cost of war of about $300 billion. However, the tax burden in Britain and other European countries was higher than that in the United States.

After the defeat of Germany and Japan in 1945 and the end of World War II, United States industry managed to switch to peacetime production without a severe recession or inflation. It continued to provide Europe and the rest of the world with vital materials and industrial products. As a result, the United States emerged as the richest and most powerful nation on earth. In June 1943, a United States proposal to form the United Nations Relief and Rehabilitation Administration (UNRRA) was accepted by 48 nations. From the $4 billion spent by this body, the United States gave $2,450 million, mainly to help feed much of occupied Europe. Lend-Lease stopped in 1945, while the UNRRA survived until 1947.

POST-WORLD WAR II COOPERATION WITH EUROPE

When World War II was over, Europe had been physically devastated, and demand for United States dollars to finance badly needed imports was great. Although most of the European nations had to depreciate their currencies to attract inflows of dollars, international deficits with the United States remained sky-high. Thus, Britain depreciated the pound from 4 to 2.80 pounds per dollar in 1947, as did other nations, but the "dollar gap" or the "dollar shortage" remained. Imports by Europe from the United States were four times greater than exports. There were widespread exchange and import controls, and primarily American aid to Western European countries went to help rehabilitate and stabilize their economies.

On June 5, 1947, George Marshall, then United States Secretary of State, in his speech at Harvard University, proposed a four-year program for the economic rehabilitation of Western Europe, initially known as the European Recovery Program (ERP), often popularly referred to as the Marshall Plan. The program was to be administered by the Economic Cooperation Administration (ECA), an agency of the United States, and the Organization for European Economic Cooperation (OEEC), representing seventeen European countries.[13] The Soviet Union and other Eastern European countries refused to participate in this program. The OEEC was later named Organization for Economic Cooperation and Development (OECD) and presently incorporates twenty-four countries, including the EC nations, the United States, Japan, Canada, and Australia.

The ERP, which had expended $12 billion in grants and loans, was liquidated on December 31, 1951, when the ECA was replaced by the Mutual Security Agency. About half of the money was used to buy industrial products, less than half for agricultural commodities, and $500 million for the European Payments Union (EPU), a clearance agency to settle trade imbalances of the member-nations. As a result of the American aid, the war-ravaged economies of Western Europe were significantly improved, especially in the production of steel, cement, aluminum, coal, and foodstuffs. It can be argued, therefore, that the impetus for European economic cooperation came primarily from the United States, while the European states were preoccupied with internal difficulties rather than with utopian projects of unification.

The main goals of the OEEC were to allocate the United States financial assistance to its members and to coordinate economic development plans. Although it had no power of its own, the OEEC was successful in bringing its members closer together as they had no choice but to agree among themselves in receiving United States assistance. From that point of view, the OEEC played an important role in creating a favorable environment for the formation of other intra-European organizations such as the European Payments Union (EPU) in 1950, the European Coal and Steel Community (ECSC) in 1952, the European Atomic Authority (Euratom), and the European Common Market or, officially, the European Economic Community (EEC) in 1957. However, the OEEC, renamed OECD, limited itself to economic research and publications of international character. The EPU, through multilateral exchange convertibility, increased trade and showed the necessity for a closer cooperation and eventual unification of Western Europe.

According to the United States Department of Commerce, aid to Western

Europe from 1945 to 1962 amounted to $33 billion, out of $83.3 billion total worldwide aid. Some $17.3 billion were nonmilitary grants, $6.2 billion were government loans, and $15.5 billion were in military grants.

In order to keep friendly relations with Western Europe and other nations, as well as to preserve international stability, the United States promulgated these foreign aid programs. Moreover, the United States fear of the spread of communism was another reason for such aid, particularly military aid. The main effect of American aid was to enable the economies of Europe to develop their resources and thereby stimulate foreign trade.

Greece, along with Turkey, received military and other aid from the United States mainly to stop the civil war and the Communists from taking over the government, as well as to avoid domination of the eastern Mediterranean by the Soviet Union which could interfere with traffic through the Suez Canal.

Under the "Truman Doctrine," the United States Congress appropriated $300 million for Greece and $100 million for Turkey in 1947. Now, both countries are members of NATO (since 1952) and receive military and nonmilitary aid from the United States (about $350 million for Greece and $500 million for Turkey, annually). There are four major and twenty smaller United States military bases in Greece and 16 in Turkey, as well as Voice of America facilities (VOA). As Walter Lippmann once remarked, these countries were selected for American aid "not because they are especially in need of relief, not because they are shining examples of democracy . . . but because they are the strategic gateway to the Black Sea and the heart of the Soviet Union."[14]

Previous European weaknesses may be considered as examples that lead to long-run and advantageous policies. On the other hand, United States emphasis on domestic economic autonomy and a disregard for its international implications may lead to disadvantageous policies concerning Atlantic and other economic relations. However, for American corporations an integrated Europe may be the most open and profitable market with which to do business, like the Balkans in previous times. Yet critics argue that the European Community could be a dog-eat-dog Darwinian nightmare with American and Japanese companies enjoying large shares of business and profits, while European workers would be squeezed and their rights trampled upon.

Important benefits of a single, unified European market can be achieved by cutting out red tape, breaking down protectionism, and removing obstacles on cross-border activities. This means economies of scale, more jobs, inflation-free growth, and healthier competition for EC and United States corporations.

NORTH AMERICAN ECONOMIC COMMUNITY

Eventually, it can be expected that the United States, Canada, and Mexico will form a common market, which may be called the North American Economic Community (NAEC) or the American Economic Community (AEC), as a counterpart of the European Community (EC) and possibly a pan-European Economic

Community. Among other things, Canada would add cheap resources to the wealth and the advanced technology of the United States, while Mexico would provide cheap labor. At the same time these three countries would compose a huge market of some 400 million people, compared to 324 million of the EC countries. Business mergers, joint ventures, a high technology collaboration, and expanded exchanges would stimulate further growth.

In response to the creation of a free-trade Europe, some people support the creation of a trans-Pacific bloc linking the United States, Japan, Canada, and Mexico. Thus, Professor Zbigniew Brzezinski, who was assistant to President Carter for national security affairs, suggests the creation of such a bloc which, in addition to the above four countries, may include Australia and other Pacific and Latin American countries.[15] Thus, in November 1989, there was an inaugural Asia Pacific Economic Cooperation (APEC) meeting of twelve nations to develop common economic positions, as a message to the EC for trade liberalization among groups of countries. It included the United States, Japan, Australia, Canada, South Korea, and New Zealand, as well as Singapore, Malaysia, Thailand, the Philippines, Indonesia, and Brunei.

The United States–Canada free trade agreement, which was approved by Congress and the House of Commons and went into operation at the beginning of 1989, is expected to increase the Canadian GNP by five percent and that of the United States by more than one percent annually in about a decade when all tariffs would be eliminated. There is no doubt that the timing of the agreement was influenced by the movement in the EC to eliminate all remaining economic and other barriers. The hope in both countries is to match the new expected competitiveness of the large unified market in Western Europe. Perhaps together with Mexico and other neighboring countries an eventual American Economic Community would be able to compete with the EC and probably with another group in East Asia in which Japan, Korea, Taiwan, and other neighboring nations might participate. Therefore, it is expected that these three economic groups or common markets would be the future competitors in the Western World. However, after a period of negotiations and adjustments, and under the aegis of the ninety-eight-nation General Agreement on Tariffs and Trade (GATT) and other international institutions, these groups are expected to move toward more economic coordination through reductions in barriers, joint ventures, mutual trade, and foreign exchange policies. Already, the United States and Canada decided on December 1989 to speed up tariff cuts in chemicals, electrical motors, printed circuit boards, and other items, covering $6 billion in trade. Moreover, entrepreneurs and multinational companies of both sides accelerated their efforts to trim costs on imported components and other products. Furthermore, expected closer cooperation between the EC and the Eastern European or Comecon countries in Europe may bring the United States and Canada closer together in the face of growing competition.

The Europeans argue that the formation of their single market aims at the revitalization of their economy and the expansion of the market for American products rather than at the exclusion of the United States and other countries. The skepticism, though, remains that Europe may practice an inward economic policy and damage American and world trade through discrimination. On the other hand, it is argued that some protectionistic actions have been taken by the United States in such products as steel, autos, microchips, and textiles.

A free trade pact between the United States and Canada, implemented on January 1, 1989, would eliminate most trade barriers over the next ten years. Formerly protected markets for many products will open and exchanges will be enhanced for both countries, which are each other's largest trading partners. More severe competition expected from the EC is a major factor for this bilateral agreement. Moreover, Japan wants closer Pacific economic cooperation and more trade with North America and Australia.

However, regional bilateralism and the formation of trading blocs may reduce the importance of the movement for global free trade under the Geneva-based GATT. From that point of view, worldwide conferences under the auspices of GATT, such as the Uruguay Round (1986–1990), may prove to be ineffective in liberalizing international trade.

Although Canada, a country 122 years old, has only twenty-five million people, it is the world's second-largest area with significant soil and subsoil resources. Together with the United States it forms the world's largest bilateral trading relationship. Canadian exports are more than $70 billion annually, while imports are about $60 billion. With a market of 260 million consumers and 5,524 miles of undefended border, the two countries will create a colossal economy. America already buys about three-quarters of all Canadian exports and Canada buys around one-fifth of all American exports, double the amount of the Japanese imports from the United States. Autos, auto parts, and trucks are the main products exchanged by both nations, about $20–25 billion annually. Canada's main exports include also newsprint, crude oil, lumber, natural gas, and wood. The main United States exports to Canada include, in addition to vehicles, tools, communication and other equipment, office machines, industrial machinery, aircraft, and chemicals.

Some Canadians feel that eventually Canada will be the 51st state and its economy will be engulfed by the United States. As previous Canadian Prime Minister Trudeau once said, it is like sleeping with an elephant in the same bed. Also, Canadians may remember that the United States twice invaded Canada and once sacked Fort Toronto or York.

There is more than $100 billion foreign investment in Canada, more than 70 percent of which is American. A growing number of American and Canadian companies and banks have business in each other's area and some of them are involved in mergers and takeovers. Scores of Canadian entrepreneurs march south to the pastures of the American markets and vice versa. Regardless of the formal agreements, the two countries are rapidly integrating their economies anyway.

Thus, the Canadian affiliates of Ernst & Whinney are planning to merge with

KPMG Peat Marwick. They are both accounting firms in the United States and Canada. With this deal, Ernst warded off the merger with Arthur Young, another big accounting firm. Finally, Ernst & Whinney merged with Arthur Young.

Campeau Corporation of Canada had two subsidiaries in the United States. One subsidiary was Federated Department Stores, which owns Bloomingdale's and Abraham and Strauss, among other department stores. The other subsidiary was Allied Stores, which owns Stern's and Jordan Marsh stores. Because these retail stores faced problems of debt payments, their underwriters (First Boston, Paine Webber, and Dillon, Reed) forced Campeau to bankruptcy in January 1990. Under a new experienced management these retail stores may reorganize and be profitable again.

Amax, an American aluminum and lead company, offered $2.4 billion to buy Falconbridge Company, a large Canadian nickel firm; Pizza Hut, a unit of Pepsico Inc., acquired 263 Winchell's Donut House restaurants from Shato Holdings of Vancouver, and so on. Furthermore, the United States–Canada agreement would eliminate the 19 percent American tariffs on fine paper, but outside nations, such as Sweden or Norway, would pay this duty. As a result, more trade and investments on paper and related industries between the two countries are expected in the near future.

Under the pressure of competition from the European community and from Japan, the United States and Canada decided to speed up economic integration. Instead of waiting for up to ten years they agreed to reduce tariffs for some products earlier than initially planned. To increase employment and business, United States trade groups and private enterprises requested acceleration of tariff reduction in some 2,000 products. Although there are frictions concerning a few commodities, such as Canadian plywood, Ontario wines and grapes, and fresh fish, the related trade commission, which meets twice a year, is speeding tariff cuts so that the two-way trade between the two countries would increase further than the present $150 billion. Under the rules of the General Agreement on Tariffs and Trade, a special panel of the trade commission solves minor problems of friction, so that integration can be achieved earlier than ten years for such products as steel, apparel, appliances, and textiles and less than five years for chemicals and subway cars.[16]

Moreover, the trend toward better United States–Mexico ties encourages the establishment of the North American Common Market. A bilateral commission for enhancing economic relations between the United States and Mexico, sponsored by the Ford Foundation, calls for the freest possible trading relationship between the two countries. This can be achieved by easing disputes regarding problems of trade in textiles, steel, automobile parts, and other products.

There seems to be a distrust of the United States by many Mexicans who consider closer ties as a new form of American colonialism. However, the largest trading partner of Mexico is the United States, while Mexico is the third-ranking partner of the United States, after Canada and Japan. New agreements would not only increase trade and cultural exchanges between the two nations, but new debt arrangements can be made, and illegal immigration and drug traffic can be reduced. For example, subsidies and other economic benefits may be provided to Mexican farmers to change cultivation of land for illicit drugs to that of other crops.[17]

Central and Latin America and East Asia are the main areas where manufacturing jobs go now. In Mexico, Hong Kong, and Singapore labor cost is about $1.50 per hour, while in the American steel and auto industries labor cost is higher than $20 per hour. In Mexico, close to the United States border, there are some 600 American-owned firms (*maquiladoras*), including Chrysler plants producing "K-cars."

More pressure in United States manufacturing regarding labor is also expected through the gradual computerization and robotization of this sector. It is estimated that the number of computers in use increased from two million in 1983 to twenty million in 1990 and robots from 6,000 to 10,000, respectively. From that standpoint, more concern with large economic groups or international aspects of trade and investment, and a more effective fiscal and monetary coordination among trade partners are needed. On the other hand, the United States and Canada, and eventually Mexico, are about to increase their discrimination in favor of each other and against the rest of the world, as the EC and probably Eastern European Bloc nations are doing, or are expected to do.

4   Economic Organization and Growth: Similarities and Differences

PUBLIC SECTOR AND PRIVATIZATION

Public enterprises are criticized as bureaucratic and inefficient. They are considered as political creatures that are influenced by pressure groups and politicians for more employment and low prices. As the critics say, the private sector is controlled by the government but the public sector is controlled by nobody. Poor management by political appointees and high costs from excessive union pressures, combined with low prices for social reasons, lead to frequent deficits and therefore to government subsidies on both sides of the Atlantic.[1]

Because of all these problems, there is a privatization drive in a number of market economies, including Britain, France, Germany, Italy, Greece, and Portugal. Similar trends of privatization or decentralization can be observed even in planned economies, such as the Soviet Union, Hungary, Poland, and other Eastern European countries.

Critics of privatization point out that there are certain industries that are natural monopolies and should be controlled by the public sector for the protection of the consumers from excessive profiteering and exploitation. Monopolies and even oligopolies are largely not under the power of the competitive market for controls in prices and quality. Nevertheless, industries that are important to national securities, such as aerospace and nuclear industries, should be controlled by the government. Another argument against privatization is that public enterprises are used to fight inflation by maintaining low prices, and to reduce unemployment by employing extra labor for economic or political reasons. Moreover, there may be cases in which the government sells public enterprises to finance budget deficits or to favor speculators who resell stocks at far higher prices to make profits. This occurred in Britain and France where traders bought such stocks and sold them at higher prices in the open market, sometimes at double prices.

Some state-run enterprises are monopolies. Privatization of such enterprises may not change their nature from the standpoint of competition and market pricing. Thus, many enterprises sold to the private sector remain monopolies and as such they resort to price fixing, supply restrictions, and other anticompetitive and antisocial measures. They become sleeping monopolies with no interest in innovations and technological advancement. As economist Professor Maurice Allais, the 1988 French Nobel Prize Winner argues, state-owned enterprises, many of which exist in the EC countries, may provide services that are socially efficient and economically viable through investment and determination of optimum prices. In that case, if there is a price change, no one can be made better off without making somebody else worse off, according to the principle of Pareto's optimality. From that point of view, performance of state-owned enterprises may be equally or more socially efficient than private monopolies. In practical terms, this depends on the efficiency of the managers involved, regardless if they operate under public or private ownership.

In the United States, Consolidated Rail Corporation, briefly known as Conrail, which was created to take over Penn Central and other bankrupt railroads, proved to be a successful case of denationalization or privatization. Since 1987, when the United States Government sold the almost bankrupt Conrail Corporation to the public at $28 a share, the company became profitable with more than $40 a share. The United States Congress prohibited Conrail's takeover and the buying of 10 or more percent of its shares after it was sold to the public. Because of capital improvements and its good performance, the company is considered a cash *cow* attractive for acquisition, as was CNW, another railroad which has been acquired in a leveraged buyout. As an anti-takeover defense, Conrail plans to establish an employee stock ownership plan, as do airline companies which are magnets for takeovers at present times. Other railroad companies, mainly Norfolk Southern, Union Pacific, and CSX railroads, as well as competitive shippers, are interested in buying Conrail.

From the EC countries, France has a high level of public ownership in a number of vital industries. It has 100 percent ownership in post offices and railways, as all other large EC countries do. Also, France, West Germany, Italy, Greece, and the Netherlands have 100 percent public ownership in telecommunications, while Spain has 50 percent ownership. In electricity, Britain, Greece, and France have 100 percent, while West Germany, Italy, and the Netherlands have 75 percent. In natural gas, France and Italy have 100 percent, West Germany 50 percent, and the Netherlands and Spain 75 percent of public ownership. About the same proportions prevail for coal where only Britain has 100 percent. In airlines, West Germany, Italy, Greece, and Spain have total public ownership, while Britain, France, and the Netherlands have 75 percent. In automobiles, Britain, France, and the Netherlands have 50 percent public ownership, and West Germany and Italy 25 percent. In steel, Britain, France, and Italy have 75 percent, and the Netherlands 25 percent. Finally, in shipping, only Britain has 100 percent public ownership, Italy and Spain 75 percent, and West Germany 25 percent. The United States has 100 percent public ownership in post offices and 25 percent in electricity and railways.

In West Germany, 9 percent of the labor force worked for government enterprises in the mid–1960s, primarily in railroads, telephone, television, radio, electricity, gas, sanitation, and water. At present, less proportions of the labor force work for government enterprises. Moreover, 20 percent ownership of Volkswagen by the federal government and 20 percent of Lower Saxony by a state government were transferred to the private sector.

In the 1980s, French legislation let employees and workers elect one-third of the directors of state-owned enterprises. This measure, which was appraised as a significant step toward industrial democracy, has had modest practical results. Although it allows the workers to participate in decisions affecting their income and employment, it may impair the technical efficiency of the enterprises affected and reduce long-run performance of the economy. Furthermore, there is criticism that if similar or more severe measures of workers' controls are applied to private enterprises, they may transform them into corporate zombies.

Over the years, British workers accumulated power, primarily through the Labor Party, but they have not achieved participation in boards of directors of enterprises as in other EC countries. However, labor leaders, together with business executives and government officials, were engaged to set up the goals of "planning by consent" in 1962 and later. These goals included: retraining of labor, modernization of industry, and economic growth. Although the planning process was abandoned later, British labor unions remained aggressive in exercising power over layoffs, hiring, promotions, and wages. However, critics have charged that union pressures contributed to incessant strikes, absenteeism, and low productivity. Moreover, whenever the Labor Party was in power nationalizations have been carried out, particularly in coal and steel industries, gas, electricity, and transportation.

ANTI-MONOPOLY CONTROLS, MERGERS AND ACQUISITIONS

To discourage monopolization of the market, special laws and regulations have already been introduced by the United States and the EC. They aim at the protection of the consumers from adulteration, pollution, resource depletion, and misrepresentation of quality and prices. In the United States, such laws include the Sherman Act (1890), prohibiting activities which restrain trade and monopolize the market; the Clayton Act (1914), forbidding price discrimination and elimination of competition between corporations through interlocking directorates and other devices; the Trade Commission Act (1914), prohibiting unfair methods of competition; the Robinson-Patman Act (1936), making it illegal to try to eliminate smaller rivals by charging unreasonably low prices and using other supply discrimination techniques; the Celler-Kefauver Antimerger Act (1950), prohibiting acquisition of real assets if it substantially lessens competition; and other laws and regulations which were enacted to achieve these goals, that is, to restrict monopoly and maintain competition. Similar antitrust laws prevail in the EC countries and aim at the protection of the consumers from unfair trade practices.

However, in spite of all these pieces of legislation and the accompanying judges and lawyers to implement them toward discouraging monopolies, monopolization and oligopolization of the American and the EC markets continue to grow. This may be due to economies of scale which large firms can achieve through concentration of capital and modern technology. As long as large monopolistic or oligopolistic firms can utilize mass production methods and reduce cost per unit, it is difficult to discourage their formation and operation through controls and regulations in the economy. The dilemma, therefore, is how to encourage competition and entrepreneurial intuition without hurting efficiency and economic progress.

Antitrust legislation may be considered as being, to a large extent, not too realistic just as are the models of competition it aims to protect. Breaking down large enterprises or prohibiting mergers and other monopolistic formations do not seem to accomplish much from the viewpoint of optimal resource allocation and entrepreneurial innovations. The problems which antitrust laws face today resemble the heads of the mythological Lernaean Hydra, for in the place of every problem solved two others appear.

Consolidations and mergers may lead to better organizations and research and lower unit costs. To break or discourage such efficient formations is to punish efficiency and success. Antitrust laws and related restrictions should probably discourage price fixing and employment malpractices rather than obstruct mergers which can improve quality and reduce the cost of production. One could argue in favor of replacing all antitrust laws with modern and simplified pieces of legislation which would recognize the present real conditions of the oligopolistic and monopolistic structure of the domestic and international markets. This is what can be observed in the EC and to some extent in the United States, particularly for firms dealing with foreign trade and investment in the face of severe competition.

Public regulations and public enterprises appeared as an alternative to the shortcomings of the antitrust legislation. The responsibility of public utility regulations in the United States is mostly entrusted to state and local agencies. However, federal government commissions have also been introduced to reinforce local and state controls, mainly during and after the Great Depression. They include the Federal Power Commission (FPC), regulating gas and electricity; the Securities and Exchange Commission (SEC), regulating stock and security markets; the Federal Communications Commission (FCC), controlling telephone and telegraph as well as radio and TV services; the Interstate Commerce Commission (ICC), regulating interstate and foreign trade movements; the Federal Aviation Agency (FAA) and the Civil Aeronautics Board (CAB), responsible for enforcing airline safety rules and economic aviation regulations, respectively. However, the CAB was abolished at the end of 1984, after 46 years in operation, and the Department of Transportation assumed some of its remaining functions.

Parallel commissions or other business control institutions exist or are at a development stage in the EC economies. Thus, the European Court of Justice upheld the European Commission's right to raid companies suspected of price fixing and other anticompetition practices. As a result, the Commission raided several European companies suspected of price fixing and inspected their books. The inspection included subsidiaries of the Dow Chemical Company and other American firms.

Excessive government interventions into the market process, especially in the EC, through regulations and controls may, however, alter entrepreneurial investment decisions and, *ceteris paribus*, retard growth.[2]

Thus, environment and health and safety regulations may require investment which might otherwise be used in plant and equipment. They may also require a sufficient workforce to operate needed control equipment and administer legal activities and office work without adding salable outputs. Nonetheless, public regulations are expected to yield contributions to total welfare, such as improvements in health and safety, that are difficult to measure and cannot be fully reflected in reported output. Thus, further research is needed and more efficient measurement of the economic impacts of public regulations on a society to determine if their total beneficial effects overpass their detrimental effects on productivity. For in general, United States antitrust regulations and similar controls in the EC nations have indirect and modest influences on private sector allocations and free market operations.

Recent efforts to remove excessively burdensome regulations from the United States and the EC economies have fallen short of the political rhetoric and limited goals have been achieved. The bulk of deregulations on both sides of the Atlantic concerns transportation, financial services, environment, energy, and communications. Implementation of deregulations, though, gave more freedom to airlines and railroads to set prices as well as to commercial banks to freely set deposit interest rates after the elimination of ceilings on such rates.

Government regulation of airlines, for example, was responsible for high labor costs and low efficiency. Since 1978, however, when the United States government's sheltering regulations of airlines was ended, increased competition suppressed operation costs including wages, which were reduced in a number of cases. Similar deregulation trends can be observed also in the EC countries. However, there is the danger that smaller companies will be swallowed up by large ones, which eventually may control the market and charge higher prices. Also, problems of proper maintenance and dangers of air accidents may appear.

Mergers and Acquisitions

Managers, people with plenty of money, banks, financiers, and numerous yuppies (some of whom were previous hippies) form groups and raise sufficient funds to acquire common shares of other companies in order to control them. This phenomenon can be observed on both sides of the Atlantic and the antitrust authorities seem to be confused and skeptical concerning this new trend of mergers and acquisitions. Scores of buyouts and friendly or hostile takeovers occur within the United States and the EC as well as between the two continents. Proposals of mergers and acquisitions are either accepted by company stockholders and managers or rejected. In the second case, corporate raiders may come back with more attractive proposals or other competitors may enter the battle offering better terms. Payments may be in cash, through loans, or based on future earnings. Competition in products turns to competition in acquisitions of whole companies and real investment in plants and equipment turns mostly to financing mergers and buyouts. Some brokers collect large fees, at times in a fraudulent manner, like Michael Milken, a former head of "junk bond" trading at Drexel Burnham Lambert, Inc. (already under bankruptcy), with $650 million in fees a year, and Alfred Elliot, a specialist in mergers and acquisitions at the law firm of Schiff, Hardin and Waite.

The main argument in favor of takeovers and acquisitions is that they are used to unseat inefficient managements and corporate bureaucracies. They result in corporate restructuring and asset redeployment for higher productivity and greater competitiveness. The takeover boom, with so many takeovers and leveraged buyouts (LBOs), mainly in the 1980s, led mostly to economic gains. As the argument goes, a number of companies on the brink of bankruptcy were saved and turned to be profitable, as happened with T.W.A. and other United States and EC firms, although sometimes with concessions by labor unions. Entrenched inefficient managers, counterproductive vice presidents, and stagnant executives, who cannot be otherwise removed easily with true elections, are changed or eliminated. This is the way to make management accountable and enterprises more productive, instead of creating a corporate welfare state by compensating mediocre executive officers according to the size of companies and not according to their profitability.

Large amounts of capital borrowed by LBOs come from pension funds with the expectations of good returns for the support of future retirees. However, pension funds could invest directly in takeovers instead of being lenders and running too much a risk. Also, with such pension funds becoming equity investors, instead of lenders, in-between dealers would not be needed, corporate debt would be reduced, managements would become more interested in enhancing shareholder value and productivity would be raised.

A serious argument against takeovers and leveraged buyouts is that they transform investment banks and financial markets into casino institutions with armies of brokers, accountants, lawyers, and arbitragers competing for short-run profits.[3] Giant leveraged buyouts and acquisitions, such as that of RJR Nabisco Inc., worth some $25 billion, by Kohlberg Kravis Roberts and Company in the United States, Rowntree of Britain, Britoni of Italy, and Nestlé of Switzerland, monopolize the market and misdirect finances from productive investment ventures into speculative bets and game activities.

Takeover bets and trades financed mainly with "junk" bonds make the capital development a byproduct of casino operations. Long-term real investments are cut back in favor of short-run risky operations, corporate assets are rearranged toward less productive ventures, and efficient managers become financial moguls and paper entrepreneurs. Less engineers and production managers, but more financial specialists and lawyers (twenty in 10,000 citizens in the United States compared to only one in Japan) are trained, and the speculative spree with borrowed money continues in a fashion similar to that of the 1920s. On the surface the economy looks strong but underneath unhealthy elements grow as corporate, government, and private debts increase, productivity slows down, and the risk of depression looms in the background.

In leveraged buyouts (LBOs) brokerage houses and their executives (the yuppies with the golden parachutes), as well as the paper-shuffling law firms, appeared to be the winners, while the little investors buying junk bonds may suffer when these paper machineries collapse. Such corporate mergers and acquisitions brought hefty fees to the law firms (some $10.6 billion by 100 United States law firms in 1988 alone). However, LBOs may be justified in case such arrangements are needed to survive competition from other countries. Otherwise, the enthusiasm for LBOs seems to have reach a peak and caution is exercised in many instances. Below are some recent cases of mergers and acquisitions.

Paramount Communications was engaged in a takeover battle with Time Inc. in 1989. Cablevision Systems Corporation was also actively engaged in a bid to acquire Time Inc. To avoid such hostile takeovers, Time Inc. merged with Warner Communications into the Time Warner Inc., which became the world's largest media and entertainment conglomerate, worth $25.2 billion. However, concerns about the monopolistic power created by the Time-Warner merger have been raised by major television networks and other entertainment firms (mainly in records, magazines, TV production, movies, book publishing, and cable programming), which expect more difficulties in future competition. Plans are for Time Warner, Inc. to create a homogeneous market everywhere, particularly in the European Community, following the empire-building process of media production and distribution, mainly by satellites, of Rupert Murdoch and Robert Maxwell.

Since Time Warner, Inc., merged in July 1989, the first joint operation of that company was announced. It involves publisher Little, Brown and Co., owned by Time, Inc., and Warner Books to produce both hardcover and paperback books.

The boom in takeovers and LBOs makes the valuing of the related companies by their cash flow (that is, net income, plus depreciations, plus depletion, plus amortization) popular. For example, Paramount Communications Inc. asked Wall Street to look at its cash flow status instead of its earnings for a related takeover.

Mergers and acquisitions became common for the United States airline industry as well, not only by foreign but also by domestic carriers. Thus, U.S. Air joined operations with Piedmont Aviation. However, hasty mergers such as that of Continental Airlines, Inc., with the failing People Express Airlines, Inc., in 1987 proved to be unsuccessful.

In 1989, UAL, the parent of United Airlines, was to be acquired by its pilots and partially by British Airlines for $6.75 billion, in competition with Marvin Davis, a Californian financier, and Coniston Partners, a New York investor group. Although not concluded, because of the refusal of United States and Japanese banks to finance the takeover, the UAL deal initiated a buyout price of $300 a share from $120 four months before. A similar buyout proposal of American Airlines by Donald Trump inflated its stock prices from around $80 to $120. However, the financing of these deals and other leveraged buyouts by junk bonds became problematic. This was the main reason for the drop in the stock market by 190.58 points on October 13, 1989, the second largest decline in history since the October 19, 1987 drop by 508 points. Percentage-wise, though, the decline was 6.9 percent compared to 22.6 percent in 1987 and 11.7 percent (or 30.6 points) on October 29, 1929.

The drug industry is also stricken with mergermania. In a recent $11.5 billion deal, Bristol-Myers merged with Squibb to form Bristol-Myers Squibb, the world's second largest drug company, with about $4.5 billion in sales and $600 million in research spending a year. Other recent deals include Smith Kline Beckman, which was bought by Beecham for $7.7 billion; Dow Chemical Company bought 67 percent of Marion Laboratories for $5.5 billion; White Knight Eastman Kodak got Sterling Drug Company for $5.1 billion; American Home Products is in the process of buying A. H. Robins for $3 billion.

A leveraged buyout of American Medical International Inc. by an investment group, which includes the First Boston Corporation and the Pritzker family of Chicago, was concluded for $2.14 billion over other less attractive proposals. American Medical, which operates some seventy-nine acute-care and psychiatric hospitals in the United States and abroad, plans to sell twenty-five of the hospitals in Europe to repay part of its debt. Also Black and Decker Corporation purchased Emhart Corporation for $2.8 billion.

Fiserv, Inc., a computer service in Wisconsin, acquired Northeast Datacom, Inc., a data processing firm in Connecticut. Another firm, though, General Business Corporation, called off a merger in which it would have 58 percent of the combined company with Adage, Inc., a computer graphics firm of Massachusetts.

The Reebok Company, known for its sport products, bought the Boston Whaler, which is specializing in fast boat engines and other sport products, at the price of $42 million, and so on. More details on mergers and acquisitions involving the EC can be found in chapter 8 of this book.

The speculation fever and the anticipation of acquisitions have driven stock prices fictitiously up. It was realized that sales of assets could not support the financing of takeovers of the companies considered, and managers of pension and mutual funds offered large blocks of stock for sale, thereby forcing prices down. Such events may end the speculative game of takeovers for the years to come through junk bonds or other financially weak instruments. Already, the fever of takeovers via junk bonds has begun to subside.

Insider-Trading Regulations

It seems that acquisition and investment scandals from insider-trading in the EC countries are modest by American standards. Nevertheless, they are spread rapidly all over Europe. Thus, speculators and investors bought some 220,000 shares of Triangle Industries, the American packaging company in France, after they learned secretly from government officials that Pechinery Metal Company, a state-owned metal firm, planned a $1.26 billion friendly acquisition of Triangle. Although the suspicious stock purchases were made in the United States through French, Swiss, and other European brokers, this became a public scandal in France, affecting François Mitterrand's government. About $10 million insider-trading profits were made by buying at $10 a share before Pechinery announced it would buy Triangle at $56 a share. That is why suggestions are being made for adopting the standards of the United States Securities and Exchange Commission (SEC) and reinforcing the power of the related French Bourse Commission. Already heavy fines and up to two years in prison are the penalties for insider-trading in France and heavier ones in Britain.

The rapid spread of telecommunications and portfolio transactions on a world-wide scale necessitates the introduction of insider-trading regulations in all countries where stock market operations occur. Such insider-trading operations in one country affect related transactions in other countries, including the United States and the European Community. Thus, the Japanese Cabinet recently approved tougher regulations concerning insider-trading as a result of the big Recruit Corporation scandal. Under the new rules that went into effect April 1, 1989, together with a 3 percent consumption tax, employees cannot trade before information related to their companies has been disseminated in two or more public forums (newspapers, televisions, radios) about events concerning the companies' revenues or assets by more than 10 percent. To avoid fraud in stock market trading, the EC countries have prepared or will prepare codes outlawing insider-trading, as the United States has done.

West Germany first drew a code to prevent insider-trading in 1970, and strengthened it in 1976, and again in 1988. The term "insider" includes not only company directors and bankers but also middlemen, accountants, and people working in the credit departments of financial institutions. Although many German executives and German companies accept the code, they still feel that self-regulation is more effective because the disgrace from improper behavior outweighs the related sanctions. In any case, companies not accepting the code of insider-trading are listed as "black sheep." Among a few insider cases were those that involved share-trading of an electrical company, AEG, and the sales of Klockner and Co. notes in the Dusseldorf stock exchange.[4]

Most of the other EC member-nations also have codes outlawing insider-trading or are in the process of drawing new ones. Belgium, Italy, Ireland, Spain, and Greece are in the stages of drawing such codes and regulations. The Commission of the EC proposed in 1987 common rules of insider-trading, which were implemented at the beginning of 1991. Although the West German government initially considered such rules bureaucratic, it started reconsidering its position. It seems that the majority of the EC members favor the introduction of insider-trading laws and the adoption of related rules similar to those of the United States.

EMPLOYEE OWNERSHIP AND SHARE ECONOMY

In recent decades a remarkable development in industrial organization has been introduced in a number of countries, signifying a deviation from both the private and public sectors. Gradually and quietly, workplace committees of workers and employees have come to play a significant role in enterprise decision making concerning wages, working conditions, investments, and similar matters. Such work groups have been developing in the EC countries and recently in the United States. In cooperation with capital, or under a system of employee ownership, they aim at stimulating incentives and improving productivity and welfare. Although they grow at the expense of the traditional labor unions, which presently behave like tamed dogs, they do not seem to raise questions of replacing the authority of owners of property and state. From the point of view of the public sector, such a trend unloads the government subsidy expenditures to moribund enterprises and undesirable controls to a new form of decentralized social activity.

In a number of instances, management encourages labor representation in enterprise decision making, especially in the EC and to some extent in the United States, so that strikes and other union disturbances may be avoided as workers become responsible for decisions affecting them. Moreover, when enterprises, public or private, are not profitable or approach bankruptcy, employees are asked, and frequently accept, to take over management to keep the firm in operation and preserve their jobs. In such cases, the government, or any other responsible authority, is not required to finance and rescue weak or bankrupt enterprises.

In prosperous times, a competitive labor market permits improvement in wages because of the increase in demand for labor relative to supply. But increase in wages and improvement in working conditions may equally or better be achieved under the system of industrial democracy than through the countervailing power of labor unions versus management. However, in times of severe recessions and automation, unemployment increases and workers and unions (with dwindling power) are unable to protect their jobs, let alone keep constant or improve real wages, as was evidenced during recent recessions in both the EC and the United States.

Incentives of participation in a democratized workplace may be able to replace conventional incentives (pay, promotion, discharge) in the market economies of the EC and the United States. Industrial democracy may strengthen and stimulate production. This is important in modern societies because of growing specialization, which makes the person feel stupid and ignorant, according to Adam Smith, and which increases nervousness and rivalry among workmates.[5] Inventiveness and accomplishment, affection, relief, and happiness in the workplace may require replacement of heirarchical and authoritarian structures in enterprises, whether private or public.

Along these lines, John Stuart Mill and Jean Jacques Rousseau believed that collective decisions and participatory democracies advance human intellect, reduce bureaucracy, and increase efficiency.[6] However, care should be taken through employees' training to make participation workable and practical, otherwise there is the danger of frustration and inefficiency which may drive communities and nations into stagnation, and keep them there. A frantic participation or apathy and too great a public preoccupation with politics may make the system unworkable and inefficient, or may lead to the creation of a professional elite in place of an old bureaucracy.

Years ago Joseph Schumpeter suggested that a new economic system, known as "people's capitalism," may combine the advantages of both capitalism and socialism. Recently, some success lessons in that direction can be observed in the United States, the EC, Japan, and other economies through the spread of ownership.[7]

The spread of ownership to employees and individuals, mainly in the EC countries, might be the answer to problems with bureaucracy and inefficiency of a growing public sector. This would be the result of the expansion of democratic ideals and widespread educational improvement. People would learn to release their talents and combine their efforts in decision making and productive cooperation for the betterment of themselves and society. They would stop worshipping the state or being directed or pressed by the authorities in their activities. On the other hand, they would resent the practice of being exploited by other people, or adhere to the myths of the economically powerful who are presented as the exclusive magicians of economic betterment. From that point of view, oppressive communism, as well as exploitative capitalism, may need modifications and reforms. Even the Yugoslav model of self-management, with a good part of state control, might not be advisable on these grounds.

The self-management or the labor-capital co-sharing system, wisely managed, can probably be made more efficient for attaining economic ends than any alternative yet in sight. The main problem of the EC and the United States economies is to work out a social organization which shall be efficient in achieving the best results with the least possible costs, without offending people's notions of freedom and a satisfactory way of life.[8]

Thus, the main question for the countries considered is how to attain acceptable material goals while preserving freedom and moral values. Rapid economic development and removal of market imperfections and state bureaucracies call for a new form of management organization. Moreover, efficient allocation of resources and exploitation of external economies may require departure from the strictures of the competitive market or state controls.

The limitations of the private and public sectors and the avoidance of extremes, or the pursuit of moderation in freedom and welfare, as Aristotle and the Pythagorians advocated centuries ago, may be achieved through a new system of employee ownership and enterprise decision making. An economic system in which working people participate in enterprise decision making, as is developing in the EC, the United States, and Japan, may be considered as a healthy basis for an effective democratic way of life with more political freedom, less inequality and higher efficiency. The proverb that "in capitalism man exploits man, in communism it is the other way around," may be avoided in such a system.

Employee ownership is a successful process which saves moribund companies, reduces unemployment, and increases investment and productivity. It is a process of democratization of capital that is growing year after year on both sides of the Atlantic. By being partners in the ownership of the enterprises in which they work, the workers benefit if these enterprises are successful and usually they preserve their jobs when they are unsuccessful. On the contrary, if the workers were not partners in the ownership of their companies, they would not benefit much in success—but they might pay with the sacrifices of their own jobs in cases of the companies' failures. Although there may be cases of confusion in wage determination and other policies when there is coincidence of management and ownership by employees, workers and employees may know more about their companies than anyone else. However, wages and salaries have to be set by competition, not in-house by employee owners who may care only for their short-run benefits.

The decline of the competitiveness of some companies usually leads to unemployment and loss of income. The question posed therefore is: Can employee ownership save such companies? Recent trends show a positive response, as more and more United States and EC companies approaching bankruptcy come under the employee stock ownership plans (ESOPs). They manage to cut costs and, as a result, to line up financial backing from banks and other institutions. However, employee ownership requires good employee-management relations, so that employee owners would not strike against management and vice versa. In many cases, though, the key to success for such companies under ESOPs is whether there is demand for their products. Demand, in turn, is normally stimulated through price decreases from cost cutting, which labor can achieve easier than management. When ESOPs lower wages, expectations are that they recoup by increased capital earnings and restored competitiveness.

Employee ownership, as practiced in the United States and the EC, is democratizing access to capital and transforms labor workers into capital workers by using corporations' credit to allow employees to buy their shares. Modern capital formation and new technology require commercial financing and insurance and not so much old-fashion saving and self-financing. Not only wealthy persons with accumulated savings or inheritances can buy companies but employees and workers can as well, through the availability of credit by financial institutions. This is the way to split ownership, instead of having wealth concentration. (For example, all non-residential productive assets are owned by only about 5 percent of American families.) In addition, productivity and competitiveness would increase by a motivated work force of employee-owners. Automation and demand stabilization require that the economy supplements labor employment with capital ownership and labor workers with capital workers—a transition and a combination essential to private property and a free market.

United States ESOPs

Employee stock ownership plans, or ESOPs, have spread rapidly all over the United States. Some 9,800 plants with about 10 million workers, compared to about half a million in 1976, are under such plans, according to the National Center for Employee Ownership. They include such companies as Phillips Petroleum, Weirton Steel (the largest completely employee-owned company), LTV Steel Company, ARCO, Dan River, U.S. Sugar Corporation, Cone Mills Corporation, Time Warner Inc., Rath Packing, O and O (Owned and Operated), Rochester Products, Fastener Industries, American Standard Co., Stone Construction Equipment, Procter and Gamble, Polaroid, Bera of Ohio, Gore and Associates, Makers of Gore-Texas, Avis, Oregon Steel Mills, Quad/Graphics, Texaco, Ralston Purina, J. C. Penney, TWA, Seymour Speciality Wire, and National Can Corporation.[9]

Although labor unions have in many cases opposed employee ownership, especially in the United States, they recently started to support the establishment of employee-owned firms, as happened in the case of United Auto Workers (UAW) and United Press International (U.P.I.). Today the employee-owned companies represent as much as 8 percent of the United States workforce and in some fifteen years are expected to increase to 18 percent, equal to the present members of labor unions.

A number of companies in the United States, and to a lesser extent in the EC, offer ESOPs for pension funds and profit sharing while others use leveraged ESOPs to avoid unwanted takeovers. Employees and workers agree to buy the firms in which they work and offer concessions to avoid buyouts by other firms. Tax deductions, up to 25 percent of the annual payroll of the company's contributions to ESOPs plans, and other incentives, are offered by the United States federal government to encourage employee ownership. Also, lenders to ESOPs in the United States do not have to pay income taxes on half of the interest they collect. Such tax breaks are estimated to be two to three billion dollars each year.

Moreover, loans and other support measures are provided particularly by the

EC member states to problematic and moribund firms. As long as the states preserve complete or partial control of such firms, these rescue operations tend to be institutionalized and introduce a modern form of undesirable fiscal activity. However, with the introduction of a share economy and the employee ownership of enterprises, such government interventions and undesirable controls can be reduced or eliminated.

Facing the possibility of takeovers by corporate raiders, a number of firms sell stocks to their employees or establish an ESOP. Thus, Lockheed Corporation, which makes cargo planes, missiles, and other military hardware, decided to put 17 percent of its shares in the hands of its employees. As a technology-rich firm with a depressed stock price, it became a target of a takeover bid. With employees and workers holding a sizeable percentage of its stock, it would be more difficult for another company or a raider to take over Lockheed.

To avoid a possible takeover by Hanson PLC of Britain, Xerox Corporation, a Connecticut-based company, decided to establish an ESOP with 10 percent outstanding shares and to repurchase 11 percent of its stock. The employee stock plan, the largest single block of voting shares, would be financed by loans from a consortium of banks led by First National Bank of Chicago. It puts employees and stockholders in the same boat, with 10 percent of the shares in friendly employee hands. Likewise, Conrail (Consolidated Rail Corporation), a United States privatized company, is considering the creation of an ESOP as an anti-takeover measure.

As mentioned previously, the United Airlines pilots' union was considering participation with British Airways and United's management to take over the UAL Corporation, the airline's parent company. The employee stake in the airline's ownership (about 70 percent) was in the wake of a takeover by Marvin Davis, a California investor. An alternative to this management-led buyout, which would include an ESOP, is a leveraged recapitalization, under which the company would make payments to its shareholders with borrowed money. However, the deal was stalled because Japanese and American banks did not finance it. Nevertheless, the union came back with new offers and labor cost saving, and the battle of acquisition continues.

Because pension funds of some 30 million employees were used to finance hostile takeovers, legislation was introduced in the United States Congress to give the employees control over $1 trillion of their pension funds. It requires the participation of an equal number of employee and employer representatives on a joint board of trustees where issues regarding corporation pension funds are discussed. This means that employees would have a voice in how these funds are invested but not in a company's contributions or benefit payments. Although corporate executives argue that employees lack the sophistication necessary to make modern financial decisions affecting the investment of pension funds, employees think that the pension funds are a form of deferred compensation about which they should have a say, instead of letting management invest these funds in "junk bonds" and other risky ventures.

The United States House Ways and Means Committee, however, is considering restrictions on current tax breaks for ESOPs, unless the participants own at least 30 percent of a company's stock. Such restrictions refer to the repeal of the tax preference that allows financial institutions to avoid taxes on up to 50 percent of the interest they receive from loans to ESOPs. Also, the committee might repeal the deduction for dividends paid on employers' securities obtained by ESOPs and require taxpayers who sell securities to ESOPs to have held them for three years before the sale in order to be eligible for tax benefits. The legislation aims at closing an "abusive loophole" and collecting revenue for the governmental budget.

At times, labor unions buy and sell companies instead of letting others do that. Also, cross-Atlantic raiders are involved in ESOPs. Thus Sir James Goldsmith, the British raider who acquired the parent Crown Zellerbach Corporation a few years ago, will keep 10 percent of the equity and the rest (about 30 percent) will go to the other union's financiers and debt holders. However, out of $6 billion in leveraged ESOPs during the year 1988 and $5.5 billion in 1987, only a few were initiated by unions.

EC ESOPs

In contrast, Britain and France have resolved, to some extent, the process of denationalization or "privatization" of state or semi-state enterprises through total or partial employee ownership. Thus, the British Telecon (the state-owned telephone monopoly), Ferranti (the industrial electronics firm), British Aerospace (the aircraft and missiles firm), Britoil, British Sugar, Jaguar (the luxury car maker), British Petroleum, Cable and Wireless, and British Airways, which were totally or partially owned by the state, have been or are in the process of total or partial denationalization (this is called Thatcherism) or have been taken to the market, with employee participations. The main reason is to encourage competition and increase efficiency. Thus, the stocks of the denationalized Telecon Co. were divided between British institutions (47 percent), Telecon employees and the public (39 percent), and foreign investors (14 percent, United States, Canada, and Japan).

Moreover, the National Freight Company (producing trucks) was sold to employees in 1981. Since then it has become profitable and is expanding for the first time. On the other hand, two private shipyards, Tyne and Scott Lithgow, agree with the workers' unions to cut wage costs and increase productivity so that they can eliminate the threat of closure.

To promote employee ownership and popular capitalism, Britain introduced recently a law that provides for the establishment of Employee Share Ownership Plans (ESOPs). The lack of a legal status and the uncertainty over tax exemption of ESOPs have discouraged British firms from establishing ESOPs in the past. Now with tax relief assured, a number of companies transfer ownership shares to their workers and employees. In a typical case, a trust or an ESOP borrows money and buys a company's equity. The company in subsequent years makes tax-free payments to the trust which repays its debt and releases equivalent amounts of shares to the employees.

Although there are only fifteen ESOPs in Britain, compared to more than 8,000 in the United States, the tax relief and other advantages they enjoy would speed their spread to other companies as well. A conventional management buyout (MBO) would enjoy tax relief only if it includes an ESOP through distribution of shares to the workers. The split of ownership through ESOPs is supported by almost all political persuasions, including the right-wing Adam Smith Institute and the left-wing Fabian Society in Britain. They are neither a capitalistic tool as wealth and power is split to many workers, nor a creeping collectivist tool as employees and workers become capital or wealth owners. The tax relief applies to those British ESOPs that distribute all shares to workers within seven years. However, the law discourages family-owned firms from establishing ESOPs as yet, because they must pay taxes on capital gains realized from sales of equity to an ESOP.[10]

Depending on the political philosophy of the British government in power, some companies were taken over by the state and later were transferred to the private sector to be taken over again by the state and so on. Thus, the steel industry was nationalized in 1949, denationalized in the 1950s, and renationalized in 1967. Similar companies, such as British Gas, the coal industry, and the public electric power corporation, as well as shipyards, airports, bus services, armament factories, hotels, ferries, public housing, garbage collection, and a host of other services are all being prepared for sale or leasing by the Thatcher government to the private sector or to their workers. Private and overseas investors, in addition to pension funds, and the employees of these companies, are expected to be the major stockholders. However, the Labor Party has pledged to renationalize some privatized companies to protect the consumers and the workers.

Along these lines, France embraces "Popular Capitalism" and it is in the process of selling off government-owned industry to employees and other private investors. The campaign of denationalizing some sixty-five public enterprises, a number of which had been nationalized by Charles de Gaulle, has been warmly received by employee-investors and other domestic and foreign financiers. They include such companies as Paribas, Saint-Gobain, Agency Havas, Compagnie Générale d'Électricité and three major commercial banks.

In Western Europe as a whole, a total of about 2,000 state enterprises, worth some $130 billion, are expected to be sold in two years. The main reason for this denationalization is to encourage competition, increase efficiency, and remove governmental subsidies.

As in all market economies, the West German economy is influenced by private and public sector activities. The social market economy (SME) of Germany is based primarily on the private sector, the free market mechanism and labor-capital management or codetermination (Mitbestimmung). However, positive governmental activities are necessary to create a healthy environment for the market system, to break monopolies and cartels (through the Law Against Limitations on Competition, which is similar to United States antitrust legislation), and to provide Social Security and welfare.

Nevertheless, public and union-owned enterprises play an important role in certain sectors of the German economy such as transportation, communications, postal services, dwellings construction and, to some extent, banking, and even mining and metallurgical operations. Union-owned enterprises, created to maximize social benefits, not profits, include Gruppe Neue Heimat, a large apartment construction company, Coop-Unternehmen, the second retail trade firm, and the Bank für Gemein Wirtschaft, an inter-regional bank, providing credit facilities all over Germany.

Through large holding companies the federal government owns stocks in more than 3,000 firms. However, the waves of denationalization and decontrolization which prevail all over Europe, including the Soviet Union, engulfed West Germany as well. Volkswagen and Veba are two companies in which privatization was carried out recently, through sales of shares to private groups, employees, and low-income persons on a preferential basis. This mixed economic system, combined with a relatively harmonious labor-capital comanagement, and a high rate of saving and investment, is mainly responsible for the post-World War II German rapid growth or the so-called economic miracle.

Employee ownership is spreading not only to large EC countries, where a number of state-owned or private enterprises are sold partially or totally to their employees and workers but small ones as well. Thus in Portugal, União Cervejeira, S.A., which makes soft drinks, sold one-third of 3.2 million shares to its employees for 2,300 escudos or $15.3 each, about one-half to the public for 2,500 escudos or $16.7, and one-sixth to small savers and emigrant workers for 2,400 escudos or $16 each.

Related legislation for the establishment of ESOPs has also been enacted in Greece since 1988. It provides for the option of giving shares to the employees and workers by the companies in which they work, instead of wage increases and other premiums. Because of the expected advantages of ESOPs, especially for weak and problematic public and private enterprises, all the political parties voted in favor of this legislation in the Greek Parliament.[11]

In order to boost the single market's "social dimension," the European Commission considers certain ways of workers' participation in the process of decision making of the companies in which they work. One way is to follow the West German model in which workers are represented on supervisory boards. Another way is that of France with separate workers' councils. Or a new system to be agreed upon by management and the work force via collective bargaining may give the workers the option to participate or not. It seems that the Commission would base its decision, regarding workers' participation, on Articles 54 and 100A of the Treaty of Rome, which allow majority voting on such matters. To smooth out disagreements, particularly from Britain, the commissioners prefer to use the term "involvement" instead of "participation." Moreover, proposals are advanced that workers would merely share information on plant closures, alliances, and other strategic decisions but not consultation on day-to-day operations. Nevertheless, the European Parliament wants some form of workers' involvement in decision making.

A company under the European statute would be subject to the EC rules not only regarding workers' involvement but on mergers, acquisitions and joint ventures, as well as a single tax code. Companies incorporating under the EC rules could be able to write off losses in one member nation against taxes in other member nations. However, a number of the EC governments object to this privilege because they fear that their tax revenue might be reduced.

A Revenue-Sharing System

Different schemes of employee participation in decision making, revenue, and ownership have been developed in a number of countries, including the EC and the United States. In the system of revenue-sharing, employees would receive a certain percentage of revenue instead of fixed wages. Paying part or all of workers' compensation in the form of periodic bonuses has the financial advantage of providing the enterprise with working capital for several months. Part of these bonuses may remain with a special fund for additional pension or for extra payment after a number of years of work.

The revenue-sharing system, in one form or another, gradually is acquiring worldwide importance. One can argue that the relaxation of the rules of wage determination through union-management negotiations in the United States and the EC countries is due to the abandonment, in many cases, of the fixed wage system. Even the non-adjustment of the United States minimum wages ($3.35 per hour for years) to inflation may be considered as an indirect way of accepting the principle of revenue-sharing.

There seems to be a built-in mechanism in the revenue-sharing system which tends to lead the economy to equilibrium at full employment of labor. On the other hand, the existing wage system may require long periods to slowly move the economy, through an invisible hand, toward full employment. Because of the inflexibility in wages and other sticky variables, only by accident may there be full employment in the economy. In a share economy, with wages determined as percentages of revenue, employers will not tend to lay off workers in recessionary periods. Rather, they will tend to employ more workers because of absolute lower wages. Likewise is the case during the upswings of the economy, when aggregate demand increases, the economy expands, and more workers and employees are expected to be employed.[12]

Nevertheless, in a stationary or unchanging economy there is not much difference between the share system and the wage system. In the real world, however, sociopolitical and economic changes are customary and unpredictable disturbances and disequilibria are expected, especially in the market economies of the EC and the United States. Therefore, a balancing or equilibrating mechanism, notably that of a share economy, may be of great importance in leading the economy to stability and full employment. The revenue-sharing system may achieve full employment without inflation. Thus, the United States, the EC, and other market and even planned economies may solve the sticky dilemma between inflation and recession with share economy. Perhaps the problem of the inflationary pressures, that the Keynesian system introduced through deficit spending, may be solved forever. The synchronization of wages with revenue may mitigate the problem of cost-push inflation without increasing unemployment. At the same time, there may be no need for raising budgetary expenditures for countercyclical purposes and the bureaucratic and inefficient public sector may be reduced or at least not increased.

The system of the share economy, practiced successfully in Japan, may provide a solution to the problem of recession or stagnation and inflation (stagflation) which have troubled the market economies of the EC and the United States for more than two decades. The dilemma of simultaneous unemployment and inflation or their alternating path in economic fluctuations may be tackled effectively with a system of labor compensation related to the motivation of the employees and the performance of the enterprises in which they work.

A system of labor remuneration, in which employees are paid a significant part or the total amount of their wages in the form of bonuses according to the revenue of their companies, instead of fixed wages, could increase incentives of production and reduce unemployment. The difference between the revenue-sharing and the profit-sharing systems is that even in the case of no profits or losses workers would receive payments based on the amount of revenue of the company.

A new method of workers' participation that attracts attention in the United States and the EC is the team production system introduced at NUMMI (New United Motor Manufacturing Inc.), the joint venture of General Motors Corporation and the Toyota Corporation in Fremont, California, and Gencorp Automobile in Indiana. The team system is shifting control from the management hierarchy down to the workers who know better how to speed production and correct defects. Also, it eliminates middle management.

WORKERS' CAPITALISM IN EAST BLOC COUNTRIES

In the efforts of Eastern Europe to change from state controlled to market economies, serious questions appear as to the transformation and the new organization these economies will take. Are small and large enterprises to be transferred from the public to the private sector and in what form? How would the transfer of ownership be achieved? Through state sales to individuals and foreign investors or by making workers and employees total or partial owners of the firms in which they work?

Although we do not have much experience in applying such economic reforms, some form of workers' capitalism or employee stock ownership plans (ESOPs) could be used in the process of privatization. This economic system avoids extreme wealth accumulation and monopolization by individuals or the state and combines advantages from both the capitalist and the socialist systems, and it is in accordance with Joseph Schumpeter's theory of "people's capitalism."

Under this system, that has been implemented to some extent by the United States, Japan, and the European Community, work incentives and labor productivity improve, strikes and other disputes are less likely since employee-owners share in decision making, and income distribution is more equitable. Thus, the saying that "in capitalism man exploits man, in communism it is the other way around" may not be relevant to a workers' capitalism implemented in the East Bloc countries that are under economic reforms.

Along with the democratization of the Eastern Bloc (Comecon) countries, there should be an establishment of proper institutions regarding property titles and mortgages for credit, as well as patent and copyright laws, to ensure an orderly transfer of ownership. Such efforts can be financed and supported by Western countries and world institutions, while international mutual funds can capitalize on Eastern Europe's dramatic changes and invest in productive ventures. As government subsidies are reduced and prices and unemployment rise, Eastern European people need Western support because it is difficult to implement such drastic changes alone. It is important to remember that, in the long run, such a policy is expected to be beneficial to the Western economies as well.

For example, in Poland the new economic plan of solidarity-led government incorporates, among other reforms of transferring state ownership to private ownership, the setting up of ESOPs. In addition, the plan sets up a stock market where the stocks of the employees and other individuals and institutions can be exchanged. Other East Bloc countries are expected to introduce similar measures in their economic reforms.

PRODUCTIVITY GROWTH

Human Resources

Both the EC and the United States are rich in human resources and advanced in skilled workers. The total population of the twelve EC countries (323.6 million in 1987) is higher than that of the United States (243.8 million). Given that the total GNP is almost the same as that of the United States, per capita GNP is lower in the EC than in the United States. As Table 4.1 shows, from the twelve EC nations, Denmark and West Germany have the highest GNP per capita (a little more than that of the United States), followed by France, the Netherlands, Belgium, Luxembourg, Britain, and Italy. Spain, Ireland, Greece, and Portugal have relatively low GNP per capita. However, depending on the appreciation or depreciation of the dollar in terms of the individual currencies of the EC countries changes in total and per capita GNP may be significant.

Table 4.1
Population, GNP (billions of U.S. dollars, current prices) and GNP Per Capita (current dollars) for the EC Countries and the United States, 1987

Country	Population	GNP	Per capita GNP
Belgium	9.9	139.7	14,090
Britain	56.9	666.7	11,723
Denmark	5.1	97.5	19,041
France	55.6	846.9	15,229
Germany, W.	61.0	1,129.9	18,526
Greece	10.0	45.9	4,584
Ireland	3.6	25.6	7,180
Italy	57.4	632.1	11,021
Luxembourg	0.4	5.0	12,500
Netherlands	14.6	213.5	14,581
Portugal	10.3	33.4	3,229
Spain	38.8	284.0	7,312
Total EC	323.6	4,120.2	12,732
USA	243.8	4,486.2	18,403

Source: United States Government, Department of Commerce. For Luxembourg, International Monetary Fund, *International Financial Statistics.*

Urban population, as a percentage of total population, remained relatively constant or increased slightly in the United States and in the advanced EC countries during the last three decades. It is 74 percent for the United States, compared to 72 percent in 1965. For France the figures are 74 and 67 percent, respectively. For West Germany, urban population increased from 79 percent of total population in 1965 to 86 percent currently; for Britain from 87 to 92 percent; for Italy from 62 to 68 percent; for Spain 61 to 77 percent; for Greece from 48 to 61 percent; and for Portugal from 24 to 32 percent, respectively.

These figures indicate that urbanization depends, to a large extent, on the level of economic development of the country. In less developed countries, more people migrate from the rural areas to urban centers. However, as the countries become more advanced the urbanization rate slows down and eventually it reaches a certain plateau.

In the United States, and more so in the EC countries, economic policies, directly or indirectly, encouraged the movement of labor and other resources to urban centers during the postwar years through infrastructural and educational facilities, credit, and other public services. The existence of high power capacity, the convenience for raw material imports, and the availability of skilled workers are additional reasons of concentration in the big cities. As a result, the gap in income and wealth distribution between the urban centers and the rural areas became larger, industrial and commercial growth flourished in urban centers, and many poor regions remained backward.

To reduce interregional differences, the governments of a number of countries, particularly France, Italy, Spain, Greece, and Ireland, provided investment incentives such as tax concessions, generous depreciation allowances, credit facilities, and even labor subsidies. However, the cost of living, especially that of housing, is higher in the large cities than in the provinces. This, together with recent problems of pollution, congestion, and crime, may lead to a gradual decentralization from the cities back to the countryside with its fresh air, natural serenity, and other amenities.

Concerning migrant workers and refugees from non-EC nations, there is skepticism that the integration of Western Europe could result in a "fortress" of a different sort. Presently, like the United States, some countries of the EC, such as West Germany, Belgium, and Britain are more open to migrant workers and asylum seekers than other countries such as France and Denmark. It is possible that the EC single market project and the process of unification may result in strict rules regarding immigration and refugee rights. Instead of using the existing flexible regulations in one or more member nations, the EC may adopt stricter rules that apply to the entire Community for demographic and security reasons.

In West Germany, there are about 4.6 million foreigners or 8 percent of its population are primarily guest workers from Turkey (637,000 in 1981), Yugoslavia (358,000), Italy (361,000), and Greece (132,000). However, with the new influx of East Germans, employment and housing problems appear.

Mainly because of low wages, particularly in the service sector, the United States has a low level of unemployment (5 to 5.5 percent). The rapid expansion of retail trade, the health care for a growing aging population, and the growth in the financial, communication-computer, and other producers of services increased low-paid service employment. United States private service workers earn 67 percent as much as those in manufacturing compared with 85 percent in West Germany and as high as 93 percent in Japan.

Competition from the EC and other countries will continue until equalization of factor prices, primarily labor prices. Under the pressure, average real wages in the United States fell by 2 percent between 1980 and 1987 and now are about 10 percent below the peak of 1972. Although the unemployment rate is relatively low, lost highly paid manufacturing jobs are ending up in low paid service jobs (hamburger flippers and the like). It is estimated that one manufacturing job lost is equivalent in pay to three newly created jobs.

According to the Bureau of Labor Statistics, hourly labor cost (wages and benefits) in 1988 varied from $18.1 in West Germany to about $16 for the Netherlands, Denmark, and Belgium, $13 for France and Italy, $10.6 for Britain, $10 for Ireland, $8.7 for Spain, $4.6 for Greece, and $2.7 for Portugal. For the United States, the hourly labor cost was $13.9 for the same year. The "charter of fundamental social rights" of the EC would force the poorer EC countries such as Spain, Greece, and Portugal to introduce minimum wages and workers' participation in corporate decisions, thereby increasing labor cost and endangering industrial competitiveness.

Labor unions of the northern EC countries fear that the complete integration of Western Europe may lead to reduction in real wages, huge layoffs, and other setbacks, because it becomes easier for employers to move production to low-wage areas such as the poorer sunbelt countries of Europe, namely Spain, Portugal, southern Italy, and Greece. Moreover, low wage workers from the south would move to wealthier northern countries to compete for higher wages and benefits, while more northerners are expected to relocate to Europe's olive belt. As a result, the wage gap among the EC members nations would be reduced.

To discourage an exodus of jobs from the rich north to the poor south, the EC is in the process of introducing a social charter for minimum work hours, decent retirement, raising the minimum working age from fourteen or fifteen to sixteen, worker's participation in enterprise decision-making, and other benefits. Although such measures are considered as back-door socialism by British and other conservatives, it seems that the Eurocrats and other supporters of labor can manage a comfortable majority in the Euro-Parliament and approve these measures. These measures refer to workers' compensation, pensions, and employee participation in corporate decisions and probably in revenue or ownership, as happens to some extent in the United States and Japan.

The rate of unemployment is higher in the EC than in the United States. After 1982, the United States unemployment declined constantly from 9.7 percent to 5.4 percent of the labor force currently, while that of the EC remained, on the average, constant at around 11 percent. Ireland has the highest rate of unemployment as a percentage of the labor force (19.75 in 1989), followed by Spain (18.75), France, Italy and the Netherlands (11–12), Britain (9.75), Denmark (9), West Germany (8), and Greece and Portugal (7–8). The total employment of the EC (127.3 million workers in 1987) is higher than that of the United States (112.4 million). West Germany has the largest number of workers in millions (27.1) in the EC, followed by Britain (25), France (21.3), Italy (21), Spain (11.4), the Netherlands (5.9), Portugal (4.4), Belgium (3.7), Greece (3.6), Denmark (2.7), and Ireland (1.1).[14]

The United States spends 12 percent of GNP on a health system that provides spotty or no service to millions, Canada spends 8.6 percent, and other Western democracies spend even less to provide some form of national health insurance to their citizens. According to the United States Census Bureau, thirty-five million Americans or 15 percent of the population lack any kind of health insurance.

Table 4.2
Average Annual Rates of Growth of GDP and Per Capita Growth for the EC and the United States

Country	Growth of GDP		GNP Per Capita Annual Growth
	1965-80	1980-87	1965-87
Belgium	3.9	1.3	2.6
Britain	2.4	2.6	1.7
Denmark	2.9	2.5	1.9
France	4.3	1.6	2.7
Germany, W.	3.3	1.6	2.5
Greece	5.6	1.4	3.1
Ireland	5.3	0.9	2.0
Italy	3.8	2.1	2.7
Luxembourg	3.6	1.9	1.6
Netherlands	4.1	1.5	2.1
Portugal	5.5	1.4	3.2
Spain	4.6	2.1	2.3
EC	4.1	1.7	2.4
USA	2.7	3.1	1.5

Source: World Bank, *World Development Report;* and OECD, *National Accounts*, various issues.

Total and Sectoral Rates of Economic Growth

As Table 4.2 shows, the rates of economic growth of almost all the EC countries were lower in the 1980s compared to those of 1965–80. Only Britain and Denmark had about the same growth rates, 2–3 percent per year on the average during the last two decades. However, all the other ten countries had higher growth rates of GDP than Britain and Denmark in 1965–80 but lower rates in the 1980s. On the contrary, the United States rates of GDP growth were lower in 1965–80 and higher in the 1980s.

Because of the huge trade surplus ($73.5 billion in 1988) of West Germany, there were complaints that its economy needed demand stimulation to increase

Table 4.3
Sectorial Average Annual Growth Rates for the EC and the United States

Country	Agriculture		Industry		Services	
	1965-80	1980-87	1965-80	1980-87	1965-80	1980-87
Belgium	0.5	2.6	4.4	1.1	3.8	1.2
Britain	1.6	3.2	- 0.5	1.8	2.2	2.6
Denmark	0.8	4.3	1.8	3.1	3.5	2.2
France	1.0	2.6	4.3	- 0.1	4.6	2.3
Germany, W.	1.4	1.9	2.8	0.4	3.7	2.1
Greece	2.3	- 0.1	7.1	0.4	6.2	2.5
Ireland	NA	2.2	NA	1.7	NA	0.0
Italy	0.8	0.8	4.0	0.5	4.1	2.9
Luxembourg	NA	4.6	NA	3.6	NA	1.9
Netherlands	4.7	5.4	4.0	0.5	4.4	1.9
Portugal	NA	- 0.9	NA	1.0	NA	1.4
Spain	2.6	0.9	5.1	0.4	4.1	2.1

Note: In some cases earlier years' data were available.
Source: World Bank, *World Development Report*; and United Nations, *Yearbook of National Accounts Statistics,* various issues.

imports and raise growth rates in other countries. Indeed, the German government used tax cuts and less restrictive monetary policies and expanded its economy in recent years. It is expected that this policy, together with higher investment in residential construction and heavy foreign demand for German goods, would continue to stimulate the economy and help high growth rates in the coming years, especially as a result of the influx of low-wage laborers from East Germany.

In most of the EC countries and the United States there was a higher average annual growth rate for agriculture in the 1980s than in 1965–1980. Also, there was improvement in industrial growth for the United States, but not much for the EC countries, except for Britain and Denmark. Moreover, all countries considered had lower rates of growth in services in the 1980s than in 1965–1980, as Table 4.3 shows.

The sectorial distribution of GDP for the United States and the advanced EC countries is very small for agriculture (mostly around 2 to 4 percent). However, for less developed Portugal, Ireland, and Greece it is 9 percent, 10 and 16 percent, respectively. For industry, the percentage share of GDP is mostly around

Table 4.4
Sectorial Distribution of GDP for the EC and the United States (percent)

Country	Agriculture		Industry		Services	
	1965	1987	1965	1987	1965	1987
Belgium	5	2	41	31	53	67
Britain	3	2	46	38	51	60
Denmark	9	5	36	29	55	66
France	8	4	38	31	54	66
Germany, W.	4	2	53	38	43	60
Greece	24	16	26	29	49	56
Ireland	NA	10	NA	37	NA	53
Italy	10	4	37	34	53	61
Luxembourg	NA	2	NA	33	NA	64
Netherlands	NA	4	NA	30	NA	66
Portugal	NA	9	NA	40	NA	51
Spain	15	6	36	37	49	57
USA	3	2	38	30	59	68

Source: World Bank, *World Development Report*, various issues.

29 to 40 percent, while that of services varies from 51 percent for Portugal to 56 percent for Greece, 60 for Britain, 66 percent for France, and 68 percent for the United States. Depending on the stage of development, more advanced countries have a relatively small and declining share of the agricultural sector to GDP, a constant or declining share of the industrial sector, and a high and growing share of the service sector, as Table 4.4 shows.[15]

Labor Productivity

In current dollars, American productivity, that is the total value of goods and services over the number of working persons, grew from about $29,000 per worker in 1959 to $37,000 in 1973. If this trend had continued from 1973 to 1988 the average productivity would have been about $48,000 instead of the actual $40,000 compared to $30,000 for the EC.

While the engine of United States economic growth has been stalled for fifteen years, Germany's labor was about 10 percent and Japan's 20 percent more productive. The lower level of research and development in the United States may be considered responsible for comparatively lower levels of inventions and innovations and lower rates of productivity growth. For example, 47 percent of United States patents went to foreigners in 1988, compared to only 19 percent in 1963. Up to 1975 the Germans were the forerunners in patents, but afterwards the Japanese became first.

The proportion of investment (gross fixed capital formation) to GDP in the 1980s was 18 percent for the United States and 20 percent for the EC, not much different from that of the previous two decades. The incremental capital output ratio (ICOR) in current dollars was 2.6 for the United States and 3.3 for the EC during the same period. If the GDP is multiplied by the ICOR, the total capital stock can be estimated. It was $11.2 trillion for the United States and $11.0 trillion for the EC in 1987. This gives a capital to labor ratio equal to $100,000 for the United States and $86,000 for the EC.

The Europeans and the Japanese use machines and higher productivity technology for work that is done by workers in the United States. For example, unattended machines sell gasoline at night in Europe. United States firms invest less capital per worker compared to other developed nations. Thus, in Germany capital investment per worker is growing twice as fast. As a result productivity growth rates in services and in the overall United States economy are lower than in the EC and Japan. The old-fashioned labor intensive process of production is rapidly being replaced by modern mechanization or robotization. The question though is whether American, European, or other foreign enterprises will do the manufacturing. It seems that the decline in the dollar's exchange rate since 1985 has been the economic offset to low level United States investment in plants, equipment, and research. If investment in innovations and new technology increases, then improvement in productivity would make the United States industries more competitive at home and abroad.

To boost the anemic savings rate for investment financing and high productivity, the United States tax code should stop favoring debt over equity. Interest payments were for years deductible for taxable income but not dividend payments. This leads to overleveraging and the extensive use of junk bonds for financing mergers and acquisitions.

The symptoms of an affluent society and consumerism are rapidly spreading in Europe as they were and still are in the United States. However, according to Stoic teachings, in order to be happy and have inner harmony, individuals should live in accordance with nature: "*Akolouthos ti fisi zin.*" On the other hand, nations, such as the United States and those of the EC, should continue to stress education for higher productivity, a better quality of life, and the "maximization" of social welfare. As Plato mentioned, education and training of members of a society should become the "principle of utmost principles."[16]

Presently, America faces the problem of low productivity growth. This is a phenomenon which seems to support the long neglected theory of stagnation.

With less then 1 percent productivity growth in each of the last twelve years, the standard of living of Americans is falling relative to those in the most advanced nations of Europe and in Japan with a productivity growth of two to four times as rapid. Already, United States average wages are lower than those in the above advanced countries.

One important reason of productivity difference between the United States and its major competitors is less investment in plants and equipment (about two-thirds that of Europe and half that of Japan, where there are ten times as many programmable robots relative to the size of the labor force). To finance such investment, more saving is required. This can be achieved mainly through reducing consumption. It is estimated that if consumption increases by 1 percentage point less than the GNP, in favor of investment, the gap can be closed in about eight years.

Another reason for low United States productivity is the lower level of investment in research and development and a neglected education. American expenditures for civilian research and development is 1.8 percent of GNP, compared to 2.8 percent for Germany and Japan, while the adult functional illiteracy rate is 13 percent, high school graduation is down to 72 percent, and workers have less training (school days are 180 a year compared to 220 in Europe and 240 in Japan).

From a technological point of view, the EC and the United States can both flourish by exploiting their own strengths and by learning from each other. It seems that they are engaging in a competitive struggle from which both are expected to win. The EC is rapidly moving forward in inventions and innovations that it may thrust ahead in the near future. This may be unjustifiably frightening to Americans who seem to be vulnerable to chauvinist calls and may consider other competitor countries, such as Europe and Japan, as economic enemies. American enterprises and policy makers should emphasize long-term investment in research and development (R&D) as well as improvement in workers' education and high capital technology.

Like the ant in Aesop's fable, Europe and Japan save and build for the future, while the United States, like the grasshopper, is singing and entertaining others passing by as if the summer fullness will continue forever. If these conditions continue and the gap in technology-intensive products increases, America may find herself in an inferior position, and the ant may say to the grasshopper, "Well, now that it's winter, why not dance?"

For an improvement in the living standard of American workers and retirees, higher productivity gains are necessary. For the last twenty years output per hour was growing by 1 percent per year, compared to 3 percent in 1948–1965. Although it is hard to isolate the factors responsible for such a productivity decline, failure to invest in new technology, declining domestic savings, and maturation of the economy may be considered as the most important factors that put America in a relatively lower position regarding modernization and global competition.

Low cost transportation, efficient new plants and, in many cases, cheap labor increased foreign competition by the EC, Japan, and other countries, and put American industries on the defensive. Also, the shift away from labor-intensive to more productive capital-intensive industries and low cost of borrowing, due to large amounts of available savings, made other countries more competitive than the United States. On the contrary, the large United States budget deficits, and the low rates of savings and the consequent high interest rates are responsible for high cost of capital and low productivity.

It would seem that fiscal and monetary policies favoring savings and investment, reducing deficits, and subsidizing private and public research and innovations in semiconductors, biochemistry, synthetic fuels, robotics, electronics, and other products of new technology would stop erosion and improve productivity in industry and services. Investment in new plants and equipment in knowledge-intensive industries and in R&D generates new technology and long-term economic growth. Encouraging long-term trading in stocks, modifying the antitrust legislation, and diversifying production are some of the additional measures needed for a highly productive and competitive economy.

The lower level of net investment that has slowed productivity is the main challenge for the United States. Total private investment is the lowest in the post-World War II period. Although gross investment, which includes depreciation or worn-out assets may be satisfactory, net private investment is very low. It is about 2.2 percent of the GNP on the average for this decade, compared to about 3 percent for the period 1950–1980.[17] From the standpoint of productivity, net investment, that is, additions to plants, equipment and other assets, counts more than gross investment that includes replacement of worn-out capital goods. Moreover, investment indexes should not include consumer durables, such as cars and televisions, because it is doubtful if such items increase productivity.

Low level of net United States investment is the result of weak domestic saving and high real interest rates due mainly to large federal deficits. More than the total amount of private saving, that is, about $110 billion (or $5,000 billion GNP times 2.2 percent), is being swallowed up by the budget deficit. Competition for funds to finance the deficit drives up interest rates and crushes investment. Less capital stock is available per worker and productivity declines. Of course, there are large inflows of capital from Europe and other countries, but this capital is largely not directed to new investment and the country is responsible for payments abroad for its servicing. Therefore it is important that budget deficits be cut, pro-investment tax cuts be introduced, and savings be encouraged by totally or partially eliminating taxation on income from savings. An increase in savings would hold down interest rates and finance investment at home and abroad.

Germany with higher wages and income compared to other EC countries, as well as the United States, has a disciplined labor force and a corporate state nature. The individual seems to be secondary to the state's preeminence. Americans are beating up on themselves because Germans are more efficient in productivity and economic performance. Similar work discipline and economic performance can be observed in Germany, compared to Eastern Bloc countries, as well as in Japan.

There are fears that slow United States productivity and the gradual loss of industrial production to the EC, Japan, and other countries may transform the American economy into a peasant economy providing raw material and agricultural products. However, reduction in domestic and foreign deficits is expected to strengthen United States industrial production and help regain initiatives in world trade and investment over the long-run cycle. Moreover, taking away regulation handcuffs from American enterprises would make them more competitive in domestic and world markets. It seems that Americans are at their best when they feel strong in competition and business expansion, Japanese when they are under pressure, and Europeans when they are under the spirit of cooperation and reconstruction.

According to the OECD statistics, United States labor productivity (private sector employment) was about 1 percent per year during the past decade, compared to 1.5 percent for Britain, 2 percent for West Germany, 2.2 percent for France, and 2.5 percent for Japan. During the period 1974–1979, the annual labor productivity was about 0.5 percent for the United States, 1.5 percent for Britain, and 3.8 percent for Germany, France, and Japan. However, in 1960–1973, labor productivity per year was 2 percent for the United States, 3 percent for Britain, about 5 percent for Germany, close to 6 percent for France, and as high as 8.8 percent for Japan.

As mentioned previously, the main reason for low United States productivity growth was low rate of investment. Thus, net investment, that is, gross investment minus depreciation, was only 5 percent of GNP in the 1980s compared with 7 percent in the 1970s. Such sluggish investment and low productivity may be considered as a prolonged wasting disease that may push the United States further toward protectionism.[18] The anorexia of investment and growth may erode future living standards and worsen the international position of the country. Moreover, if foreigners, who finance about half of United States net investment, reduce or stop the inflow of savings, then investment would be even lower. Therefore it seems that the long-run sluggish investment and the low level of productivity may be a bigger threat to the United States economy than a sudden financial heart attack from another stock market crash similar to that of 1987.

In the index of entrepreneurial confidence, Germany is the first in the EC (0.5), followed by Britain (0.2), France (−0.1) and Italy (−0.2). In the United States this index is almost equal to that of Germany.

In manufacturing productivity, Britain is the front runner followed by Italy, France, and Germany. Output per man hour increased by 50 percent in the 1980s for Britain, about 40 percent for Italy, 35 percent for France, and 25 percent for Germany. For the United States, such productivity increased by 35 percent during the same period.

From that standpoint, the concept of Eurosclerosis is gradually changing, particularly regarding Britain and Italy, which are considered the superachievers of Europe in the 1980s. Comparatively low business taxes in Britain are facilitating manufacturing and fast-improving productivity.

Regional Disparities and Urban and Environmental Problems

A serious problem of the European integration is the great disparity in regional economic development among EC member nations. Differences in regional or territorial development can be seen not only among member nations but also in each nation. Certain regions are less advanced than others with regard to economic, sociocultural, and technological development.[19] Previous government policies, particularly in France, Italy, Spain, Portugal, and Greece, have not much discouraged the trend toward regional concentration through public services, credit facilities, and capital investment. The result has been a rapid growth in certain industrial and urban areas and a "backwash effect" in other areas. On the other hand, the beneficial "spread effects" from the rich and dynamic regions to the poor regions have not been working well for many areas all over Europe. That is why regional development programs have been advanced by the EC but without much success up to now.

Together with economic growth come urbanization, pollution, and other side effects. Urbanization, a global phenomenon, presents serious problems in the economies of the EC and the United States. Industrialization and agricultural mechanization continue in all the economies considered, and they seem to ensure that urbanization would remain one of the main characteristics of our civilization for years to come. Although there are serious urban problems such as crime and vice, debilitating congestion, extremes of wealth and poverty, and sometimes ethnic discord, the influx of people into the cities continues while the population of the agricultural sector shrinks. A number of development programs enacted for urban improvement have limited impact on the plight of the cities.

As a large group in the international arena, the European Community should further its efforts and implement comprehensive policies on: greenhouse effect warming, ozone depletion, fossil fuel and chemical waste pollution. In cooperation with the United States, Comecon and other groups and individual countries, it should introduce measures to avoid the warming of the earth's climate and melting its polar ice caps that may threaten to submerge populated coastlines. Also, it should make efforts to curb chlorofluorocarbons that deplete the stratospheric ozone layer, which results in skin cancer in humans from exposure to the ultraviolet sun rays, as well as to avoid nuclear accidents, such as that at Chernobyl in April 1986, with potential catastrophic consequences for large segments of the population.

There seems to be a conflict between clean environment and wealth accumulation through rapid economic growth and material well-being. Among other

EC member nations, Italy as well as Greece face the most serious environmental problems.

Many marble columns, cathedrals, old palaces and statues in European cities, particularly Athens and Rome, are sickly gray because of air pollution, chaotic traffic, and public indifference. This is particularly so with the fifth century B.C. Acropolis in Athens and the second-century statue of Marcus Aurelius in Rome, and many other monuments. It is suggested that some original statues be stored in museums and copies be put in their place for public display. Other measures include protecting the statues with glass screens. In any case, keeping Athens, Rome, Paris, and other tourist cities and their ancient monuments in shape requires a Sisyphean task and heavy public-sector expenditures.

Most of the large cities in Europe show signs of physical and spiritual uniformity. As a result, urbanists and tourists have begun to look toward smaller, neglected cities for a sense of history, continuity, and old-world cultural and social manners. Primarily because of economic backwardness and political neglect, many of these lesser cities remain intact. Gradually, economic development and the process of European integration is expected to change the old characteristics of many of these cities. Nevertheless, measures should be taken by EC member-nations to preserve and even to improve their historical and touristic elements through environmental protection rules and quality city planning.[20]

Low Performance in Eastern Europe

According to United States government statistics, East Germany had the highest per capita gross national product in 1988, followed by Czechoslovakia and Hungary, as shown below.

	Per capita GNP ($ thousands)	Population (millions)	Foreign debt ($ billions)	Cars per 1000 people
E. Germany	12.5	15.6	19.5	209
Czechoslovakia	10.1	15.6	6.1	173
Hungary	8.7	10.6	18.0	145
Bulgaria	7.5	9.0	7.1	120
Poland	7.3	38.2	38.5	105
Rumania	5.5	23.2	2.2	11

Poland has the largest external debt, followed by East Germany and Hungary. However, Hungary has the largest per capita foreign debt ($1,700), followed by East Germany ($1,250), Poland ($1,000), and Bulgaria ($790). Rumania has a very small amount of external debt because of the payments of previous loans in recent years. This resulted in severe austerity measures that may be partially responsible for the insurrection of the Rumanian people and the December 1989 ouster of Nicolae Ceauşescu, a communist dictator for twenty-four years.

On the average, per capita GNP in East Bloc countries is lower, about half, than that of the EC. The average annual growth of GNP for 1980–89 was slow. It varied from 1.7 percent for East Germany, 1.5 for Czechoslovakia, 0.8 for Hungary, and only 0.7 percent per year for Poland.

To overcome shortages, Eastern European nations, notably Hungary and Poland, are aggressively seeking venture partners mainly in the EC and the United States. Their slow economic growth (from 3–6 percent, on the average, in the 1960s and 1970s to only 0–2 percent in the 1980s) and their heavy foreign debts (currently varying from about $50 billion for the Soviet Union, $40 billion for Poland, $20 billion for Hungary, $8 billion for Bulgaria, and $7 billion for Czechoslovakia) foster dramatic changes towards a free market system. However, long job security, state-guaranteed wages, and equal incomes across most of society—which characterize planned economies—would make drastic changes difficult in the short run.

Out of a $18.7 trillion worldwide GNP in 1988, the United States' share was 26 percent, that of the EC 22 percent, that of the Soviet Union 14 percent, and that of the other Eastern European countries only 6 percent. To improve economic performance and to modernize their production units, East Bloc countries need foreign capital and the relevant know-how. At the same time, managers of state-owned enterprises and collective farms, coming mainly from the party elite or the "nomenklatura" of the communist world, should adjust to the new managerial market techniques and eliminate their improper privileges, or be replaced.

5   *Related Fiscal and Monetary Policies*

This chapter deals with similarities and differences in fiscal and monetary policies of the United States and the European Community (EC). It examines governmental expenditures and taxation and their changes over time, as well as the relationship of money supply and credit to inflation, interest rates, and other related variables.

With a growing public sector in the United States and the EC economies, fiscal policy acquires great importance not only on matters of financing governmental expenditures but also on matters of countercyclical policy. General government expenditures include central or federal, state, and local government spending. The federalism of the United States and, to some extent, Germany, establishes a division of powers between the national and the state governments, in contrast to other non-federal countries such as Britain, France, Italy, Spain, Greece, and Portugal. Governmental spending involves payments for goods and services and other transfers and intergovernmental activities.

Monetary policy in the United States is exercised primarily by the Federal Reserve Bank (Fed), which is largely independent of the government in managing money and credit. The seven members of the board of governors of the Fed are appointed for fourteen years by the President with the consent of the Senate. On the contrary, the central banks of the EC nations are mostly under the control of the government and the political party in power. The managers of these banks are appointed by the government and are largely following its policy directives. The main economic problems of the central banks are the financing of budget deficits in a noninflationary way and the stimulation of the economy in cases of recession.

Figure 5.1
The Growing Public Sector in the United States and the EC

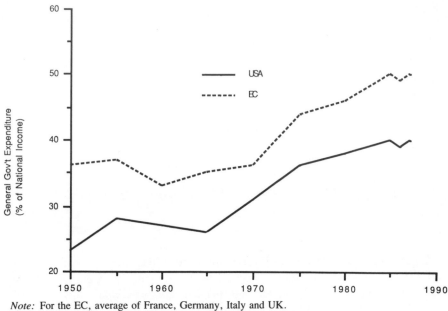

Note: For the EC, average of France, Germany, Italy and UK.
Source: OECD, *National Accounts*, various issues.

DIFFERENCES IN GOVERNMENT EXPENDITURES

Unlike the European nations, where power is concentrated mainly in the central government, the United States federal system of government, with a number of independent state governments, provides for regional diversity and preserves liberty. Except for some important federal government activities, such as creating money, collecting taxes, regulating trade, and conducting wars, all other powers and controls were left by the United States Constitution of 1788 with the individual states, which drew their own constitutions, collected their own taxes, and exercised their own policies and controls.

As Adam Smith suggested, "Public works . . . are always better maintained by a local or provincial revenue . . . than by the general revenue of the state."[1] However, to encourage specialization and promote positive externalities and lower production costs, some restrictions on the United States state governments have been introduced regarding freedom of trade across state lines. A similar policy of free trade movement across member-nations is presently followed by the EC for larger markets, economies of scale, and diffusion of technology.

The United States and the EC public sectors have grown proportionately at a faster rate than the overall economy in the long run. As Figure 5.1 shows, United States general government expenditures increased from 23 percent of national income in 1950 to 40 percent currently. For the EC countries (average of Britain,

France, Germany, and Italy), general government expenditures increased from 36 percent of national income in 1950 to 50 percent currently.

The expansion of the public sector, or the growing average propensity to spend, is the result of ever increasing demand for government services, including those of regional and local units of government, which in turn leads to high elasticities of government expenditures with respect to national income. Such elasticities, that is, the percentage change in government expenditures over the percent change in national income, were high (varying from 1.2 to 1.4), meaning that for each percentage increase in national income there was a higher than 1 percentage increase in general government expenditures, for the United States and the EC, particularly after 1965.

As economic development continues, public expenditures on goods and services such as defense and internal security, social security, post-office operations, sanitation, health, education, fire fighting, parks and environmental protection, and other urban and social services increase more than the overall economy. This trend verifies the argument of Adolph Wagner, a German political economist, who argued, about a century ago, that social progress in industrializing nations causes a proportionately higher growth of government than growth of the overall economy.[2] However, because of the bureaucratic and inefficient government activities, a number of EC countries started denationalizing or privatizing a number of national industries.

Although there is a great gap in the per capita GNP among the EC countries, the differences in government outlays are not as large. As Figure 5.2 shows, Spain, Greece, and Portugal with relatively low per capita GNP have general government expenditure varying from 40 to 44 percent of national income, compared to 50 to 57 percent for Germany and France. The ratio of government outlays of the EC (average of Britain, France, Germany, and Italy) is close to 50 percent and that of the United States is 40 percent. The advanced EC countries with a larger public sector than the United States are taking measures of denationalization and relative reduction of government expenditures. As a result, the proportion of national income spent by the government may be the same or lower for the EC and the United States in the near future.

To achieve less intervention, less spending, and more competition, the EC reduced and even abolished governmental subsidies that were given to some industries in accordance with Article 92 of the EC. They are about 82 billion ECUs or $90 billion per year. Italy holds the first place in such subsidies followed by Germany, France, and Britain. However, subsidies are permitted for poor regions, for social policy, for programs of economic importance for the EC, and for cases in which free trade is not interrupted.

Central government expenditures, as percentages of GNP, are lower in the United States than in the EC countries. They vary from around 23 percent for the United States to 30 percent for Germany, 35 for Spain, 40 for Britain, and 45 percent for France. For the United States, the largest part of such expenditures goes to housing, social security, and welfare (about 30 percent), followed by

Figure 5.2
Relationship of Per Capita GNP to General Government Expenditures as Percentages of National Income (1987)

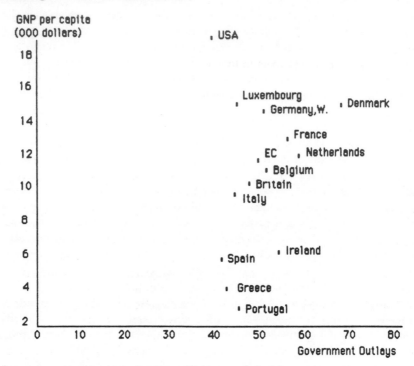

Note: In some cases closest years' data available were used.
Source: World Bank, *World Development Report*; OECD, *National Accounts*; United Nations,
    Statistical Yearbook, all various issues.

defense (25 percent) and health (12 percent). Mostly, EC countries have higher proportions of central government expenditures going to housing, social security, welfare, and health. In education, the proportions are about 2 for the United States, Britain, and Germany, 7 for Italy, more than 11 percent for Ireland and the Netherlands, and 15 percent for Belgium.

Because overcentralization and bureaucratization kill initiatives and create unhealthy economic dependencies, decentralizing trends continue and local governments are strengthened particularly in the United States, France, Greece, and Italy. Countries with decentralized public sector activities or federations have large proportions of state and local government expenditures as a proportion of total government spending. They vary from 40 percent for the United States and Germany to 32 percent for Italy and 28 percent for Britain. France and Belgium have low levels of state and local government expenditures (13 percent and 11 percent, respectively) and therefore a high concentration of the public sector mainly because of their institutional structure. Also for countries with relatively lower per capita income such as Portugal, Spain, and Greece, these expenditure ratios are low, varying from 4 percent to 10 percent.

The social security program was introduced in Europe in the 1880s, first by Germany, and during the Great Depression (Social Security Act, 1935) in the United States. As life expectancy has improved steadily, the social security benefits paid by the government have increased. In 1900, for example, the average American could expect to live for 47.3 years. Presently, life expectancy at birth in the United States is 75 years (71 for males and 79 for females). In France, Italy, Spain, and the Netherlands, it is 77, in Greece 76, in Ireland 74, in Portugal 73, and in all other EC countries 75 years. This trend, along with declining birth rates, leads to what is known as the graying of America and Europe.

The proportion of national income absorbed by social security varies from about 8 percent for Britain and the United States, 14 percent for Italy, and as high as 18 percent for Germany and 22 percent for France. Payroll taxes for social security are relatively low in the United States: 15.3 percent (7.65 percent for the employee plus 7.65 percent also for the employer up to $52,000) than in the EC countries (around 30 percent of earnings). However, social security benefits are relatively higher in Europe (around the basic salary at retirement) than in the United States (about $500 monthly on the average). Moreover, almost all people in Europe are covered by national health insurance but, according to the United States Census Bureau, 35 million Americans (30 percent Hispanic, 22 percent blacks, and 14 percent whites) lack any kind of health insurance. The largest proportion of insured population in the United States (75 percent) and, to a lesser extent, in Britain has private health insurance.

With the ideological walls crumbling all over the world and the evolution of Western Europe toward a unified market, greater competitiveness in production and distribution, less government spending, and sustained economic growth for higher standards of living are the objectives of national economies. Socialist governments in France, Spain, Italy, and Greece and other countries adopted programs geared to free market economies and international competition. Although in these and other Western European countries government expenditures are higher than those of the United States, emphasis is placed more and more on the private sector as the main driving force of employment and growth. Similar policies of reduction in government expenditures and privatizations are implemented more emphatically in Eastern Europe.

As nationalistic and ideological differences are withered away, more productive investments are financed by worldwide reduction in defense spending. Moreover, gradual elimination of traditional borders in capital markets between the United States and the European Community stimulates transactions and increases interdependence. From that point of view, domestic fiscal and monetary policies should be formulated within a global framework, while national security and economic policies should be interwoven with international policies. This is particularly so for the United States with large domestic and foreign debts which

Table 5.1
Military Spending for the United States and the EC Allies, 1986 (current dollars)

Country	Spending (billion $)	Percentage of GNP	Spending per person ($)
France	28.5	3.9	514
Germany (West)	27.7	3.1	454
Britain	27.3	5.1	481
Italy	13.5	2.2	235
Spain	6.0	3.1	156
Netherlands	5.3	3.1	365
Belgium	3.4	3.0	345
Greece	2.4	6.1	243
Denmark	1.6	2.0	322
Portugal	0.9	3.2	91
Luxembourg	0.1	1.1	145
EC	116.1	3.4	360
USA	281.1	6.8	1,164

Source: United States Government, Department of Defense; and OECD, *National Accounts*, various issues.

may lead to a gradual loss of the preeminent role the country played in this century.[3]

The twin deficits in the federal budget and the balance in foreign trade increased United States claims concerning military spending share by Western European nations and other NATO (North Atlantic Treaty Organization) member-nations. The argument is that the United States spends more for common defense than all members of NATO together including the EC countries, Japan, and Canada. It is suggested by the United States policy makers that all partners share in the expenditures of mutual defense according to their economic conditions, which have been largely improved lately. Each American spends for common defense twice as much as any allied citizen in the EC and the other partners in the alliance.

As Table 5.1 shows, the United States spends close to 7 percent of its Gross National Product (GNP) for defense. The EC countries (except Ireland) spend altogether half of that of the United States. As a percentage of GNP, Greece is second in military spending (6.1 percent of GNP) in the NATO alliance, mainly because of conflicts with Turkey over Cyprus, followed by Britain (5.1), France

(3.9), West Germany, Spain, and the Netherlands (3.1 percent each), and Italy (2.2).

Japan, with a per capita income close to that of the United States, spends only about 1 percent of its GDP for defense, Canada spends around 2 percent, Turkey about 5 percent, and Norway 3 percent, compared to 12 percent for the Soviet Union and 7 for China. As a percentage of total expenditures of the central government, annual defense spending is about 26 for the United States, 13 for Britain, 12 for Greece, 9 for Germany, and 5 each for Belgium and Denmark.

Large EC nations, such as Britain, France, and Germany, are able and willing to share more toward a defense cooperation that could reduce the United States burden and strengthen the union of the European Community. At the same time, a shift in the balance of decision-making power in favor of the Western European Community could take place in the future, while the United States could divert more attention to the economic development of third world nations. Such a geopolitical re-orientation is also greatly supported by the new economic and political reforms implemented presently in the Soviet Union. Moreover, because of the dramatic changes in the communist Eastern European countries, the new "guns and butter" battle might change in favor of more butter and less guns in the near future. Already, the United States agreed to withdraw 30,000 American troops from Western Europe in return for a reduction of 375,000 Soviet troops from Eastern Europe to leave 275,000 soldiers from each superpower in Europe, while negotiations continue for further troop reductions.

SIMILARITIES IN TAXES

Total revenue of general government (state and local government included), as a percentage of national income, increased for the United States from 13.3 percent in 1929 to 29.0 percent in 1950, 33.6 percent in 1960 and 37 percent currently. United States federal taxes account for about 20 percent and the remaining 16 percent are state and local taxes. Higher United States federal expenditures (about 15 percent of tax revenue) are covered by borrowing.

For the European Community, general government taxes, on the average, are higher (around 50 percent of national income) than those of the United States and close to those of Canada. Comparing the main EC countries with the United States, we can see that France has the highest percentage of income absorbed by taxation, followed by Germany, Britain, and Italy. From 1960, they increased from 34 to 56 percent of national income for France, from 31 to 51 percent for Germany, from 31 to 49 percent for Britain, and from 29 to 44 percent for Italy.[4] These figures show that in all countries considered there was an upward trend of taxes to income ratios during the years since 1960. Such increases in tax revenue, which are larger than those of national income, indicate that the public sector is growing more than the private sector.

Direct and Indirect Taxes

Direct (or income and profit) taxes that are imposed primarily on individuals absorb relatively higher proportions of income in the advanced economies of the EC (except the Netherlands) and the United States than in the less developed economies of Greece, Portugal, and Spain. Likewise, they account for higher proportions of the total tax revenue for the advanced EC and United States economies, compared to the indirect taxes (or taxes on goods and services), as Figure 5.3 shows.

Tax revenue from social security is relatively higher in France, Germany, the Netherlands, Spain, Greece, Belgium, Italy, and the United States than in Denmark, Ireland, and Britain. For the other countries of the Organization for Economic Cooperation and Development (OECD), Turkey, Finland, and Canada have low social security taxes. Figure 5.4 shows the differences in various types of taxes between the EC countries and the United States and changes in receipts as percentages of tax revenues in the last two decades. In all countries considered property taxes are relatively small while payroll taxes are very small or non-existent.

Empirically, the United States direct tax flexibility in relation to national income (marginal direct tax) is around 20 percent, compared to 15 percent two decades ago. In relation to total revenue of general government, though, United States direct taxes are 66 percent, and are more or less constant during the last three decades. The same trends almost prevail in EC countries, particularly in Britain, Germany, France, and Italy. The sizable growth of direct taxes, including social security contributions, is primarily responsible for the increase in taxation in the United States and the EC. Income elasticities of direct taxation were higher than 1 in the 1980s, and more so in the 1970s. Ongoing high rates of inflation, which raised the rates of progressive income taxes, seemed to be responsible for this upturn for the marginal rate of direct taxes.

For the United States, personal income taxes account for about 40 percent of the federal government revenue, social security for 30 percent, and corporation income taxes for 8 percent. As a percentage of national income they are about 15 percent for the United States, 16 percent for Britain, 14 percent for Italy and Germany, and 7 percent for France. Presently, the United States personal tax rates are 15 percent for a single person's taxable income up to $17,850, 28 percent for $17,850 to $43,150, 33 percent for $43,150 to $100,480, and back to 28 percent for higher income. This is a drastic reduction from 70 percent in 1981 and from 50 percent in 1986.

These three progressive income tax rates were very similar to those introduced in ancient Greece (*pentacosiomedimni*, knights, *zeugites*) by Solon's Laws (594 B.C.) or perhaps later (428 B.C.). The lowest-income class (*thetes*) was exempted from taxation. Plato, it seems, supported this form of progressive taxation as simple and fair.

United States corporation income tax rates are 15 percent for taxable income

Figure 5.3
Tax Revenue of Main Headings as a Percentage of Total Tax Revenues of the United States, the EC, and Other OECD Countries, 1985

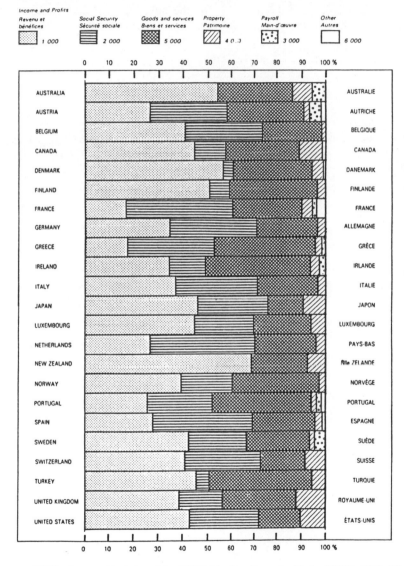

Source: OECD, *Revenue Statistics of the OECD Member Countries* (Paris: OECD, 1986), 20.

Figure 5.4
Receipts as Percentage of Total Tax Revenues

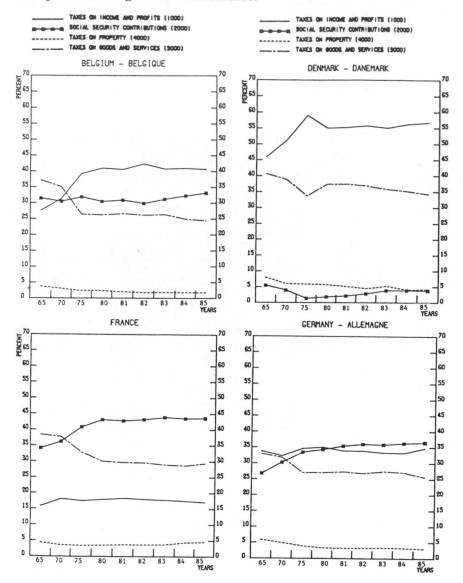

Figure 5.4 (continued)

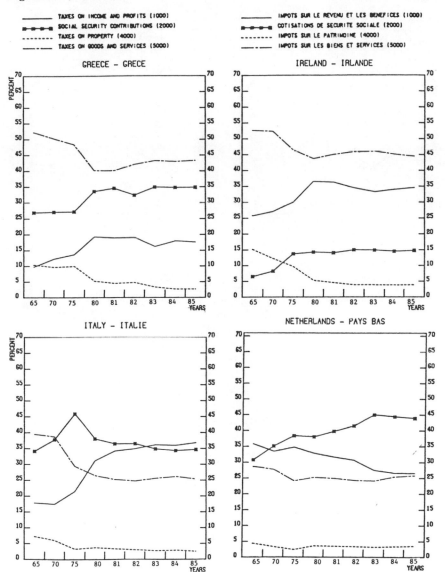

91

Figure 5.4 (continued)

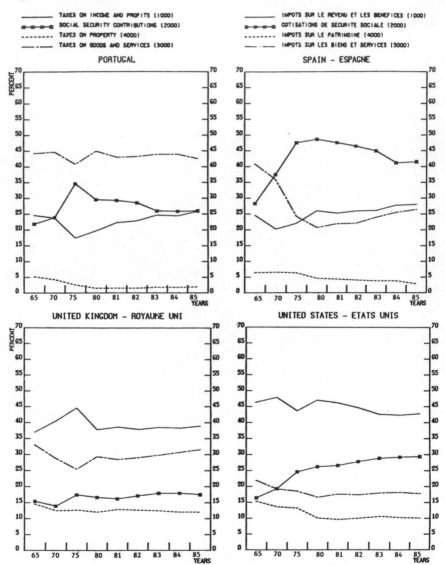

Source: OECD, *Revenue Statistics of the OECD Member Countries* (Paris: OECD, 1986), 24–28.

up to $50,000, 25 percent for income from $50,000 to $75,000, and 34 percent for taxable income over $75,000. With the Tax Reform Act of 1986, the number of corporate income tax brackets was reduced from five to three, and the maximum tax rate from 46 to 34 percent.[5] As a percentage of GNP, the United States corporation income tax is 2.4, compared with 3.3 percent in-1970, 4.4 percent in 1960, and 5.4 percent in 1953. In the EC it varies around 3 to 4 percent of the GNP.

The tax system of the individual EC countries is based mainly on a progressive income tax on individuals and corporations and on value added taxes, replacing previous complex turnover taxes. There is also a small property or real estate tax collected by local authorities in the EC countries and a relatively high one in the United States.

On both sides of the Atlantic, the corporation income tax has been criticized on the grounds that it taxes corporations as independent entities without considering the tax brackets of individual shareholders and that it leads to a low level of business investment. Consequently, reforms have been suggested to integrate corporation and individual income taxes, thus making the corporation a withholding unit for individual income taxes. Some people have even called for the abolition of the corporate tax altogether. Already, other industrial democracies, except the United States, Sweden, and the Netherlands, integrate the two taxes on corporate income and shareholders' dividends at the corporate or individual level.

United States income tax rates are far lower than those of the EC, as are the tax brackets. In recent years, though, Britain cut its top marginal income tax from 83 percent to 60 percent; Italy from 72 to 62 percent; Portugal from 80 to 69 percent; Ireland from 77 to 65 percent; Sweden from 87 to 80 percent; and Greece from 63 to 50 percent. Further tax cuts are considered by some of the above and other nations for work stimulation and higher productivity.

When assets or investments increase in value over their original cost, capital gains rise and taxes are paid for gains realized. For the United States capital gains taxes are 28 percent, for Britain 30 percent, for France 16 percent, and for Italy 2–25 percent. Germany has a tax on capital itself (assets) of 0.70 percent. The United States has estate taxes varying from 18 to 55 percent, Britain from 30 to 60 percent, France from 0 to 60 percent, and Germany from 3 to 70 percent. Belgium has inheritance taxes varying from 3 to 80 percent, Italy from 0 to 31 percent, and the Netherlands from 5 to 68 percent. For the United States, gift taxes are the same as estate taxes, for Britain they vary from 15 to 30 percent, for Belgium from 3 to 80 percent, and for the Netherlands from 5 to 68 percent.[6] However, exemptions are provided for a certain amount of property inherited. Thus, for the United States, in up to $600,000 of inherited property, no taxes are paid.

In general, the EC countries do not have interest income taxes. Recently Germany switched position regarding EC-wide withholding tax on interest from supporting to opposing it. Britain also previously opposed this idea.

Figure 5.5
Indirect Taxes as Percentage of National Income

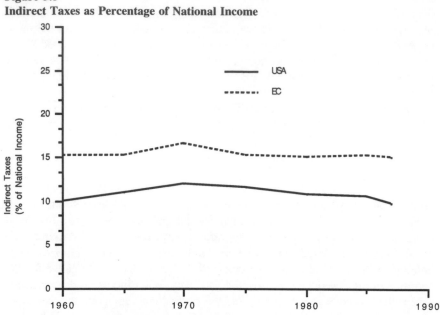

Source: OECD, *National Accounts*, various issues.

Both the United States and the EC do not have high proportions of indirect taxes relative to national income. Indirect (or consumption) taxes, that are imposed initially on objects (in "rem" taxes) and include excises (mainly on fuel, beverages, tobacco, travel), sales taxes, value-added taxes, stamps and tariffs and are levied against goods and services independently of the owner's ability to pay. In the United States, they are levied primarily by individual states and localities, but in the EC mostly by the central governments. Figure 5.5 shows that indirect taxes were constant and around 10 percent of national income for the United States and 15 percent for the EC from the 1960s onward.

Indirect taxes, as percentages of total taxes, are higher in low income EC countries such as Greece, Ireland, and Portugal than in the advanced EC countries and the United States. From that standpoint and as a result of the EC integration, a relative decrease in indirect taxes and structural changes in both direct and indirect taxes are expected to occur in the near future in the above low-income countries. In EC countries with high indirect taxes, reduction or elimination of excise taxes and tariffs, according to the directives of the EC, would reduce tax revenue and exert pressure on domestic industries producing the same goods or close substitutes to imported goods. However, such a competitive process would reduce inefficiency, despite the expected detrimental effects on employment conditions.

The elasticities of indirect taxes, with respect to private consumption, imports, and Gross Domestic Product (GDP), for the periods 1950–60 and 1960–70, were greater than 1. In the 1970s, however, the elasticities were less than 1 and lower in the United States than in the EC. These results indicate that, during the 1970s, the relative growth of indirect taxes in the United States was lower than the growth in the other variables (private consumption, GDP, and particularly imports). The dramatic increases in the value of oil imports, without a similar increase in tariffs on imported oil and contrary to what is customary in the EC and other countries (where oil prices are more than double those prevailing in the United States), seemed to be responsible for the differences. In the 1980s, the elasticities of indirect taxes, with respect to private consumption, imports, and GDP, were all close to 1. For correlations of direct and indirect taxes with private consumption, imports and inflation, see Appendix A.[7]

The value added tax (VAT) is primarily a consumption tax and as such is included in indirect taxes. The VAT, which has been introduced by the EC member states, is a proportional tax on the value of all goods and services included in the firms' invoices, reduced by the amount of previous VAT liability. As the supporters of VAT argue, this tax is simple: it reduces consumption expenditures, decreases tax evasion, improves the flexibility of the tax structure, and stimulates investment and economic growth. As a tax upon the difference between the total value of output minus the value of purchased material inputs, it helps policy makers determine whether demand for consumer goods is growing in an inflationary way. From that point of view, the VAT can be used to regulate demand. However, additional value added taxes, when first introduced, would more likely pass on to the consumers by means of rising prices.

Policy makers and economists in the United States and other countries started contemplating the introduction of VAT as a substitute for personal income taxes. It is argued that by shifting the nation's tax burden away from taxes on income and profits, and toward sales or value added taxes, production incentives would be stimulated and consumption expenditures would be discouraged. However, care should be taken to avoid overburdening the low and middle income people upon whom consumption taxes primarily fall. This can be achieved by providing tax exemptions for the necessities of life, such as food, modest rental payments, or a small home and the like. Also, a VAT can be coupled with a rebate on low incomes and exports.

Multiple rates of a VAT can be used to eliminate the regressivity likely to be associated with a single rate of such a tax. However, this increases administrative complexities, compliance costs and distortions in consumption to an extent that is probably unjustified.

In the United States most states levy sales taxes at widely different rates. However, in other countries circumstances are different either because VATs have either replaced inefficient turnover or cascade taxes (e.g., in France, Germany, and the Netherlands), or have been required for EC membership in the Community. The VAT was introduced in France in 1954. Presently, it raises about 50 percent of tax revenue in that country. In Germany, the VAT was proposed in 1918, and introduced in 1967. There it provides 13 percent of government revenue. In Britain, it provides 15 percent, and in the EC 10 percent of the overall tax revenue.

The revenues of the EC countries as a group come primarily from value added taxes (VAT) (one percent of the VAT collected by the member nations), customs duties, and special levies on agricultural imports (including sugar duties). Revenue from VAT is about 50 percent of the total revenue of the EC, as a unit separate from that of the individual member countries.

Most of the collected revenues are spent for the support of prices of agricultural products by a special EC fund known as FEOGA (Fond Européen d'Orientation et de Garantie Agricole) (about two-thirds); around 10 percent for the regional development of backward areas; and the rest for social policies, research, energy, and for aid to third world countries (about 6 percent). Greece, Italy, Portugal, Spain, and to some extent France are the main recipients of subsidies for agricultural products and regional development.[8]

The EC VAT rates vary from 6 percent for basic goods to 16 percent for most goods and services, and up to 38 percent for luxury goods. However, the sixth directive of the EC provides that enterprises with sales less than 10,000 European Currency Units (ECUs) are not liable to pay VAT. Moreover, there are special treatments for special small enterprises and those involved in agriculture, travel, and petroleum products. Also, exports and capital goods are normally exempted from taxation, so that investment and domestic production will be stimulated. There is discussion, though, to reduce and harmonize the value added tax to 14–20 percent for most goods and to lower the rates to the range between zero to nine percent for "social sensitive" items. Most of the member-countries are willing to go on zero-rating taxes for food and children's clothing.

Related Eastern European Fiscal Systems

Because of the closer relationship of the East Bloc countries with the EC and the United States, as a result of the cosmogonic economic and political reforms implemented recently, a brief review of their fiscal system is needed.

The tax system of the Eastern European nations relies heavily on turnover taxes to provide revenue and to balance supply and demand. When the policy makers want to avoid shortages and rationing, they impose turnover taxes to move prices close to the equilibrium of supply and demand and to collect revenue to finance subsidies and other expenditures. The turnover taxes therefore play a distribution role by discriminating between necessary goods (housing, transportation, medical care, education, books) for which there is a small or no turnover tax, and luxury goods (cars, videos, liquor) with high taxes. Usually manufacturing is favored over the agricultural sector, as are other social services (health, education, the arts) through inexpensive credit, tax reduction, and undervalued foreign currency. To correct severe shortages of some goods and sectoral imbalances, rationing and tax-cum-subsidy measures are used. That is the way to avoid extensive productivity losses due to misallocation of resources and effective protection from imports.

In order to encourage domestic and foreign private enterprises the tax laws of Eastern European countries should be changed. Not only turnover and other indirect taxes should be reduced but progressive income or direct tax rates, which are as high as 90 percent for the Soviet Union and other East Bloc countries, should be changed and adjusted to those of the EC and other Western countries.

Total direct taxes in the East Bloc countries are relatively small. As percentages of government revenue, they vary from 20 to 30 percent, while indirect (mainly turnover) taxes account for 70 to 80 percent. The ratio of direct/indirect taxes is only about 30 to 40 percent, compared with 90 percent or more in the EC and far higher in the United States. Although recent reforms tend to reduce the fiscal role of turnover taxes in favor of new taxes on income, profits of enterprises, and capital charges, they still continue to be relatively large, mainly because it is easier to collect them compared to other forms of taxation. General government tax revenues in the Eastern European countries are mostly 60 percent or more of national income, compared to about 35 percent for the United States and 45 percent for the EC.

COORDINATION OF MONETARY POLICIES

In the United States there was a significant increase in the money supply after 1980, which is related to the increase in the nominal Gross National Product (GNP), that is, the real GNP plus inflation. Velocity of money, the speed by which the average dollar is changing hands in a year, was declining or relatively constant and around 6 in the 1980s. However, there was a gradual increase in velocity during the 1960s and the 1970s.

As Figure 5.6 shows, the velocity of money, that is, the ratio of GNP over money supply, increased gradually from 3.5 in 1960 to 6.8 in 1981, that is, by 94 percent. This supports the argument that the velocity of money is not constant over time as the monetarists argue. From that standpoint inflation, during that time and particularly in the 1970s, was largely due to the increase in velocity of money, which is mainly the result of fast spending promoted by advertisement and the United States advanced monetary system.

What happened to the relationship of the United States money supply and the velocity of money in the 1960s and 1970s can be observed in Britain as well. As Figure 5.7 shows, the velocity of money increased from 3.9 in 1960 to 7.4 in 1980, but it declined thereafter. Likewise, money supply increased slowly from 1960 to 1974 and rapidly thereafter. However, velocity of money remained relatively constant for France for the last three decades and declined slightly for Germany and Italy. This means that both Germany and Italy, as well as Britain after 1980, financed their nominal GNP (real GNP plus inflation) through increases in money supply.

On June 27, 1989, the twelve EC nations accepted in Madrid the first stage

Figure 5.6
Money Supply (M_1) and Velocity of Money ($V = GNP/M_1$) for the United States (in billions of dollars, end of period)

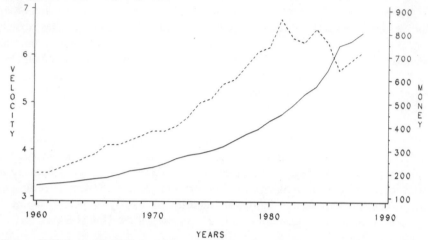

YEARS

Source: IMF, *International Financial Statistics (IFS)*, various issues.

Figure 5.7
Money Supply (M_1) and Velocity of Money ($V = GNP/M_1$) for Britain (in billions of pounds, end of period)

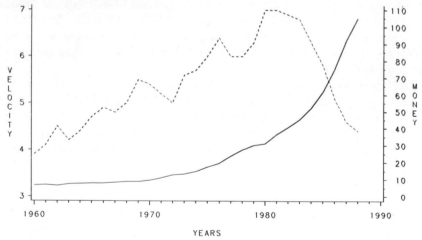

YEARS

Source: IMF, IFS, various issues.

of the monetary union plan, which would end exchange controls and other restrictions in banking and insurance services. The first stage, that started on July 1, 1990, would be followed by two further stages which would involve the acceptance of a common currency and the establishment of the central European bank. Prime Minister Margaret Thatcher of Britain, under the pressure of the possible election defeat of her party, and not to be left out of the trend toward a European integration, accepted the first phase of the plan but still presents objections regarding the other two phases.

An intergovernmental conference would deal with the other two phases of the EC monetary union. Also, it would consider modifications of the initial charter of the EC (the Treaty of Rome of 1957) toward full economic union. In the process, Britain, Greece, and Portugal are expected to join the European Monetary System, while France eliminated foreign exchange controls and restrictions on capital movements on January 1, 1990.

The EC controls about 20 percent of world trade, the United States 15 percent, and Japan around 10 percent. Although Japan controls around 47 percent and the United States 32 percent of the financial capital of the world, a significant expansion of related EC companies is expected to increase European financial controls on an international level.

The United States' addiction to domestic (public and private) debt as well as to external debt affects the economic power of the country and increases its financial dependence upon the EC and other countries. Internal United States government debt increased from $1 trillion in 1980 to $3 trillion currently, while the United States net international investment position changed from a positive balance of $106 billion in 1980 to a foreign debt of more than $700 billion now. At the same time, United States nonfinancial companies rely more and more on borrowed money, including Eurodollars and some $200 billion "junk bonds," while their equity to debt ratio declines. Presently, United States banks and corporations are at a disadvantage, compared to the European and Japanese banks and corporations, mainly because of the depreciation of the dollar. For the EC and other foreign corporations American assets are far cheaper in terms of their currencies than are European assets in terms of dollars. In connection to that, the Eurocurrency market plays a significant role in acquisitions and transfer of assets.

In addition to the serious debt exposure with developing countries, big American banks face another important exposure with leveraged buyouts (LBOs). Some fourteen large United States banks have about $50 billion LBO exposure. Manufacturers Hanover Trust ($5.1 billion), Bankers Trust and Citicorp ($4 billion each), Wells Fargo, Chase Manhattan, and Chemical Bank (from $4 to $4.5 billion each) have the largest LBO exposure. They are followed by Security Pacific, Bank of Boston, Bank of America, and five smaller banks with LBO exposure varying from $1.3 billion to $3 billion each. Moreover American banking is in trouble as saving banks are in the red for some $500 billion.

So far similar LBO exposures with EC banks are limited because of related controls by central banks and governments in Europe. However, as such transactions are expanding rapidly in the old continent, LBO exposure of EC banks would follow, more or less, the example of the United States banks.

An additional reason for the continuation of the large United States trade deficits and the sizable depreciation of the dollar is the lack of vigorous expansionary policies in countries with large trade surpluses, such as West Germany and Japan. If fiscal stimulative measures are not undertaken, easy monetary policy may be implemented through short-term increase in money supply and reduction in interest rates. It is estimated that a reduction of interest rates by 1 percentage point increases real GNP by ½ to 1½ percent in Europe and Japan and by approximately ½ to 1 percent in the United States after some two to three years.[9] However, it must be recognized that monetary easing should be temporary, because extended monetary growth, *ceteris paribus*, may lead to a rise in inflation.

High interest rates in one country attract capital inflow from other countries and affect exchange rate fluctuations. Typically, interest rates are raised to keep inflation checked. Recently Germany raised the discount rate from 4 to 4.5 percent, which is still lower than that of the United States (7 percent). This is the rate commercial banks pay for borrowing from central banks. Also, the short-term (Lombart) rate was raised from 6 to 6.5 percent. The main reason for these raises in interest rates is to keep inflation at the present rate (2–3 percent), although it is still lower than in other countries, notably the United States (4–5 percent). Other EC countries such as Denmark and the Netherlands joined Germany in raising interest rates, while Britain and France are expected to follow.

As a result of interest rate increases the value of the dollar is expected to decline while that of the German mark and other related EC currencies are expected to increase. Although a similar increase in interest rates by the Bundesbank was criticized for contributing to the crash of the stock market in October 1987, the new increase is not related to the same variables of that time, the main one of which was the overinflated prices of stocks.

The drastic reforms in Eastern Europe and the economic union of West and East Germany attract capital investment and financial aid that put strains on the EC and the United States credit markets. Competition for funds raises interest rates in Europe and the United States and reduces bond prices. For example, interest rates on ten-year German bonds (8.5 percent) rose above United States rates for the first time in more than ten years.

Countries with trade deficits such as Britain, France, Greece, Portugal, and the United States would face more serious problems in financing their deficits and external debts. Funds previously headed for these and other countries in financial need would shift to East Bloc nations, particularly Hungary, Czechoslovakia and Poland. The drain of capital from the West would lead to fears of inflation, higher interest rates and lower economic growth across Western Europe and the United States. It is estimated that the cost of rehabilitation and development of East Bloc countries would be $300 billion to $500 billion over the next decade or so.

Financial Services

Strong ongoing competition between the EC and the United States is expected to continue, particularly after the welding together of the twelve European national economies into a single market and a closer cooperation with the East Bloc countries. The 1986 Single European Act provides for the free movement not only of goods and persons but also of services and capital. Although financial and banking services have not benefitted to the same extent as manufactured goods, they are expected to play a major role to the improvement of other sectors of the Community's economy. Already, direct and portfolio investment have been liberalized in the 1960s and similar measures were adopted for deposits and credits later. The EC financial sector accounts for about 7 percent of the Gross National Product and represents more than three million jobs or 3.5 percent of total EC employment.[10] Projected harmonization of national laws concerning banks, insurance policies, and stock exchanges, as well as expansion in Eastern Europe, will greatly improve the services sector.

In spite of the fact that a number of banks and financial institutions operate on both sides of the Atlantic, there remain important obstacles in serving foreign markets primarily because of different national regulations of banking and financial operations. The next frontier for trade liberalization is international services in general and financial services in particular. This is important because of the growth of trade between Europe and the United States, as well as investment and other transactions that require the development of banking and financial services to facilitate and lubricate such transactions. As the services sector is rapidly growing in domestic economies, likewise financial and other services are expected to grow rapidly in a global scale, so that capital movements, information and security services, and other activities can move quickly between continents. Already, many securities are listed on the stock exchanges of both the EC and the United States.

The spirit of harmonization of financial regulations includes the reciprocity provision concerning banking services, portfolio management, and stock transactions. The banking directives allow banks, which pass guidelines, to receive a single banking license and enable them to operate throughout the whole European Community. However, foreign banks should receive these rights on the basis of reciprocity, that is, only if EC banks have equal access to other partner countries' markets. This reciprocity principle includes life insurance and investment services, particularly portfolio management activities. On these grounds, the Shareholder Disclosure Directive stipulates that an owner who sells or buys at least 10 percent of a company's total stock must notify that company and the company, in turn, must inform the public through the responsible authorities.

With a unified European monetary system linking domestic money markets, the stronger EC countries would largely influence monetary conditions in other member countries. The Eurodollar market played a similar role in affecting, directly or indirectly, national monetary policies in Europe and linking such policies with those of the United States. Thus a policy to tighten monetary conditions in a country would lead to an increase in borrowing by commercial banks or individuals from other countries. This money would be converted into local currency and affect money supply and credit policy, thereby nullifying partially or totally the restrictive policy of the country in question. However, flexible exchange rates are expected to correct the situation through adjustment in the par values. Also, tax and expenditure policies can be used to supplement monetary policies toward domestic economic stability. Moreover, coordination of national policies and cooperation among central banks can prevent large-scale movements of capital, in the short run, in response to changes in monetary policies and interest rate differences.

The introduction of a European monetary system could eliminate large fluctuations in exchange rates and enhance convertibility in national currencies. Even common rates of money growth could be established. If member nations attempt a divergent monetary policy, this will result in payment imbalances that will force them back to monetary harmony. Again, coordination of national economic policies is required to avoid disturbances from budgetary deficits and other misguided financial policies. A limited pooling of reserves with some form of joint management would provide the first step of an EC monetary union and facilitate credit extension among members, and between the EC and the United States. The First EC Banking Directive of 1977 provided for the coordination of national laws and regulations, and the Second Banking Directive of 1988 introduced a single banking license valid across the EC.

With amendments to the second banking directive of the European Commission, the European Parliament introduced controls regarding banking permits for new banks and takeovers of EC banks by other banks outside the Community. The controls are referring to the suitability of the shareholders of more than 5 percent of the assets of the banks. Such supervisory controls cover branches of non-Community banks as well. Some exemptions from the regulations of this directive were extended for Greece and Portugal until the end of 1992, instead of 1989.

In the banking sector, the EC permits the establishment of banks by other countries under the principle of reciprocity. Also EC banks can participate in other nonfinancial companies up to 25 percent of their own capital.

To make the banking sector more competitive to other European and international banks, Spain approved the merging of Banco Español de Credito and Banco Central to create the biggest commercial bank in Spain and the twentieth in the world in capital and reserves. The combined profits of the two banks are more than 60 billion pesetas (120 pesetas to the United States dollar) per year. Their total assets are more than 7 trillion pesetas, deposits about 5.5 trillion, and equity 530 billion pesetas.

Under pressures for growing world trade, many countries, such as Germany, France, Britain, the Netherlands, and other industrialized countries, reduced or are in the process of eliminating obstacles to foreign banking activities. However, requirements of national or reciprocal treatment still remain in force for most of the countries. The United States government prefers national treatment for its subsidiaries in other countries. The common EC rules on banking operations, though, would be easier and less costly than adjustment to each of the twelve different EC nations. Then serving the United States multinational companies on their efforts to increase trade and investment in continental Europe would be more efficient and less expensive.

Financing growing stock market operations in the EC is another field that needs attention, especially in Britain, the Netherlands, and France. The recent removal of the last foreign-exchange controls on businesses by France and its successful policy of disinflation would make the Eurofranc Market an important source of credit and investment. Moreover, individuals are permitted to have foreign-currency accounts or to hold a foreign account in France. France, with a high withholding tax on investment income, is expected to adjust to the harmonizing EC investment rules and remove related controls and regulations.

To raise funds quickly, aggressive corporate raiders prefer syndicated loans mainly in the Eurocurrency market. Lenders also prefer to give acquisition-related loans because the average spread on Eurocurrency loans is about 0.5 percent above LIBOR, the rate at which British banks lend to each other. Moreover, loans for acquisitions and leveraged buyouts in the United States can bring up to 3 percent more than those in Europe. Such syndicated loans, associated with mainly United States mergers, were $34.5 billion or more than 30 percent of all new borrowing on the world's capital markets in 1988, compared with $8.3 billion or 12 percent, respectively, in 1987. These figures are expected to be higher in the future considering the loans or their selling to be enacted by such big leveraged buyouts and buy-ins in Europe and the United States.

In relation to that, the banks which lent money to Kohlberg Kravis Roberts to buy RJR Nabisco for $25 billion plan to sell $14 billion of loans to mainly European banks. Also, European firms use the syndicated loan market to buy other European or American companies. For example, Grand Metropolitan, a British hotel group, borrowed some $6 billion to acquire Pillsbury, a food and restaurant company. Total syndicated loans were $127 billion and new issues of Eurobonds reached $175 billion in 1988.[11] American and European investors are lining up to use such syndicated loans, although more and more European companies are moving towards leveraged buyouts and buy-in deals as the EC gradually becomes integrated into a single market. However, extensive use of "junk bonds" for leveraged buyouts may be risky, as happened with the bankruptcy of Drexel Burnham Lambert Inc., a large United States investment firm that laid off 5,400 employees (in February 1990) in the United States and Europe.

In order to discourage takeovers on both sides of the Atlantic, it may be suggested that short-term capital taxes be raised. But for long-term investment, indexation of capital gains is needed so that the effects of inflation be eliminated. Such measures would discourage leveraged buyouts and megamergers for short-run profits and stop the unhealthy and superficial growth of the economies involved.

To encourage more banking business in the United States and to attract capital inflow, the Federal Reserve approved in 1981 the creation of international banking facilities (IBFs) which accept foreign deposits. Because they were not subject to domestic regulations and taxes, they became successful in attracting foreign deposits, which exceed $300 billion. They are treated like foreign branches of United States banks and are not subject to reserve requirements and other restrictions. They are mostly exempted from state and local taxes as well.

There are more than 500 offices of foreign, mainly European, banks in the United States with over 20 percent of total United States banking activities. They may operate as agency offices of foreign banks that are not subject to United States regulations or as branches of foreign banks bearing their names and usually enjoying full-service offices. Finally, they may operate as subsidiary United States banks which are subject to United States regulations but they are owned by foreign banks. Foreign banks can form IBFs and Edge Act corporations, which are special subsidiaries created by the Edge Act of 1919, engaged mainly in international banking and are exempted from certain regulations such as those not permitting the opening of branches across state lines.

Liberalization of banking and financial services is also required to speed up monetary unification of the EC member countries. In the process, painstaking negotiations may be needed to reconcile differences and to avoid embarrassing interest groups that may feel threatened. It is difficult, though, to completely eliminate banking and financial regulations on a national level and achieve a completely free banking on the EC or international level. Restrictions exist even on interstate levels, as in the United States, for example, and more so on an international level. Thus, in Britain, banks based outside the EC must include a warning in their advertisements about the absence of deposit insurance, and transfer risks. Also, the Netherlands requires certain conditions for non-EC banks to use the word "bank" in their titles. In many cases permission of establishment is required and certain activities such as deposits and loans, managing securities issues, or underwriting bond issues are prohibited.

As America's external trade deficits shrink, imbalances within the EC continue. While trade deficits in Britain, Greece, and other EC members are getting worse, Germany's surplus is growing (from less than 10 billion in 1983, to about 140 billion marks or $81 billion in 1989, compared to $77 billion for Japan. If such imbalances continue, the planned monetary union of the EC may be in jeopardy. To reduce or eliminate imbalances, surplus countries like Germany should stimulate their economies and import more from their deficit partners. However, differences in inflation and competitiveness and therefore in real exchange rates seem to be the main reasons for trade imbalances. Nevertheless, it is expected that adjustment in the related currencies, together with flexible monetary and fiscal policies, would reinforce monetary stability in the European Monetary System and help achieve monetary integration, along with trade and eventual political integration among the European nations. It seems, though, that barriers in financial and banking services have not generated as much concern as trade transactions.

The Eurodollar Market

Although the Eurodollar Market began its expansion in the late 1950s, some form of foreign currency existed even before World War I in London, which was the international financial center. In 1957, the Moscow Norodny Bank of the Soviet Union deposited dollars in its branch in London and to another Soviet bank in Paris (the Banque Commerciale pour l'Europe du Nord) whose telex was "Eurobank." The main reason for the removal of the Soviet balances from New York to a British-chartered Russian bank and to Paris was the fear of possible freeze or confiscation of Soviet funds by American authorities during the cold war. The example of the Soviet Union was followed by other Eastern European countries and later by American and other banks and corporations. These Eurobank dollars or Continental dollars were and still are called Euro-dollars.

The first Eurodollar business was on an $800 million loan on February 28, 1957, by the Moscow Norodny Bank in London which was borrowed and repaid in dollars outside the United States banking system without any interference. The Sterling crisis of 1957 encouraged the British Banks to turn to such dollars for the financing of foreign trade. Other Western European banks continued the practice of accepting dollar deposits and lending them out to other European banks and corporations, thereby financing world trade in dollars outside of the United States.[12] The European banks are able to take deposits and lend out dollars with more attractive interest rates, compared to their American counterparts, because they are not under restrictions and regulations such as reserve requirements or exchange controls.

The development of the Eurodollar Market, particularly after 1963, was the result of the efforts of the banks to escape national controls whenever their cost outweighed benefits. In order to regulate United States banks participating in this market, the Kennedy Administration tried to enforce the Interest Equalization Tax, taxing the differences in interest, but the result was the opposite with a large outflow of dollars from the United States to Western Europe. Similar outflows of dollars occurred in the 1960s as a result of exchange controls introduced by the Voluntary Foreign Credit Restraint Program and the Foreign Direct Investment Regulations. Such controls and regulations required foreign investments to be financed mainly from abroad. As a result, United States banks increased their operations in Europe where they established branches to tap the Eurodollar market. Although these regulations and controls were removed in 1974, exchanges in dollars in Europe continued to thrive. The same thing can be said about Regulation Q of the United States Federal Reserve Bank (Fed) requiring that member banks pay the lower interest rate on time deposits fixed by the states where they operate. But Regulation Q did not apply to deposits outside the United States and investors looking for higher interest rates deposited and redeposited their money in the Eurodollar Market.

There are arguments that the Eurodollar Market may be responsible for stimulating world inflation. Although the Eurodollar multiplier is not expected to be large, there is some influence upon inflation depending on the velocity or the speed of Eurodollar transactions. However, it is difficult to measure such a velocity and the related influence upon inflation, because, among other reasons, controls and supervisions of the market by central banks are limited or nonexistent. Moreover, domestic monetary policies become, to some extent, ineffective, especially in countries whose currencies are involved. Such countries include the United States with dollars (Eurodollars), Germany with marks (Euromarks), France with francs (Eurofrancs), and Japan with yens (Euroyens). Thus, if the United States Fed attempted to absorb dollars by selling bonds domestically, this policy might be undermined by domestic banks through loans from the Eurodollar Market, thereby nullifying partially or totally the results of contraction of money and credit. In addition, more and more United States corporations and investors become foreign holders of dollars and this means less business and profits for United States banks and other companies. To such fears, expressed mainly by David Rockefeller and other bankers, one can advance the argument that deposits of dollars abroad are, to a large extent, transfers to the same or another American bank or even to a non-American bank still in dollars that remain primarily with the American banking system. Overall, in spite of some problems with the central banks, the Eurodollar Market is beneficial to the world economy, particularly to the EC, making accessible loans, facilitating transactions among nations, and advancing the international financial markets.

A growing Eurodollar Market in a more unified Europe would make EC banks stronger than their American counterparts, while their influence on the World Bank and other international institutions would be more significant. However, the establishment of United States banks or their subsidiaries and other industries into Europe would enhance their ability to influence events in the old continent and help avoid serious impediments to American economic and defense policies in this part of the world.

The real political power in the world is related to economic, technological, and financial power. Banks and other financial intermediaries, along with advanced telecommunications, play a significant role in the transmission of such power from country to country and from continent to continent.

Foreign exchange markets, where monies are traded, exist to facilitate currency transactions and international payments. The terms Eurocurrency market and Eurobanks signify international monetary exchanges, deposits, loans, and credit in general not only in Europe but also to offshore banking activities in the Bahamas or Hong Kong and elsewhere. The reserve status of the dollar and the dollar deposits in the European banks created the sizable Eurodollar market. Because of controls and regulations in domestic banks, Eurobanks or offshore banks are able to offer higher deposit and lower loan interest rates, thereby narrowing the difference (spread) on dollars.

Eurobanks are largely unregulated regarding reserve requirements, credit allocations, credit and interest rate controls, and deposit insurance. Although in some countries domestic regulations apply to the Eurocurrency transactions, such transactions are considered riskier compared to domestic ones in United States dollars. The United States deposit rates provide a floor for the Eurodeposit rate and the United States loan rates a ceiling for the Euroloan rates, in the sense that supply of deposits and demand for loans would fall to zero outside the United States spread. However, the LIBOR (London Interbank Offer Rate) is mostly used for Eurodollar transactions, that is, the interest rate at which six big London banks would charge to each other every morning. The size of the Eurocurrency market was $2.2 trillion or 75 percent of the gross market size in 1981, and $4.1 trillion or 67 percent in 1986.[13]

The European countries and perhaps the entire world have an interest in preserving the health of the United States economy. At the same time, the United States should encourage saving for investment. Its policy of dependence on Eurocurrencies and foreign savings to finance budget and trade deficits and domestic investment is gradually wearing away its economic strength and world influence. Although this policy is not expected to lead to a collapse or a "heart attack" of the United States economy in the short run, it may lead to a gradual weakening or a "cancer" in the long run.

There are large amounts of Eurodollars deposited in European and other banks that affect the economies of the United States, the EC, and other countries. At present, many multinational corporations deposit their surplus funds into European and other banks instead of preferring the United States banks. Eurodollar deposits became more attractive because European banks are permitted to pay interest in very short-term deposits and no reserve requirements and other restrictions exist. This new money supply outside the United States makes the United States monetary policy less effective and the United States dollar an important component of the international monetary system. Therefore, a synthesis of domestic monetary policy and international monetary and trade transactions would improve economic stability at home and abroad.[14]

Banks and trust companies from the United States, Britain, and other countries move operations to Bermuda, the Bahamas, and the Caribbean islands, among other offshore centers. They are now looking to the European Community to pick up more business, particularly as closer integration is advanced. Instead of farming investment management out to managers in Europe or in the United States, they increasingly offer it to their global investors in these places where they enjoy more freedom and flexibility regarding taxation and other restrictive measures.

There are more than 1300 captive insurance companies or offshore banks or trusts in Bermuda alone, about half of the world's captives, that resemble their competitors in Luxembourg and Switzerland. More than $8 billion premium income was attracted by Bermuda's insurance companies in 1987, $1.1 billion by those in the Cayman Islands, and $200 million by those in the Bahamas. United States corporations and associations of lawyers, doctors, and other professionals who have difficulties in getting insurance coverage onshore move their money offshore. In addition, there are reasons of tax and time-zone convenience for money movement and premium payment there.[15]

The United States Tax Reform Act of 1986 is taxing all investors, wherever they are, and does not allow exceptions for investment in Eurodollars. This reform act and the easing of related regulations by some states made it more attractive for onshore captives. International companies partly owned by a United States company can use Eurodollars and enjoy previous benefits. From that point of view, the Europeans are expected to make up for the offshore operations lost because of the new United States regulations.

Inflationary Pressures

Comparatively speaking, inflation in the EC, on the average, was higher than in the United States during the last two decades, as Table 5.2 shows. After 1986, however, the United States inflationary rates were slightly higher than those of the EC. From the EC member-nations, Greece and Portugal had high rates of inflation, followed by Italy, Spain, and Britain. The Netherlands, Germany, Belgium, and France had low rates of inflation in recent years and the other EC members were in between. In the two decades before 1986, the United States and the EC had relatively high rates of inflation, but due to disciplinary economic policies on both sides of the Atlantic those rates were reduced significantly. Presently, though, inflation (the Consumer Price Index) started rising again to annual rates above 4 percent in the United States and close to 4 percent in the EC.

A coordinated monetary policy and eventually a single currency with a central bank in the European Community, along with a common economic policy, would reduce inflation differentials in the EC countries and help stabilize their economies. Although this would involve a transfer of national sovereignty, as the British officials argue, it would stop substantial differences in economic policies by individual EC member-nations and reduce frictions on exchange rates among European currencies as well as between them and the United States dollar.

In the market economies of the EC and the United States, increase in prices is primarily the result of excess demand over supply (demand-pull inflation) or increases in wages or other factor prices at rates higher than the rates of productivity (cost-push inflation). An increase in spending, stimulated by budget deficits, may be considered as an important reason for demand-pull inflation in the United States and some EC countries. On the other hand, because of the strong labor unions in Greece, Portugal, Spain, and, to a lesser extent, in Italy, Britain, and France, increases in wages and labor benefits result in cost-push

Table 5.2
Inflation in the EC Countries and the United States (differences in percentages from previous periods)

Country	1967–76	1976–85	1986	1987	1988
Belgium	6.8	6.4	1.3	1.6	1.2
Britain	10.8	10.1	3.4	4.2	4.9
Denmark	8.2	9.2	3.6	4.0	4.6
France	7.8	10.1	2.7	3.1	2.7
Germany, W.	4.8	3.9	– 0.2	0.2	1.2
Greece	8.9	19.0	23.0	16.4	13.5
Ireland	11.6	12.7	3.8	3.2	2.1
Italy	9.1	15.1	6.1	4.6	5.0
Luxembourg	6.1	6.3	0.3	– 0.1	1.4
Netherlands	7.4	4.7	0.1	– 0.7	0.7
Portugal	12.6	22.9	11.8	9.4	9.7
Spain	10.0	15.1	8.8	5.3	4.8
EC	7.9	9.4	3.3	3.1	3.4
USA	6.1	7.3	1.9	3.4	4.1

Source: OECD; and Pavlos Klavdianos, "International Inflationary Trends Continue," in Greek, *Oikopnomikos Tahydromos*, August 17, 1989, p. 75.

inflation. In the United States, though, where employee stock ownership plans (ESOPs) have been established that include more than 10 million workers (approaching the numbers in the labor unions), sharing in corporate decision making reduces pressures for increases in wages higher than productivity rates. A similar expansion of employee-sharing in decision making and co-management of labor and capital (mainly in Germany) is partially responsible for antiinflationary trends in the EC. Another reason for less pressures of wage increases, especially in the United States, is the dwindling power of labor unions which, lately, behave like tamed dogs.

Although both fiscal and monetary policies are used to curb inflation by the governments considered, more emphasis is placed on monetarism and supply-side economics, particularly in the United States. Sometimes, though, reduction in government expenditures or tax increases are used to reduce inflation. This is particularly so in countries with large budget deficits such as the United States and most of the EC countries. The idea is to reduce spending and aggregate demand, thereby supressing inflation which started growing again.

Tight monetary policy by the central banks of the EC and the United States to fight inflation usually pushes yields of short-term debt securities above those of long-term bonds and produces a slowdown in the economy. Such a policy, which was implemented in the early 1980s when rates of inflation were high, pushed real interest rates up high and produced a severe recession in the United States, the EC, and other Western economies.

The United States and EC monetary authorities then have to consider seriously these developments in determining money supply for financing real GNP and for reducing inflation. Because, when the velocity of money (V) and the money supply (M_1) grow over and above the real production (Q) then prices (P) grow accordingly. This is so, because, according to the classical equation of exchange, the percentage change in money supply ($\Delta M_1/M_1$) plus the percentage change in velocity ($\Delta V/V$) is equal to the percentage change in the price index ($\Delta P/P$) plus the percentage change in real GNP or the change in the quantity of production ($\Delta Q/Q$), that is $\Delta M_1/M_1 + \Delta V/V = \Delta P/P + \Delta Q/Q$. For example, if money grows by 8 percent, velocity by 2 percent, and real production by 4 percent, then inflation is 6 percent ($0.08 + 0.02 = \Delta P/P + 0.04$ and $\Delta P/P = 0.10 - 0.04 = 0.06$).

Unlike some EC countries with high inflation, notably Greece and Portugal, which finance public sector deficits in an inflationary manner, the United States borrows money from the general public to finance budget deficits. It does not increase the money supply for that purpose. From that point of view, there seems to be a close relationship between budget deficits, changes in money supply, and the rates of inflation in countries that finance budget deficits by printing additional money. In such cases, public sector deficits, including those of public enterprises, should be responsible for inflation.

Although financial markets in the United States and Britain are efficient in transmitting savings into investment, lately they channel savings largely in financing acquisitions and takeovers and not much in financing investment in new plants and equipment. Moreover, the governments and the central banks of the EC and the United States can cause a new surge of inflation by bailing out savings banks or other enterprises. Such bailing out of troubled banks, with uncovered debts of more than $150 billion, occurred recently in the United States. Inflationary pressures are also expected from financing the weak economies of the Eastern European countries.

To deal with inflation and recession, central banks or monetary authorities on both sides of the Atlantic, explicitly or implicitly, use the following version of the quantity equation of exchange

$$P^* = (M_2 \times V^*)/Q^*$$

to forecast inflation. In this equation, M_2 stands for the money supply that includes not only the cash in the economy and deposits in checking, but also travelers checks, savings accounts, and deposits in money market and mutual funds. V^* stands for the long-run velocity of M_2, that is, the speed with which money changes hands in the economy. Q^* is the potential value of production or real GNP (Gross National Product). Finally, P^* stands for expected future prices.

Since velocity is considered constant (according to monetarists) and Q^* is regarded as a predictable figure, the eventual price level will depend on the manipulation of the money supply by the central bank. If P^* is compared with P (the current price level) then inflationary trends can be predicted. If P^* is higher than P, then future inflation will exceed current inflation and vice versa. For example, $P^* = (\$2,200 \text{ billion} \times 3)/\$6,000 \text{ billion} = 6,600/6,000 = 1.1$. That is, if M_2 (money supply) is \$2,200 billion, V^* (velocity) is equal to 3 and Q^* (predicted real GNP) is \$6,000 billion then P^* (expected inflation) will be 10 percent.[16] Although additional measures of fiscal and income policies are also important, monetary measures, based upon the above equation, play a vital role in dealing with inflation or deflation, particularly in the United States and Britain and to a lesser extent in France, Germany, and other EC countries. However, our empirical findings do not support constancy in money velocity over time, making predicitions on inflation doubtful (see Figures. 5.6 and 5.7).

As the dollar becomes stronger, the EC monetary authorities are under pressure to raise interest rates to avoid an increase in inflation. The question is: What are the causes that determine the value of the dollar and how it affects trade balances? It seems that psychological reasons affect the ups and downs in the short run, while interest rates, inflation, saving rates, budget and trade deficits, and economic growth affect the value of the dollar primarily in the medium term. However, in the long term the purchasing power of currencies plays an important role in the determination of their relative values. It may be argued, though, that all these factors, one way or another, affect the dollar up or down regardless of the longevity of time.

In the process of monetary adjustment and policy harmonization, some flexibility should be allowed for the EC member countries to adjust their fiscal and monetary policies to new conditions of monetary integration. Individual governments should be permitted, within specified limits, to finance budget deficits through domestic credit creation, that is, through their central banks. Nevertheless, budget deficits should be financed primarily by selling securities (bonds or bills) to a Community-wide market. Thus, each member-nation can achieve monetary expansion by selling government securities to other member nations with available capital, thereby curbing inflationary pressures and contributing to regional economic stabilization and growth. Such securities can be sold also in local currency but guaranteed by European Currency Units (ECUs), as happened recently in some cases. However, the EC should develop a mechanism for effecting transfers of funds among its different regions, supplemented by related subsidies.

Currently problems of monetary stability are appearing regarding the inconvertibility of the currencies of the East Bloc countries. For example, questions are raised as to the exchange rates of the currencies of Eastern European nations in terms of German marks, United States dollars, or other hard currencies and their effects on interest rates, inflation, and economic growth.

6 Trade Relations

EXPORTS, IMPORTS AND TRADE DEFICITS

This chapter deals with trade relations between the EC and the United States. The possibilities and the difficulties of closer cooperation are also examined. Trade and other relations between the two have been strong throughout history. In a way, it can be said that the relations of old Europe and young America have been and still are similar to those of a mother and a daughter, not only on economic but also on socio-cultural and other matters. However, the integration movement of the European Community presents problems of trade and investment adjustment between the United States and the EC. In the short run, there may be conflicts regarding exports of certain products and services but in the long run their mutual needs for trade and investment will necessitate closer cooperation and mutual dependence.

Subsidies and other measures are frequently used by both the EC and the United States to stimulate production and to increase exports, as well as to protect certain domestic industries or products. In many instances, though, agricultural and industrial expansions create unneeded and duplicative projects with idle capacity that threaten to initiate slumps on both sides of the Atlantic. To grasp foreign markets and increase employment and income at home, the governments of the EC and the United States resort, from time to time, to protectionistic measures that stifle competition and restrict free trade between them.

As in 1492, when Christopher Columbus expanded European trade by discovering North America, so 500 years later, in 1992, a new European odyssey of economic expansion is in the making. The new integrated Euromarket of the twelve EC nations, as Jean Monnet and Robert Schuman advocated in the 1950s, arose high hopes about the great opportunities expected to be opened to domestic and foreign enterprises. Although member nations are slow in yielding sovereignty, the pressure for economic improvement, via the free movement of people, goods, and money, generated cooperation in removing nationalistic and other obstacles and creating a single market and a closer partnership.

Europe realizes that it cannot compete with the United States and Japan without dismantling trade barriers and restructuring its economic and political institutions. The complete economic unification of the EC countries and eventually all of Europe is an ambitious plan, similar to that of Napoleon the Great, but it must be voluntary, not forced. A united Europe will reduce internal national conflicts and strengthen democracy. Extreme right or left governments will be discouraged as resources and investment will quickly move to other EC and East Bloc countries. However, there is skepticism in the United States and other nations that European enterprises, exposed to greater competition internally, may press for protection against their American and Asian counterparts. There is a risk that restrictions on trade, investment, services, and other economic activities may take place.

Some American economists and politicians feel that the European integration may lead to protectionism, introducing preferences for European firms and European goods and services and adversely affecting United States companies and United States products. This may be particularly so for food products, pharmaceuticals, and services. Although the European policy makers argue that there is a commitment not to create additional barriers, some United States companies invest inside Europe to hedge against probable protectionism. Nevertheless, free trade arrangements between the United States and the EC can be made, before the European train leaves the station or at least in the next station, without challenging the EC integration and identity. Until recently Washington was slow to react but now is trying to catch up by working toward a more equal Atlantic relationship.

The fear of reciprocity, though, would rather force Europe to promote trade liberalization and more openness. It would seem that Europe needs America as America needs Europe for more trade and investment. Through negotiations and mutual concessions, less protection and more cooperation, under the umbrella of GATT, could be forthcoming. Both the United States and Europe are large markets and an American-European corporate alliance can further promote economic prosperity on both sides of the Atlantic.

As Table 6.1 and Figure 6.1 show, the United States has had large trade deficits with the EC in recent years. However, for almost all post-World War II years until 1982, it had trade surpluses. On the average United States exports to the EC are about one-fourth of its total exports, while its imports from the EC are about one-fifth of total imports. After World War II the devastated economies of Europe needed the American consumer and particularly capital goods for their development. In recent years, though, Western Europe has managed to advance enough to sell more products to the United States annually than it buys.

Imports from and exports to the United States by the individual EC member-

Table 6.1
Exports and Imports of the United States to and from the EC (billions of U.S. current dollars)

Years	Exports		Imports		Balance
	value	% of total	value	% of total	value
1968	11.7	24.8	11.5	25.0	0.2
1969	13.0	25.4	11.5	23.0	1.5
1970	15.4	26.1	12.7	23.1	2.7
1971	11.1	25.2	10.4	22.9	0.7
1972	11.9	23.9	12.5	22.5	− 0.6
1973	16.7	24.0	15.6	22.6	1.1
1974	22.1	22.9	19.2	19.2	2.9
1975	22.9	21.7	16.7	17.6	6.2
1976	25.4	22.6	18.1	15.0	7.3
1977	26.5	24.6	22.4	16.1	4.1
1978	31.4	23.7	31.1	18.0	0.3
1979	41.0	25.1	35.7	17.2	5.3
1980	52.5	26.2	38.0	15.8	14.5
1981	50.0	23.5	43.6	16.8	6.4
1982	50.8	24.1	46.4	18.3	4.4
1983	47.4	23.8	47.8	17.8	− 0.4
1984	49.0	22.7	63.0	18.6	− 14.0
1985	48.1	22.7	71.3	19.9	− 23.2
1986	52.1	24.6	78.7	20.6	− 26.0
1987	59.4	23.5	84.6	20.0	− 25.2

Source: United Nations, *Yearbook of International Trade Statistics*, various issues; United States Government, Department of Commerce; and OECD, *National Accounts*, various issues.

nations are presented in Table 6.2, while Table 6.3 compares imports of the EC countries from the United States with those from the non-EC countries. Britain and West Germany have the largest volumes of trade with the United States, followed by France, Italy, and the Netherlands. Moreover, West Germany has a very large trade surplus with the United States, as do Italy and Britain, while the Netherlands, Spain, France, and Ireland have relatively small trade deficits.

Figure 6.1
United States Exports and Trade Balance with the EC

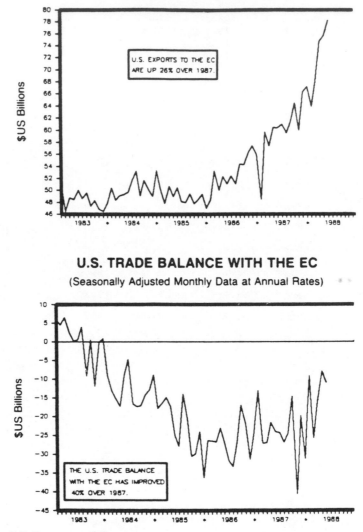

U.S. EXPORTS TO THE EC GROWING RAPIDLY

(Seasonally Adjusted Monthly Data at Annual Rates)

U.S. EXPORTS TO THE EC
ARE UP 26% OVER 1987.

U.S. TRADE BALANCE WITH THE EC

(Seasonally Adjusted Monthly Data at Annual Rates)

THE U.S. TRADE BALANCE
WITH THE EC HAS IMPROVED
40% OVER 1987.

Source: U.S. Department of Commerce.

Almost all EC countries have higher percentages of exports to, and mostly lower percentages of imports from, the United States than a decade ago.

Table 6.4 shows total trade of the EC countries with the rest of the world and trade proportions with the rest of the EC nations. West Germany has consistently

Table 6.2
Trade of the EC Countries with the United States (in billions of U.S. current dollars), 1986

Countries	Imports(C.I.F.)		Exports(F.O.B.)		Trade Balance
	billions of $	% of total	billions of $	% of total	
Belgium-Luxembourg	3.4	5.1	3.6	5.2	0.2
Britain	12.5	10.0	15.2	14.2	2.7
Denmark	1.1	4.8	1.7	8.4	0.6
France	9.5	7.4	8.8	7.4	-0.7
Germany, W.	12.3	6.5	25.3	10.4	13.0
Greece	0.3	3.0	0.4	7.1	0.1
Ireland	1.8	15.8	1.1	8.7	-0.7
Italy	5.4	5.7	10.5	10.7	5.1
Netherlands	6.0	7.9	3.8	4.7	-2.2
Portugal	0.6	6.8	0.5	7.0	-0.1
Spain	3.3	9.8	2.5	9.2	-0.8
Total	56.2	7.3	73.4	9.3	17.2

Source: United Nations, *Yearbook of International Trade Statistics* (New York: United Nations, 1988).

more exports than imports, ending up with large surpluses. The Netherlands, Italy, and Belgium-Luxembourg have relatively smaller trade surpluses, but Britain, Greece, Spain, and Portugal have trade deficits. The other EC nations have small surpluses, while the EC as a unit has sizable annual trade surpluses.

Trade between the EC nations has increased significantly more than trade with non-EC nations. Britain, Greece, Spain, and Portugal have higher proportions of exports to the rest of the EC nations than a decade ago, but even higher proportions of imports. All the other EC countries have about the same or somewhat higher proportions of exports to the other EC nations. Among the EC nations, except for Ireland, the proportions of imports from other EC nations increased during the last decade by 1.5 percent for West Germany, 7.1 for France, 10.4 for Italy, 10.1 for Portugal, 11.3 for Britain, 13.8 for Greece, and as high as 16.1 percent for Spain.

These trends indicate that as the European Community moves toward more integration, trade between member-nations increases at the expense of the non-EC nations, including the United States. From that point of view, the United States fears of lower exports to the EC are justified, at least for the short term.

In the long run, though, a unified common market of Europe would increase trade opportunities not only among EC member-nations but between EC and non-EC countries, primarily with the United States. Free movement of goods

Table 6.3
EC Imports from the United States and from Non-EC Countries (in billions of U.S. current dollars), 1987

Countries	Imports from the United States	Imports from non-EC countries
Belgium-Luxem.	3.9	23.0
Britain	15.1	74.3
Denmark	1.2	12.0
France	11.3	53.5
Germany, W.	14.2	103.1
Greece	0.3	5.5
Ireland	2.3	3.8
Italy	6.7	53.9
Netherlands	6.6	36.7
Portugal	0.7	4.9
Spain	4.0	20.8
EC	65.7	391.6

Source: United States Government, Department of Commerce.

and services, without national regulations and border restrictions, a uniformed business code, and a more homogeneous consumer population would facilitate transactions between the EC and the United States.

Table 6.5 shows total exports and imports of the EC with the rest of the world. Although there were trade deficits in a few recession years in the 1960s, 1970s, and early 1980s, mostly trade surpluses prevailed in the EC during the last three decades. However, large surpluses can be observed after 1982. This trend encourages rapid integration of the European Common Market, as well as closer cooperation with non-EC trade partners, particularly the United States and the East Bloc countries.

As Table 6.6 shows, the United States has large trade deficits, particularly after 1980. This is due primarily to big increases in imports compared to comparatively lower increases in exports. For more than fifty years before 1971, United States exports were higher than imports, leaving surpluses in the balance of payments. The steep rises in oil prices in the 1970s were a severe burden on the economies of the United States and the EC. Moreover, the appreciation of the dollar in the first half of the 1980s and the federal budget deficits may be considered as the main reasons for the large deficits in the United States balance

Table 6.4
Total Exports and Imports of the EC Countries (in billions of U.S. current dollars), 1988

Countries	Exports		Imports		Trade Balance
	billions of $	% with the EC	billions of $	% with the EC	billions of $
Belgium-Luxembourg	100.0	73.3	95.8	72.8	4.2
Britain	192.6	48.1	224.6	52.0	-32.0
Denmark	34.0	45.3	30.9	51.7	3.1
France	200.7	57.9	199.5	60.0	1.2
Germany, W.	384.9	50.9	317.7	52.4	67.2
Greece	11.6	63.6	15.1	58.6	-3.5
Ireland	17.5	72.0	15.5	67.3	2.0
Italy	149.0	53.6	143.3	56.1	5.7
Netherlands	122.4	74.9	114.6	63.9	7.8
Portugal	12.5	68.3	14.8	58.9	-2.3
Spain	68.2	60.3	72.1	50.4	-3.9
EC Total	1,293.4	-------	1,243.9	------	49.5

Note: In some cases, earlier years' data were available. Exports and imports in national currencies were changed to dollar values at year end exchange rates. Percentages of trade with the EC for 1986.

Source: Organization for Economic Cooperation and Development (OECD), *National Accounts*; and United Nations, *International Trade Statistics*; and International Monetary Fund (IMF), *International Financial Statistics*, various issues.

of trade. However, the depreciation of the dollar thereafter is expected to reduce trade deficits, although with a delay. This is indicated by lower trade deficits that can be observed in recent years.

Efforts of the United States monetary authorities to drive the dollar down aim primarily to reduce imports from and to increase exports to the EC and other countries. For instance, there is a decline in United States car imports of some $10 million annually, mainly because of the depreciation of the dollar. Depressed sales can also be observed in German cars, such as Audi, Porsche, and even Mercedes-Benz, which has had a near monopoly in luxury cars for some thirty years, with an annual production of 550 thousand cars. However, BMW, a strong competitor of the United States Pontiac Fiero cars, with an annual production of about 500 thousand, is maintaining ever increasing sales in the United States and other countries including Japan. It seems that the recent increases in discount interest rates in Germany (from 4 to 4.5 percent) and Japan (from 2.5 to 3.75 percent for the first time in nine years) would curb inflationary pressures

Table 6.5
Imports and Exports of Goods and Services of the EC (at current prices and current exchange rates, billions of U.S. dollars)

Years	Imports	Exports	Balance
1960	55.6	57.6	2.0
1961	59.4	61.6	2.2
1962	64.5	65.3	0.6
1963	71.9	70.9	-1.0
1964	80.7	79.1	-1.6
1965	87.4	87.4	0.0
1966	94.8	96.4	1.6
1967	99.0	102.0	3.0
1968	107.9	112.4	4.5
1969	125.5	129.3	3.8
1970	146.3	150.5	4.2
1971	164.8	172.6	7.8
1972	196.9	206.4	9.5
1973	272.2	275.6	3.4
1974	368.9	357.7	-11.2
1975	382.4	387.2	4.8
1976	426.8	421.4	-5.4
1977	479.6	487.3	7.7
1978	563.9	589.8	25.9
1979	737.2	737.4	0.2
1980	881.3	850.4	-30.9
1981	791.3	787.6	-3.7
1982	755.3	757.2	1.9
1983	718.9	738.2	19.3
1984	726.4	749.9	23.5
1985	750.6	786.3	25.7
1986	900.6	973.3	72.7
1987	1171.5	1106.8	64.7

Source: Organization for Economic Cooperation and Development (OECD), *National Accounts*, various issues.

but they would reduce somewhat the huge industrial expansion these countries achieved in the 1980s.

Countries with surpluses in their trade balances, such as Germany, often do not want their currencies to appreciate much because it makes their products more expensive abroad and foreign products cheaper at home. On the other hand, countries with trade deficits, such as the United States, frequently do not want their currencies to depreciate much because it can stimulate inflation as prices of imported products are rising. Although the demand and supply mechanism of currencies should be free to correct imbalances, in many cases coordinated policies of concerned monetary authorities may intervene in money markets to influence currency prices one way or another.

The establishment of pan-European standards and regulations in product testing and certification, safety and quality requirements, telecommunications and marketing, financial services and public sector procurement would harmonize and reduce national differences and encourage internal and international competition.

Table 6.6
Imports and Exports of Goods and Services of the United States (at current prices and current exchange rates, billions of U.S. dollars)

Years	Imports	Exports	Balance
1960	22.6	26.7	4.1
1961	22.4	27.3	4.9
1962	24.7	28.7	4.0
1963	25.9	30.7	4.8
1964	27.8	34.6	6.8
1965	31.2	36.7	5.5
1966	36.7	40.4	3.7
1967	39.5	43.0	3.5
1968	46.1	47.3	1.2
1969	50.0	51.4	1.4
1970	55.2	59.1	3.9
1971	61.7	62.3	0.6
1972	73.5	70.0	-3.5
1973	90.4	93.8	3.4
1974	125.6	124.2	-1.4
1975	120.6	136.4	15.8
1976	148.5	146.6	-1.9
1977	179.1	155.7	-23.4
1978	208.2	182.0	-26.2
1979	248.2	223.6	-24.6
1980	288.1	273.4	-14.7
1981	310.5	293.0	-17.5
1982	295.1	270.9	-24.2
1983	319.8	264.0	-55.8
1984	389.4	283.3	-106.1
1985	400.0	281.0	-119.0
1986	429.3	290.2	-139.1
1987	484.5	332.0	-152.5
1988	537.9	430.9	-107.0

Source: Organization for Economic Cooperation and Development (OECD), *National Accounts*, various issues. For 1988, International Monetary Fund, *International Financial Statistics*, October 1989.

Thus, wasteful duplication would be avoided and investment and trade would rise on a European-wide scale.

To take advantage of this large European market and the liberalized trade regulations, the United States is proceeding aggressively with plans to improve exports and investments into Europe. Thus, the "Europe now" and "export now" programs have been initiated to highlight the advantages of exporting to and investing in Europe. To support these programs and help United States companies penetrate the European markets, a number of services are offered by such institutions as the U.S. and Foreign Commercial Service (U.S. and FCS), providing information on customs and exchange rates (with about 250 trade professionals in Europe and specialists in sixty-six major United States cities); the International Trade Administration (ITA) of the Department of Commerce, offering counseling services; and the Trade Development (TD) unit, assisting

United States exporters and investors to promote exports through successful marketing and effective competition. Also, trade fairs and exhibitions or pavilions in Europe are used to promote United States products and to attract potential customers and qualified distributors and European trade agents.

Competition between the EC and the United States is becoming strong not only on commercial goods and services but also on military weaponry. The European Community is successfully challenging the United States arms industry in such weapons and military hardware as missiles, aircraft, and tanks.

United States financial deregulation, though a meritable idea, has not proven effective in correcting unbalanced transactions between the United States, the EC, and Japan or other countries. Perhaps its timing and implementation were not proper, exposing financial markets to great uncertainties and risks. Thus, the weaker dollar has not done much to improve the United States trade balance, probably because of the existing inflexibility in trade and financial markets.

Business fluctuations and other external factors affect economic trends in the EC. Since 1945, and until the oil crisis in 1973, Western Europe had a satisfactory economic expansion. Thereafter, a severe recession followed until the middle 1980s, when an upturn in economic growth and foreign trade could be observed again.

Figure 6.2 shows the interelationship of EC entities affecting European trade and investment standards.

In the process of harmonizing rules and removing barriers, there are complaints, mainly from Britain and West Germany, against France and Italy, that they favor maintenance of trade barriers to outsiders. There is a serious question, though, whether American or Japanese cars and other goods with European content be considered as foreign and subjected to tariffs, quotas, and other restrictions. Thus, executives of Fiat S.p.A. in Italy and Renault and Peugeot in France maintain that if the EC content of Bluebirds (cars) are more than 50 percent Japanese and less than 50 percent British they must be subject to import quotas (no more than 3 percent of the domestic market in France). The same thing can be said about the EC imports of Honda cars assembled in Ohio. It is argued, however, that this policy would reduce or discourage American, Japanese, and other foreign investment in the EC.

In the European countries, entrepreneurs and business people in the automobile and other industries express their solid support for the single European market, expecting to increase trade and investment. They began to overcome their earlier indifference to the expected European integration and to grasp its implications on their enterprises. The feeling is that they have to adapt rapidly to the new economic and political environment in order to survive in a more competitive, larger market. This is particularly so because of the new conditions created in the reformed economies of Eastern Europe.

There are complaints in Europe that American performance in restraining demand to reduce imports and increase savings is inadequate. Excessive spending and the rise in exports lead to pressures on productive capacity and feed infla-

Figure 6.2
Interrelationships of Entities Influencing the Development of European Standards

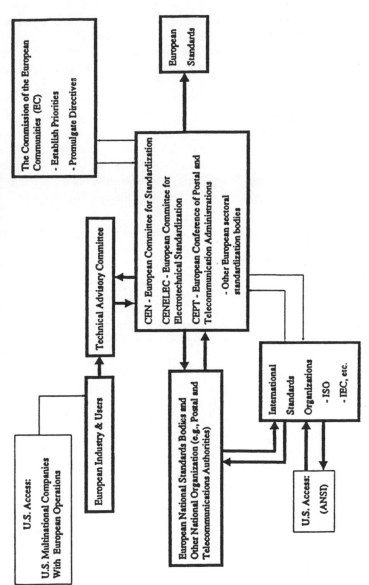

Source: United States Government, Department of Commerce.

tionary expectations. On the other hand, the United States criticizes West Germany for not doing enough to stimulate demand and increase its rate of economic growth, which would encourage investment, reduce unemployment, and increase tax revenue. From that point of view, a better coordination of economic policy between the United States and the EC to prevent it from turning into a fortress group and to preserve open economies on both sides of the Atlantic would increase free trade and keep Europe and the United States from turning against each other with all the consequent detrimental effects for their economies and their people.

The percentage increase of imports related to increases in income (income elasticity of imports) was higher in the United States than in the EC for the last three decades. Thus, the income elasticity of imports was, on the average, 1.97 for the United States for 1960–1980 and 1.29 for the EC during the same period, while for the 1980s, it was 1.03 for the United States and only 0.82 for the EC. This means that the United States spent proportionally higher percentages of income increases for imports than the EC during the last three decades.

PROBLEMS OF COMPETITION AND PROTECTIONISM

As mentioned earlier, historically the United States had high tariffs. The duties collected as a percent of dutiable imports varied from 45 percent in 1820, to 64 percent in 1833 (Compromise Tariff Act), about 25 percent in 1857, some 18 percent in 1860, around 50 percent in 1900, 12 percent in 1920, 60 percent in 1930 (Smoot-Hawley Act), about 15 percent in 1967 (Kennedy-Round Reductions), and around 7 percent now (Uruguay Round).[1] Recently it seems that the United States, along with other members of GATT, took a number of steps to promote free trade by reducing tariffs and eliminating trade barriers.

However, there exist quotas on certain products, based mainly on voluntary restraint agreements, among the United States, Japan, some EC countries, and other nations. Thus, to protect the American steel industry against imports from some 29 nations, imports are limited by the United States to 20 percent of domestic steel consumption. Such quotas are the result of the flood of imports and the big losses by steel companies in the early 1980s. Steel companies argue that foreign governments subsidize steel that can be sold in American markets at prices lower than the cost of production. Similar voluntary restraints prevail for cars, textiles, and other products that are considered to be under conditions of unfair competition. There are complaints though by some 400 United States companies which buy steel that, as a result of protection, shortages appear and prices go up. This is why they try to influence Congress not to extend such protective measures. Also, imported vehicles classified as trucks are subject to 25 percent duty, instead of 2 percent for other imported cars—a measure that affects United States imports mainly from West Germany, Britain, and Japan.

In a customs union like the EC, where no tariffs or other barriers on trade among members are allowed and trade policies are harmonized with the rest of the world, trade creation and trade diversion may occur. Trade is normally created and welfare increased among member nations of the customs union. But trade diversion and welfare reduction can be expected to occur in non-member nations because of the less efficient use of their resources as a result of the formation of a customs union. When part of domestic production is replaced by cheaper imports from another member of a customs union, then trade creation occurs. Moreover, the welfare of non-member countries may increase through higher imports from them as a result of the increase in real income of the members of the union. As long as a customs union, like the EC, does not raise tariffs or other trade barriers to outside nations, then the reduction of barriers among members would normally increase trade and welfare, not only for members but for non-members as well. Nevertheless, there may be reductions in the union's demand for imports from and its supply of exports to the non-member nations and an improvement in its collective terms of trade, depending on the relative elasticities.

Since 1980, protectionist barriers have gone up on both sides, the EC and the United States. A real appreciation of the currency of a country, *ceteris paribus*, leads to a worsening of the balance of foreign trade and therefore to the economic and political pressures for protection. On the contrary, a real depreciation of a currency leads to the improvement of the balance of trade and the relaxation of protectionist pressures or even the reduction of trade restrictions. Thus, the sizable depreciation of European currencies from 1980 to 1985 (by 43 percent for the mark, 57 percent for the franc, and 62 percent for the pound) improved the EC trade balance accordingly (from $3.1 billion to $23.5 billion).

Deregulation in air and surface transportation, financial markets and communications, oil prices, and stock exchange brokerage has intensified price competition and spurred efficiency in those industries. Moreover, proposals for regulatory reforms have been made in Europe and the United States for further deregulations in banking and natural gas prices, deposit insurance and private pensions, nuclear licensing, trucking and railroads, and environmental restrictions. However, in some cases deregulations led to overlapping markets, turbulent entry of new firms, and maneuvers toward price discrimination.

Regarding foreign trade deregulation, United States restrictions on color television sets and nonrubber footwear, mainly from South Korea, Taiwan, Italy, and Brazil, were lifted and quotas on copper were not imposed in spite of the cries of domestic industries for protection. However, for a number of products, such as steel, cars, and cloth, "voluntary" quotas were introduced to reduce imports. Such quotas, though, may be considered detrimental to EC-United States competition and universal free trade. They seem to be worse than tariffs because they make it difficult for foreign competitors to increase sales and reduce prices. As a result, the United States trade policies seem to be moving gradually in a protectionist direction, despite the cries for deregulation and the support of the free market mechanism in international transactions.

United States exporters and subsidiaries sell a total of about $600 billion in the EC, while EC exports and subsidiary sales of EC companies in the United States amount to about $400 billion. Through the elimination of border controls and harmonization of product standards the EC production and market would expand for both domestic and foreign companies. It is estimated that the removal of internal barriers would result in a 5 percent increase in EC gross domestic product, that is, by more than $200 billion.

By establishing new "European" rules and eliminating conflicting procedures of individual member states, the Internal Market Program of the EC may offer good opportunities for United States business firms located in or exporting to Europe. However, in implementing internal market reforms, it is expected that the EC would not discriminate against foreign companies by transforming internal barriers into external barriers around the whole Community. The new rules should not impose limits regarding fair competition from United States and other external firms but they should introduce a true liberalization spirit for trade and investment for outsiders as well. In any case, United States businesses should be familiar with the Internal Market Directives of the EC concerning trade regulations, restrictive provisions, reciprocity requirements, product testing and specifications, public procurements, tax harmonization, new standards in the areas of services and products, and capital movements. They should consider competition more with "European Companies" and not so much with British, French, German, or Italian enterprises separately.

The Internal Market Directives, some 200 of them already adopted by the EC and another eighty-five to be adopted soon, deal with the removal of physical, technical, and fiscal barriers among member nations. As a result of the removal of physical barriers, border controls on vehicle safety, and veterinary or phytosanitary controls would be eliminated. Technical barriers to be removed include restrictions on capital movements and trade services as well as differences in industrial and competitive standards. Removal of fiscal barriers means harmonization of the tax systems, particularly value-added and excise tax systems. Already customs documents have been the same in all member countries, so that duplications and bureaucratic confusion for goods shipped to or within the EC are reduced or eliminated. However, variations for health and product safety requirements by member states are allowed within certain limits.

American companies conducting business with the EC, which is America's largest commercial partner, should be familiar with the new industrial standards and regulations covering thousands of products and business activities. They should adapt their production and marketing policies to a European-wide environment with large economies of scale, a huge market and tougher competition from their European counterparts. United States exporters and United States affiliates producing in the EC should be familiar with EC common trademark and copyright laws, the EC-wide standards of testing and certification, common public procurements, new rules on pollution (air, water, land, noise), and a variety of other regulations and directives relative to their operations.

Fair Trade Practices

Maintaining fair trade between the United States and the EC or any other group or country may require countervailing duties and antidumping measures. The United States shows a reliance on both antidumping actions and countervailing duties, but the EC is resorting mainly to antidumping actions. Thus, during the period 1980–85, there were 252 countervailing duties in the United States and only 7 in the EC, compared to 280 antidumping actions for the United States and 254 for the EC, respectively. These measures that have been accelerated substantially in the late 1970s and later are used by pro-trade governments, such as those of the United States, Australia, Canada, and some of the EC member nations, to cope with domestic protectionist pressure.[2]

Because of the large trade deficits and the unfair trade practices from some other partners, the United States introduced the Omnibus Trade and Competitiveness Act of 1988. This Act and particularly Super 301 provision, which builds on Section 301 of the Trade Act of 1974, provides a method for the United States trade representative to negotiate reduction of unfair trade practices with the EC and other counterparts. Once a country is put on the list, negotiations must be made within eighteen months. If no results appeared for an open market within three years, then the United States may close its market for certain products of the offending country. However, retaliation should occur against products with an alternative domestic supply and not against imported products that have significant United States content. It seems that the crowbar of Super 301 is a useful provision as it is backed up with a significant stick and a carrot. Under such conditions, it is difficult for trade partners to circumvent related measures and to work around specific actions, as happened with a 100 percent duty on D-Ram chips that turned out to be a failure. Instead of stopping D-Ram Japanese dumping and giving United States semiconductor companies higher share in business, it shifted production to circuit boards which include D-Rams. Because of the accumulation of more than $400 billion of Japanese trade surplus with the United States, disputes and negotiations between these two partners and, to a lesser extent, between the EC and Japan continue.

Because of large trade deficits, pressures are building in the United States for quantity import restrictions. Thus, the so-called Super 301 provision of the new Omnibus Trade and Competitiveness Act mentioned above provides for retaliations against unfair trade practices by the United States trade partners. For example, as a result of this scarecrow measure, the United States trade policy makers are after West Germany on Airbus subsidies. Also, they are against the EC for its restrictions on beef with hormones, Canada for fish exports, and Japan for using United States technology in building a new fighter plane. In such and other related matters and because of the United States pressures, compromises are reached. For example, in the case of Japan half the work on the plane would be done in the United States.

Strict interpretation of the Super 301 provision would mean situations against the EC not only for Airbus but also for European practices in trade in oilseeds and other products. Moreover, Japan's unfair exclusion of American supercomputer makers as well as Brazil's and India's unfair trade practices regarding intellectual property (patents, copyrights, and trademarks) are under review. However, Korea and Taiwan were excluded from the unfair list because of their recent trade liberalization policies. Thus, Korea adopted more liberal measures for foreign investment and under pressure from the United States agreed to open its markets in pharmaceuticals, food, travel, and cosmetics.

The EC warned, however, that if the United States persists in accusing it of unfair trading practices, it would challenge the United States law before the General Agreements on Tariffs and Trade (GATT), which serves as a global trade charter of ninety-eight nations and an agency resolving trade disputes. However, despite the disagreements, the representatives of both sides agreed to arrange a serious dispute over EC subsidies that limit imports of American soybeans, as well as United States restrictions on sugar imports. This is the proper way to avoid retaliations and re-retaliations that cause contraction of world trade.

The United States Omnibus Trade and Competitiveness Act of 1988 stipulates that sanctions can be imposed if other nations restrict imports of American products. As a result, the EC and South Korea were considered for reprisals for restricting imports of United States telecommunication products, such as digital switching devices, big switchboards, and many other related products for which the United States has a comparative advantage. West Germany and France were the main EC countries considered for sanctions. West Germany absorbs more than $100 million and France about $40 million American exports of telecommunication products annually.

If foreign products are sold in the United States at less than their fair value, the United States Department of Commerce can impose antidumping duties to eliminate price differentiation. If such imported products harm or threaten to harm American firms producing similar products then duties could be collected by the Customs Service to eliminate the difference between cost of foreign products and the lower prices at which they are sold in the United States. Such United States duties were proposed on Japanese cars, varying from 8.5 percent for the Yamaha Motor Company to 14.1 percent for the Suzuki Motor Company, 32.9 percent for Honda Motor Company, 35.4 percent for Kawasaki Heavy Industries Ltd. and 24.6 percent for other companies.[3]

On May 25, 1989, United States President George Bush singled out a number of countries as practicing unfair trade for certain products and violating intellectual property rights. Japan, Brazil and India were named as unfair traders. Some twenty-five other countries were considered violators of copyrights, patents, and trademarks. They included Brazil, China, India, Mexico, Saudi Arabia, South Korea, Taiwan, and Thailand. There was discussion of including the EC as an unfair competitor as well. However, it was not included in the final list probably because a similar EC list would name the United States as a trade violator for a number of products or because of political and strategic reasons.

There is a great deal of criticism against these United States measures on the grounds that they were used to divert attention from the macroeconomic responsibilities of the United States which lead to budget and trade imbalances. It is argued that the United States is shifting from a policy of economic internationalism to a more parochial economic nationalism. In the name of free trade it moves more and more to protectionism. Specifically, the EC argues that such unilateral measures violate the General Agreement on Tariffs and Trade and are against the global negotiations of the Uruguay Round in 1986–1990 for trade liberalization.

The main purpose of citing countries for unfair trading is to encourage free trade through cutting barriers in finance, insurance, construction, and other services as well as ending restrictions on foreign investment, imports through licensing and procurement, and other policies that suppress international transactions. To achieve this goal, the United States is prepared to cut restrictions on steel, textiles, sugar, and dairy products. If negotiations for mutual reduction of trade barriers fail, then world trade may be organized under preferential blocs, such as the EC, North America, and perhaps a Pacific trade group.

Similar efforts of reducing import restrictions are made by some 1200 steel-using companies, organizations, and lobbying political groups to eliminate steel import quotas which started in 1984. The group of companies that oppose import quotas includes Caterpillar Inc., which makes machines, White Consolidated Industries, which produces home products, National Refrigerator and Air Conditioning Products Inc., Bakers Pride Oven Company, and many other firms which complain that such quotas raised cost prices, in some cases as much as 75 percent. On the other side of the aisle, there are steel-producing companies which support the import quotas or the voluntary restraint agreements that limited the amount of imported steel to about 20 percent of domestic consumption. Imported steel was 26.4 percent of domestic consumption in 1984 compared to about 18 percent currently.[4]

The main steel companies which support the maintenance of restraints are USX Corporation, Bethlehem Steel Corporation, LTV Corporation, and many other steel companies which argue that they need import quotas and protection from competition with subsidized EC and Japanese steel producers in order to continue making progress and maintaining profitability. More details on steel trade are presented in a later section of this chapter.

The EC complains that the new United States trade law that permits the President to order 100 percent tariffs on imports from countries considered as practicing "unfair" trade restrictions is risky. It is an arrogant and dangerous policy that makes the United States an almighty judge of what is fair trade. It may lead to more restrictions and perhaps to a global recession as other countries may use the same technique to curb United States products entering their markets. Already, the EC has published a list of forty-two unfair United States trade

restrictions. They include high tariffs on textiles, shoes, onions, and other agricultural products, export subsidies, and import quotas for certain products,
"buy American" rules for a number of goods, and other restrictions including
the unfair-practices procedure mentioned above. The Europeans argue that what
Washington is doing is contrary to its international obligations.

A recent study of the International Monetary Fund revealed that United States
non-tariff restrictions were equivalent to 25 percent tariffs in such products as
textiles, cars, and steel. Barriers in textile imports alone reduce imports by about
$25 billion. There are some sixty-two United States "voluntary" restraints on
imports, including forty trade barriers listed by the EC that are estimated to cost
American consumers about $50 billion. In spite of the free trade rhetoric, United
States barriers on imports increased by 23 percent during the last decade. However, the overall level of protection for agriculture is higher in the EC and Japan
than in the United States. The producers' subsidy equivalent is around 35 percent
for the United States, 50 percent for the EC, and as high as 75 percent for
Japan.[5]

As mentioned earlier, the EC absorbs the largest amount of United States
exports. Out of a total $320.4 billion United States exports in 1988, 23.7 percent
went to the EC, compared to 21.6 percent to Canada, and only 11.8 percent to
Japan. Not only in commodity exports is the EC important to the United States,
but in such services as television programming for which American producers
have increased their revenue from sales in the EC by six times in this decade.
However, there are complaints that the largest eight EC countries require that
some degree of programming be European-produced and that there are plans to
set quotas on American television programming in the entire EC. Although there
are no restrictions in the United States, some countries, including Canada, have
such limitations to preserve their cultural sovereignty by limiting foreign films
and television material. About two-thirds of foreign program sales of American
entertainment producers, such as Fox, Columbia, Paramount, Warner, and Universal, of more than $600 million annually are made in the EC.

The EC is restricting United States and other television shows, such as "Dal-
las" and "Roseanne," not only for the commercial protection of European
producers but perhaps to preserve its society's culture. The Europeans seem to
value culture much more than Americans and allocate far larger amounts of
public funds for its maintenance compared to those of the United States. It is
argued that some form of protectionism is needed to resist the rapidly expanding
United States cultural imperialism in the European Community. The United
States, though, is fighting such EC cultural protectionism via the GATT, arguing
that it is a violation of its regulations.

There is a trend and even a war among mass media firms for the domination
of the markets on both sides of the Atlantic. Mergers, acquisitions, and friendly
or hostile takeovers lead to the monopolization of the information markets. Fewer
and fewer people control radio and television stations, satellite channels, video-
cassettes, cable systems, movies, theaters, book publications, magazines, news-

papers, and other media which influence and even direct public opinion. This concentration of media, that is, the monopolization or oligopolization of producing and distributing information, reduces critical reporting and public access to independent production, and endangers the democratic process. The relaxation of antitrust legislations and even the support of cartelization and concentration of media in the United States, and more so in Europe, reduce diversity and genuine competition and may misdirect information that feeds the human mind.

In a recent decision the EC reached an agreement to open its television frontier to other people's broadcasts. Programs in one EC country would be transmitted to other member countries, and eventually to East Bloc countries, under certain rules of advertisement and moral standards. However, a quota restriction for programs made outside the EC was kept, although far below the 40 percent quota France and Italy requested.

Spending for research and development (less than 2 percent of GNP in the United States, Britain, and France and close to 3 percent for Japan and West Germany) is responsible for innovations and new patents. It seems though that United States firms emphasize short-term profits and not long-term research and development in recent years.

There seems to be a foreign push for United States patents. The annual number of United States patents generated by the EC countries remained about the same for the last two decades. West Germany counts for some 9 percent and Britain and France for 3 percent each. Other EC countries had lower percentages of United States patents per year. Japan, however, has the highest proportion of United States patents issued to foreign residents (21 percent in 1988 compared to 4 percent in 1963–1976). Overall, foreign investors received 48 percent of the 77,924 United States patents issued in 1988, compared to 18.1 percent in 1963.

The main EC companies that received United States patents were Philips of the Netherlands (581 patents in 1988), Siemens and Bayer of West Germany (562 and 442, respectively). Hitachi, Toshiba, Canon, Fuji Photo Film, and Mitsubishi Denki are the Japanese firms with high shares of United States patents. In the United States, General Electric (including RCA acquired by G.E. in 1985), and I.B.M. are the more efficient companies in receiving patents, mainly in photocopying, optical and phonographic recording, photography, electronic plotters, magnetic disks, and tape recording, games, and so on.

The percentage of patent filings by non-residents was 92 (in 1987) for the Netherlands, 91 for Canada, 78 for France, 71 for Britain, 56 for West Germany, 49 for the United States, and only 10 for Japan. United States residents file for about 10,000 to 12,000 patents per year in Britain, France, and West Germany as well as about 12,000 to 13,000 in Japan and Canada and about 8,000 in Italy. German residents file for about 10,000 patents a year in the United States, followed by the British (4,000), the French (3,000), and the Italians (1,000). Japanese residents file for more than 20,000 U.S. patents annually and Canadians for only about 2,000.[6]

The EC, with a higher percentage of farm population (8 percent) compared with that of the United States (3 percent), presents objections to substantial cuts in farm support programs. That is why it seeks a slower pace of change and not drastic reductions of agricultural support programs in the form of subsidies or the use of variable levies that curb imports. EC farmers, mainly in France, Italy, Spain, Greece, and Portugal, are expected to present severe oppositions to cuts in or elimination of farm support. Similar opposition to the curbs of agricultural support is expected by United States farmers, chiefly by the producers of dairy products and sugar, as well as by Japanese rice growers, for which high prices and tough barriers to market access are maintained.

TRADE DISPUTES

Due to the rapid growth of the EC and the reduction of tariffs as a result of the negotiations under GATT (Kennedy, Tokyo, and Uruguay Rounds), trade between the EC and the United States is expanding. However, there is some trade diversion in agricultural products, especially United States grain, because of EC tariffs to equalize import prices to common farm prices established by the EC (variable import levels). The high prices of supported agricultural products lead to large surpluses of these products in the EC.

A serious dispute between the United States and the EC involves the agricultural support programs, guaranteeing prices above market levels, buying surplus products, and sometimes dumping them at lower prices. Such programs cause distortions in the world markets and lead to retaliations. During the General Agreement on Tariffs and Trade (GATT) recent negotiations of ninety-eight member-nations (Uruguay Round), the EC proposed a freeze in state support prices at the 1984 levels. Cereals, dairy products, beef, vegetable oil, sugar, and rice are mainly the products included in this proposal.

The United States, Australia, and other producers suggested that all subsidies stop by the year 2000. However, the EC proposed that reductions can gradually be negotiated but rejected complete elimination of subsidies. On the other hand, United States payments to farmers to reduce land cultivation or herds, as well as output quotas, are not included in the freeze proposal.[7] Although consumer-oriented subsidies help the increase in the production of food and other agricultural products, they also contribute to slow economic growth and increase inflation through rising government expenditures.

As a result of United States retaliatory pressures and the costly subsidies of about $120 billion annually, the EC agreed to eliminate soybean and other oilseed subsidies. The EC accepted the findings of a GATT panel that such subsidies lead to economic disadvantages to United States farmers and exporters that amount to hundreds of millions of dollars. From the late 1960s, when such subsidies began, the support of oilseeds (soybeans, sunflower and other seeds) increased, especially for France and Italy, where soybean subsidies reached $12 a bushel, or more than double the prices in the United States. At the same time, protection of the United States sugar farmers is expected to end, as the GATT rules require.

Serious financial problems appeared with the EC budget with about two-thirds of its annual receipts spent for farm subsidies. The countries of the north, primarily Britain and, to some extent, West Germany, object to farm subsidization and they ask for a revised farm policy to eliminate food surpluses which are then sold on world markets. Australia, the United States, and other countries, which export farm products, complain that the agricultural policy of the EC leads to unfair competition against their own products.

Moreover, Britain wants to reduce its net cost of EC membership from about 2 billion dollars presently to about 500 million dollars a year. Also, West Germany, paying currently about 2 billion dollars a year more than it gets, wants its share of Common Market expenditures to be kept under control in the future. The southern EC regions, including Southern Italy, Greece, Spain, and Portugal, press for better agricultural subsidies. Northern EC countries, such as Denmark, Belgium and the Netherlands, producing large amounts of cattle-raising products, also collect sizable subsidies. For milk only, subsidies amount to about 30 percent of the total agricultural subsidies.

The EC provides subsidies to various agricultural and dairy products, mainly by minimum guaranteed prices. Essentially, it buys such products at determined prices and sells them to the manufacturers and sellers at auction. Because of the complaints by the people who process these products that the minimum guaranteed prices rose over time and are no longer competitive outside the EC, subsidies are provided primarily on the sale of these products.

Olive oil, along with seed oils from corn and soybean, is an important product included in the EC subsidies. The current subsidy levels for the three basic types of olive oil sold in bulk, packaged products, and for export, vary from 50 ECUs (European Currency Units) per 100 kilograms for extra-virgin (nonrefined) oil to around 100 ECUs for type A and 63 ECUs per kilogram for type B oil. Type A oil is refined to reduce acidity and to improve flavor, color and smell. Type B oil is made from the pomace remains of the first pressing of the olives. The pulp subsidies vary from about 30 to 50 percent of the values of oil. Mediterranean oil producers, primarily in Italy, France, Spain, and Greece, are the main receivers of olive oil subsidies. Berio and Bertolli are the largest producers of type A olive oil imported in the United States from Italy.

Farm support policies are wasteful, inefficient, and damaging to the economies of the countries involved. The origins of agricultural protectionism are primarily caused nationally by domestic pressures to provide support to farmers. The impact of a reduction or elimination of agricultural protectionism is expected to be beneficial to the American and EC economies. It is estimated that the ending of such protectionism will reduce the United States trade deficit by more than $40 billion and create about three million new jobs in the EC. Moreover, it would increase incomes in developing nations by $26 billion and reduce their debt by 5 percent annually.[8] However, to avoid sharp ups and downs in prices of farm products in a cobweb fashion, some form of protection or other kind of price support may be needed.

In its efforts to liberalize global trade in farm products, the United States proposed to the Uruguay Round of trade reform talks a system of fixed tariffs instead of quotas, licensing, and variable levies. United States producers in highly protected sectors such as dairy products, peanuts, and sugar became uncomfortable but American farmers in general offered their cautious support to the proposal. The EC commissioner for agriculture, though, expressed opposition to the idea, while Japan, with rice prices ten times higher than the world level, is not enthusiastic about the proposal. In July 1990, unexpectedly, the EC proposed a 30 percent cut of subsidies to farmers over a decade. This covers the period 1986 to 1996 and includes cuts that already have been implemented.

Moreover, to avoid increases in budget spending and reduce overproduction of milk and other agricultural products, the EC Farm Ministers periodically urge the Commission to draw up rules concerning quotas and price determination for such farm products. France and other member states support such rules of fixed prices and quota packages as long as they do not send the wrong signals to EC farmers. These measures bring some relief to West Germany which allocated high quotas to its farmers.

Hormones and Trade War

As part of the serious battle against possible European protectionism from the EC internal unity, the United States used trade sanctions against European food products in retaliation for the EC ban on imports of meat that contains growth hormones. The ban is universal and is justified on health grounds, especially for children. It applies to all countries outside the EC. Also, European farmers are not permitted to use hormones, which increase the normal weight of animals by as much as 20 percent. The movement against hormones was started by consumer activists in West Germany and Italy who argued that they are carcinogenic. Already, Australia, Argentina, Brazil, New Zealand, and other meat producing countries agreed to ship to Europe only hormone-free meat.

The United States, though, objected to this ban and retaliated by imposing 100 percent tariffs on such EC products as tomatoes and tomato sauce, boneless beef, instant coffee, certain alcoholic drinks, fresh and concentrated juices, pet food, and certain pork products. Similar objections were expressed by Canada. The United States trade sanctions against the European Community were estimated to cost $100 million, an amount about equal to the loss of United States exports to the EC because of the ban. The EC retaliation was expected to include American walnuts, dried prunes, peaches, papayas, and apricots. There were fears that this might lead to a trade war as Brussels threatened counter-retaliation and Washington re-retaliation, *ad infinitum*.

The United States argued that there is no scientific basis for such claims. Although there is not agreement among scientists regarding health hazards from growth hormones, there is a desexing, calming effect on animals leading to unnatural, quick growth, especially when the hormones are overused. It is estimated that a single $1 hormone can save $20 in quick fattening cost.

The problem started in Italy in 1981, and later in West Germany and Holland, after the carcinogenic synthetic estrogen diethylstilbestrol, or DES, was found in baby food. As a result, infants of both sexes developed breasts and DES was banned. American breeders are permitted to shoot the hormones into cows' ears, but Europeans used to inject them into the skeletal parts of the cattle. The beef dispute would affect not only exports to the EC but also to Japan, which buys the largest amount of United States beef.

The EC ban on beef raised with growth hormones (imposed on January 1, 1989) forced United States meat producers to seek alternative markets, especially in Japan, Mexico, and Egypt. Livers, hearts, kidneys, tongues, and other specialty meats are more popular in Europe, Japan, Mexico and other countries than in the United States. Meat manufacturers, packers, and exporters predicted the ban and searched for other markets. The Japanese market, which absorbs $250 million worth of United States beef annually, has an increasing taste for processed meats and hot dogs, while the Mexican government made meat imports easier by lowering tariffs. Thus, American beef producers expect to replace part of the EC beef sales of some $130 million per year.

However, the Europeans accept hormone-treated meats for pet food, worth some $30 million annually, but not to be used by people because it is harmful to humans. Nevertheless, the United States reduced import restrictions on British pork and pork products because of the elimination of the danger of hog cholera, a contagious disease of swine.

On the other side of the Atlantic, European farmers and policy makers present proposals to ease the dispute by allowing larger import quotas for American meat free of hormones. Otherwise, there is fear that retaliations and counter-retaliations can seriously damage the $150 billion annual trade between the EC and the United States. It is better to negotiate than to fight. That is why the EC postponed for some time any retaliation against American tariffs on its food products.[9] At the same time, American beef producers, especially from Texas, put pressures on Washington to comply with the EC directives and certify meat for exports to be free of hormones, accordingly.

This dispute of the United States versus the EC over American beef with hormones resembles a similar dispute a century ago. In the 1880s, the German Empire, under Chancellor Otto von Bismarck, and other European nations banned United States pork products due to the presence of trichina worms. American pork raisers and other pressure groups argued that this was a protectionist measure. But the Germans counter-argued that they required inspection of their own pork for public health purposes. Finally, threats of retaliation and re-retaliation stopped when the United States Congress passed a microscopic inspection law in 1891, the Europeans lifted the ban, and the 1880–91 pork war was over.

It is expected that the 1988 Omnibus Trade and Competitiveness Act and especially Section 301, under which the beef retaliation was justified, will be used aggressively as an instrument of harassment of European and other trading rivals. It urges the United States president to respond to unreasonable and unfair trade practices of other nations. However, it is argued that this leads to unilateral decisions, regardless of contractual rights and obligations under the General Agreement on Tariffs and Trade (GATT). This practice makes the above competitive act anticompetitive and protectionistic. Moreover, Europeans and others accept the United States bans on such products as nonpasteurized cheese and some drugs.

It seems that, with the rapid growth of international transactions, it becomes inevitable that other nations would rise and share prominence in world trade. The acceptance of this principle would save the Uruguay Round of international trade talks on agricultural subsidies, and it would not jeopardize the EC common agricultural policy (CAP) and protect consumers all over the world, especially in Japan where farm products are very expensive.

Steel Problems

On both sides of the Atlantic, the steel industry has been in difficult conditions, particularly since the peak production of 1974. Whereas in 1950, the United States produced about half of the world's steel, today its share is only about 10 percent. The United States net imports are around 25 percent of its steel output. On the other hand, steel production in the EC was tripled from 1950 to 1970, but it was reduced thereafter, although net exports have been and still are realized. Out of a world total annual steel production of about 800 million tons, the United States is producing around 85 million tons, while the EC is producing about 140 million tons or 18 percent, compared to 26 percent in 1950. West Germany, with about 40 million tons of steel production, is the main EC producer, followed by Italy (25 million tons), France (20), Britain (15), Belgium (11), Netherlands (6), and Luxembourg (4 million tons). Other nations, primarily Japan (with about 15 percent of the world's production and net exports of more than 30 million tons annually), Brazil, and South Korea emerged as major steel producers.

Comparitively speaking, total cost per ton of steel is higher in the United States ($403 in 1984) compared to that of the EC ($314) and Japan ($302). The United States cost of labor ($170 per ton in 1984) and energy ($76) is higher than that of the EC ($97 and $48, respectively), while the cost of coal and ore ($102) as well as capital (around $60) is about the same. Relative decline in United States productivity and rise in wages are mainly responsible for labor cost differences. In the middle 1960s, the average American steel worker produced twice as much steel per hour as his German, French, and British, as well as Japanese, counterparts. However, by 1982, the productivity of the German steel worker was 108, compared to an index of 100 for the United States worker, 100 for the French worker, 71 for the British worker, and as high as 141 for the Japanese worker. Wages of United States steel workers increased to about double of those of the average manufacturing workers in the 1980s compared to less than 50 percent higher in the 1960s. But the differences in the EC nations are not as much. Thus, hourly compensation costs for production in iron and steel manufacturing are $26 in the United States, $21 in Japan, $20 in West Germany, and $16 in Britain.[10] For the other EC countries, hourly labor cost is between that of West Germany and Britain. With the unification of Germany and the reforms of the East Bloc economies related EC labor costs are expected to be reduced.

To protect the domestic steel industry till it becomes competitive, the United States introduced protective trade measures, such as the voluntary restraint agreements (VRAs) with the EC and Japan in 1969, and the trigger-price mechanism (TPM) in 1978. In 1982, the United States signed a VRA with the EC to restrain steel imports. In 1984, and under section 201 of the Trade Act of 1974, VRAs were made to reduce United States imports from the EC and other countries from around 25 percent to 18.5 percent. It was estimated that over the five-year life of the VRAs the cost to the United States consumers was about $1 billion per year and $114 thousand for every of the 9,951 jobs temporarily protected.[11] Similar results were estimated from the renewed VRAs for another 2.5 years since September 30, 1989, because of the pressures of United States steel industries for further protection, although they lately neglected to do their part regarding reinvestment and modernization. Moreover, the TPM, not permitting imports below an established minimum price, led to a relative increase in steel prices, estimated at about 10 percent.

The increase in steel prices induces the use of alternative materials and increases imports of manufactured products with steel as their component. In addition, such quotas and restrictions encourage companies that use steel to operate outside the United States. Therefore, in the long run such restrictions are expected to turn against the steel industry they aim to protect.

The Commission of the EC has primarily imposed domestic controls on steel prices, output, and investment. Thus, the Davignon Plan of 1977 introduced mandatory minimum prices on steel bars and guidance prices for other steel products. Further production quotas were imposed in 1980, while minimum prices were extended to most strip products, cold- and hot-rolled sheet, and beams. In August 1981 a regulation of national subsidies was initiated to stimulate reorganization and modernization of the EC steel industries. Nevertheless, efficient steel industries primarily in Germany objected to minimum prices and quantity controls on the grounds that they deprived them of market competition by prohibiting them from charging lower prices, thereby turning them into sleeping monopolies.

In addition to domestic controls on prices and production, the EC introduced in 1977 import price controls on steel similar to the trigger-price mechanism of the United States. This means that import prices could not be less than the basic prices established by the EC. Otherwise, antidumping procedures were to be enacted and imports were to be excluded from the Common Market. However, exemptions were permitted for countries negotiated with the EC (VRAs). Some fifteen countries, primarily Eastern European as well as the European Free Trade Association (EFTA) countries negotiated and achieved such exemptions, which have been renewed periodically.[12]

After many complaints from United States steel producers, an antidumping and countervailing investigation was started by the Department of Commerce in 1982. Many large steel companies in almost all EC countries were charged for subsidization and dumping operations as were some Japanese companies as well. This was particularly so for Italian, French, British, and Belgian steel companies with subsidies varying from 11 to 26 percent. Most German firms, though, were found not to be subsidized and were opposed to subsidies by other EC nations. Some big EC steel producers, such as Usino and Sacilor of France, Italsider of Italy, Cockerill-Sambre of Belgium, and the British Steel Corporation, did not like to lose their United States market and pressed their governments to enter into agreements with the United States to arrange the antidumping and counter-vailing duty problem.

The agreements and arrangements between the United States and the EC, as well as other countries, reduce price controls and quotas and encourage competition in favor of the consumers of the countries concerned. On the contrary, restrictive measures protect inefficiency, discourage productive investment, and penalize consumers concerning prices and quality products. Moreover, reduction or elimination of subsidies reduces budgetary deficits and stabilizes the economies on both sides of the Atlantic. Actually, coordinated policies between the United States and the EC may be needed to counter expected penetration of their markets by low-cost producers from Japan, Brazil, South Korea, and other nations with growing steel industries.

A serious problem for the economy of West Germany is the declining steel industry. The huge Krupp steel plant in the Ruhr Valley near the River Rhine, which was established about a century ago (1894), has been deemed uneconomical. High labor cost, about $22 an hour, and stiff international competition are mainly responsible for the decline of the steel industry which once was the pride of Germany's economy. The Rheinhouse Mill, for example, operates at about half of its annual capacity of four million tons and a labor force of about one-sixth of that before World War II. The number of employees in the steel industry declined from 400,000 in 1965 to about 150,000 at present.

Other steel mills, such as Mannesmann A.G. and Thyssen A.G., face similar problems and, together with Krupp, they are in the process of reconstruction through labor cuts or readjustments. It is a phenomenon similar to that in Pittsburgh, Pennsylvania, where some 100,000 jobs have been cut. The hope, though, is with additional jobs created in service industries. Nevertheless, Chancellor Helmut Kohl and other politicians promised to support the redevelopment of the Ruhr valley and other regions which suffer because of the declining steel industry. It is expected that less expensive labor from East Germany would reduce cost and make the steel industry of Germany more competitive.

As a result of the United States quotas against imported steel, import market share was reduced from 30 percent in late 1984 to less than 20 percent today. At the same time, through industry's reinvestment and restructuring, man-hours per ton were reduced to a lower level than in West Germany and Japan and labor productivity was improved. It is estimated that the United States auto companies pay $100 per ton less for domestic steel than their counterparts pay in Japan. However, this is due mainly to the recent significant depreciation of the dollar and not so much to higher productivity and lower cost in the United States steel industries.

It is argued, though, that a robust demand for steel, in addition to cost cutting and the declining dollar, made the United States steel industries competitive and profitable. In 1988, the industry's profits reached $2.2 billion and the mills worked almost at full capacity. Nevertheless, steel-using manufacturers complain that they face higher costs, delays and shortages, and expect damages in their international competitiveness and eventual losses. Steel prices they have paid were more that 20 percent higher than in West Germany and elsewhere from 1969 to 1985. It is estimated that for every job saved from the protective steel quotas, three jobs are lost in other industries. Thus, according to a recent study the quotas have saved 17,000 jobs in the steel industry but have cost 52,400 jobs in other sectors of the United States economy. For the auto industry, steel prices went up by 15 percent since 1986, and as much as 40 percent for other companies.[13] Quotas are considered as medicine: boosting one industry in the short run but making many others sick in the long run.

In a serious effort to end subsidies to all industries, the United States agreed with the EC and six other countries (Japan, South Korea, Brazil, Mexico, Australia, and Trinidad and Tobago) in December 1989 to terminate subsidies to steel producers. A similar agreement to end subsidies is pursued with three other steel-producing countries (Austria, Finland, and Yugoslavia).

At the same time, by March 31, 1992, the United States would end its quota program which keeps imports below 20 percent of the quantity sold in the country. Under the new quotas, the EC and sixteen other countries would export to the United States 19.1 percent of the United States domestic market and Japan's share would be only 5 percent. Each percentage point involves about one million tons of steel and the total amount permitted into the United States is around 18 million tons.

Such agreements of cuts in subsidies are the results of the Uruguay Round of talks (1986–1990) and the adjustments that the International Monetary Fund works out with Mexico, Brazil, and other countries. These steel-producing countries realized that trade liberalization would reduce the cost of taxpayer support of industry and benefit the consumers.

There are complaints, though, in recent GATT reports, that although the United States economy is generally open to imports, certain of its sectors, including steel, textiles, sugar, dairy and other agricultural products, semiconductors, automobiles and machine tools, enjoy high protection.

7 Capital Flows and Currency Realignment

EFFECTS OF CAPITAL FLOWS

A currency, such as the dollar, appreciates when demand for it in the foreign exchange increases. In the case of the United States, this occurs because foreigners feel that their money is best served in the form of dollars, mainly because they like the stability and security of the dollar or they are looking to make greater profits because of higher United States interest rates compared to other countries.

In the long run, the inflow of large amounts of capital from the EC and other countries into the United States may lead to an increased control of the national economy by foreign investors. If efforts are made to prevent them from pulling their money out of the United States markets, this would lead to serious negative implications as it weakens greatly the economic and possibly political independence of the country. For the time being, in America, everyone (government, business, and consumers) is on the same side of the financial boat, that is, on the side of debt, and in an economic downswing the boat may be overturned.

A serious reason why an appreciating dollar is dangerous in the United States economy is the fact that it serves to increase the already huge trade deficit. An appreciating dollar means that the prices of United States goods relative to others will rise. Consumers will then buy less American goods and more foreign goods, since they are cheaper. Exports will drop and imports will rise. This increases the foreign trade deficit.

Reviewing the related statistics, we see that after 1980 the trade deficit was an ever growing problem. It continued with a dramatic rise through 1987, and has slowed slightly since then. This problem occurred because of the tremendous increase in imports relative to exports during this time. The large appreciations of the dollar in the early 1980s allowed foreign products to be competitively cheaper than United States products and, consequently, relatively more imports entered the United States.[1] The slight decrease after 1987 probably shows the small effect that the depreciation of the dollar had thereafter.

The change in the United States interest rates at the beginning of the 1980s and, thus, the change in real exchange rates were mainly responsible for balance of payment deficits. Other related policies of reducing inflation, cutting taxes, and increasing spending increased budget deficits and, in turn, trade deficits. Inflation was a major issue at this point because the country had come out of an inflationary rate that peaked at 13.5 percent in 1980.

The United States clearly wanted interest rates to rise in the 1980s, primarily to stop inflation and also to attract money from abroad to finance its debt. A rise in interest rates will always bring about more capital inflow because it will then pay to invest more in the United States. There is no doubt, then, that the budget policies of the early 1980s played a major role, probably the largest role, in the appreciation of the dollar and the consequent trade imbalance.

As a result of external trade deficits and the capital inflow, the United States became the largest debtor country in the world. It is predicted that the United States net foreign debt will soon pass one trillion dollars. On the other hand, foreign governments try, at times, to support the dollar so as to prevent further appreciations of their own currencies, which would damage their exports. At the same time, EC and other foreign investors continue to have confidence in the growing and open American economy. As a result, capital inflow remains strong, despite the severe stock market fluctuations, while foreign assets in the United States continue to grow larger and larger.

According to recent statistics, external United States liabilities are growing by larger amounts than United States claims, leaving an ever growing negative balance. This means that the obligations or the debts of the country are increasing, mainly because of capital inflow. Such inflow of foreign capital helps improve the United States economy in the short run. However, in the long run, problems of servicing the debt may appear. Moreover, as the debt of developing countries is also growing, the accumulated international debt may lead to a worldwide financial crisis and an instability of the world economy.

On the other side of the Atlantic, in order to improve monetary cooperation, as the EC moves toward unification, a committee of central bank presidents and experts was established in June 1988, when the rotating six-month EC presidency of West Germany was expiring. Although Britain opposes the creation of a single European central bank and the establishment of a common currency, the irreversible process toward European unity acts as a magnet for a closer monetary cooperation. Jacques Delors, the president of the executive commission of the EC, is also the head of the above committee, which will consider the long-run prospects of the European monetary integration.

On June 13, 1988, the twelve members of the EC reached an agreement to allow free capital movements, while the most advanced members agreed to lift foreign exchange restrictions by mid–1989. However, Greece, Ireland, Spain, and Portugal, being at a lower level of development, were permitted to remove restrictions later. This was considered as the largest deregulation program in history.[2]

An important reason for the relatively high United States interest rates and the capital inflow is the huge budgetary deficits of the United States government. These deficits increase the external trade deficits and necessitate capital inflow for their financing. The accumulation of the budget deficits increases the interest-bearing federal debt, which increased from 906.4 billion dollars in 1980 to more than 3.0 trillion presently. Reducing or eliminating the budget deficit would help increase United States savings to make up for a possible reduced supply of foreign savings.

After 1984, the dollar took the opposite route and began to decline. This gradual depreciation was to reverse the trend of accumulated external trade deficits. The largest devaluations of the dollar occurred with the currencies of the countries with which the United States had the largest trade deficits, notably Japan and West Germany.[3] Thus, the value of the dollar dropped from around 260 yens in 1984 to about 125 in 1988. During the same period, it declined from around 3.2 to 1.7 Deutsche marks, respectively. In 1990, the value of the dollar was around 155 yens, 1.7 German marks, 0.6 British pounds, 5.7 French francs, 1,240 Italian lire, 107 Spanish pesetas, 165 Greek drachmas, and 0.8 European Currency Units (ECUs). (ECU is a monetary unit determined by a basket of European currencies.)

These sizable depreciations made United States exports relatively cheaper for foreign consumers and imports more expensive for American consumers. Assuming other things to be the same, this was expected to improve the balance of payments. However, large trade deficits persist as yet. On the other hand, foreign capital continues to flow into the United States, thereby financing the United States foreign trade deficits as well as budgetary deficits. As a result, there are record increases in foreign holdings of United States financial assets. Presently, private foreign capital moves primarily into purchases of corporate equities and in direct ownership of real property, and to a lesser extent to investment in government and corporate bonds and other fixed-income instruments.

Foreign central banks are now playing an increasing role in United States capital inflow. They purchase United States Treasury securities, while private foreign investment in such securities fall. Already the total United States government securities held by the Federal Reserve of New York for foreign central banks reached the amount of about $230 billion. The risks for another fall of the dollar and expectations for rising long-term interest rates may be responsible for the retreat of private foreign investors from United States government securities.

The depreciation of the dollar in terms of foreign currencies in recent years has intensified the inflow of foreign capital into the United States. With about half of the money that was necessary a few years ago, Europeans and other foreigners can buy American property, shares of United States corporations, and even whole companies. Although this is beneficial to the American economy in the short run from the point of view of investment and sustainable economic growth, in the long run severe problems may appear.

The United States becomes economically and politically more and more dependent on creditor nations, mainly because of foreign trade and budget deficits. Such a dependency requires extraordinary efforts of cooperation between the United States and the EC, Japan and Canada. From that standpoint, United States fiscal and monetary policies should be closely coordinated with foreign policy. United States trading partners would watch and judge related American economic policies. If such policies are irresponsible it would be difficult for European and other partners to step in and help stabilize the United States dollar and its economy. They may object to buying dollars when their value is declining and selling dollars when their value is unjustifiably moving up, thereby crippling related United States economic policies.

It would seem that the real increase in the dollar's value in the early 1980s by 65 percent was mainly responsible for the subsequent United States trade deficits. Likewise, it was the decline of the dollar by some 50 percent since early 1985 that has been responsible for the shrinking of the trade deficits in recent years. Perhaps another decline of the dollar's value by some 15 percent would be needed to correct the United States imbalance in foreign trade.

However, exchange rate fluctuations, or the ups and downs of the dollar in terms of EC and other currencies, are more closely related to short term financial flows than to trade balances. Moreover, total world trade is about $2 trillion per year, while capital flows are about $30 trillion or fifteen times of total goods exchanged.

EXCHANGE RATE DETERMINATION

To understand the monetary evolution in the enlarged EC and to see its interdependence with the United States economic policies it is necessary to review the relationship of the European currencies with the dollar. On August 15, 1971, the United States declared that the dollar would no longer be freely convertible into gold. Also, an additional 10 percent tariff was imposed on all dutiable imports. Domestically, wage and price controls were introduced for the first time since the Korean War of 1950 and the Second World War. These measures initiated substantial changes in the Bretton Woods system of 1944, which introduced fixed exchange rates, and in the General Agreement on Tariffs and Trade (GATT), which deals with reduction in tariffs and other trade restrictions.

Expanding transactions among the United States, the EC, and other nations require growing international reserves for their support, in the form of gold or other hard currencies; or finally an internationally accepted instrument, such as the Special Drawing Rights (SDRs) issued by the International Monetary Fund

(IMF). However, worldwide growing demand for gold for additions to monetary stocks as reserves would present problems of potential inflation and huge gains for gold-producing countries (the Soviet Union, South Africa). More importantly, under a gold standard there would be extensive waste of resources transferred from other productive endeavors just to dig gold from one place to bury it in another place (in the vaults of central banks).

The commitment of the United States Treasury to convert dollars, used as reserves, into gold presented problems as the ratio of reserve dollars to gold increased significantly. As a result, the dollar was disconnected from gold, and other major nations, in turn, decided to "float" their currencies against the dollar. The European countries and Japan agreed to a dollar standard and pegged their currencies against the dollar. Although the sterling of Britain and the franc of France were used as reserve currencies in areas associated with these nations, the United States dollar was and still is the predominant reserve currency all over the world. However, reserves are used to finance residual imbalances, beyond private financing and trade credit, and international reserves need not grow as much as foreign transactions. Moreover, rapid adjustments to trade imbalances reduce the need for reserves, while the use of Eurodollars and other instruments of private finance increase liquidity and facilitate rapid transactions.

Periodic meetings and agreements between the United States and the major EC countries, as well as other industrial nations such as Japan and Canada, aim at the reduction or elimination of trade imbalances and currency disturbances. Such agreements in the recent past refer to problems of currency depreciations, use of interest and other financial measures for stimulative purposes, and synchronization of trade and capital flows to stabilize the international economy.

Differences in real interest rates between the EC and the United States affect the value of their currencies. Growing interest rates in the United States, relative to those of the EC, lead to the appreciation of the dollar and vice versa. With the narrowing of interest rate differentials between the EC and the United States, the dollar, vis-à-vis the EC currencies, comes down.[4] At times, the central banks of the major industrial countries intervene in the financial markets to push a currency up or down. However, depending on the conditions of supply and demand, such interventions may not have significant effects on changes in currency prices. If the money supply in the EC were to grow by more than in the United States, *ceteris paribus*, there would be a shortage and therefore a revaluation of the dollar and vice versa. In such a case, it would be difficult for the intervening central banks to influence the value of the dollar toward the opposite direction.

To correct unexpected and undesirable appreciations or depreciations of the dollar, the central banks of the countries involved, mainly those of the United States, West Germany, and Japan, are engaged in coordinated policies through selling or buying dollars to correct unwanted exchange rate fluctuations. For that purpose, formal meetings and conferences are periodically conducted with the above three nations and Britain, France, Italy, and Canada (the Group of Seven) to decide on corrective measures to be implemented so that financial and economic crises be avoided. Thus, to stop a further rise in the dollar and to avoid inflation, West Germany agreed to follow the United States and increase short-term interest rates. Such moves are usually matched by other EC countries, particularly France and Britain, to avoid pressures for currency realignment in the European Monetary System.

In order to stabilize the price of the dollar in terms of the EC and other currencies, the United States Federal Reserve Bank (Fed) intervenes into the market, from time to time, selling dollars to stem the rise in prices or by buying dollars to avoid driving the dollar down. The largest intervention of the Fed was in the second quarter of 1989, when it sold $11.9 billion worth of dollars, followed by another sale of $5.8 billion in the August-October period. Another large dollar selling occurred in August-October 1985. Moreover, a big dollar buying of $6.86 billion took place from November 1978 through January 1979 in implementation of the then dollar rescue policy. Although similar commitments of currency stability were and still are taken by economic allies, coordinated changes in economic policy, such as changes in interest rates, are needed for long-term exchange rate stabilization.

Western European deficit nations were reluctant to devalue their currencies in the past, considering that action a sign of weakness. However, from 1950 to 1971, and under the pressure of large deficits, France devalued its currency in 1957 and 1969, West Germany in 1961 and 1969, and Britain in 1967. The United States, Italy, and Japan never changed their par values officially, while Canada maintained flexible exchange rates from 1950 to 1962 and again in 1970 and thereafter.

Reasons and Effects of the Dollar Depreciation

Beginning in 1985, the United States dollar has been depreciating substantially. Since this process began, in fact, the dollar has depreciated by 50 percent or more compared to the EC and other major currencies of the world. A currency depreciation has many implications on the different economies involved and on the world trade situation as a whole.

In a floating rate system, a particular currency, the dollar for example, goes through a depreciation when there is an excess supply of that currency, in this case dollars, in the foreign exchange market. When this occurs, and supply is greater than demand, the value of the dollar relative to the other currencies falls. The dollar is then cheaper than those currencies and United States products valued on the dollar become more competitive internationally. As a result, United States exports become more attractive and, conversely, the imports into the United States less attractive.

A depreciation of the dollar has both good and bad effects on the economy. The good effect, as indicated above, is that it appears to improve the competitiveness of United States products both domestically and abroad. Obviously, this helps the trade balance as exports increase and imports decrease. This occurs since relative prices of exports fall when compared to foreign products. Also it helps increase European and other tourism in the United States particularly in Florida and California.

Nonetheless, there are also adverse effects to a depreciation. When the dollar is depreciated, United States products and the economy as a whole do improve but this occurs at the expense of the trading partners. As foreigners buy more United States exports, they will buy less of their own products. In addition, United States citizens will purchase less imports in favor of the cheaper domestic products. Hurting EC and other foreign economies will eventually come around and catch up with the United States economy as well. In the current international system, where there is a great amount of interdependence amongst economies, if any large economies are hurt, it will, over time, spread to the others. Also, if other countries feel a United States dollar depreciation is hurting their economy, they would probably retaliate either by depreciating their own currency or by imposing protectionist measures against United States exports. Either of these policies would cause a negative impact on all economies as all countries' exports fall and, *ceteris paribus*, their GNP and employment move downward as well.

Nevertheless, the dollar has fallen substantially in the last few years. This depreciation of the dollar has been caused largely as a result of the United States fiscal and monetary policies in the early 1980s. From 1980 to 1985, the dollar appreciated enormously. This was due mostly to United States policies concerning interest rates. The United States government implemented programs to raise interest rates, which created massive capital inflows and appreciated the dollar. Thus, the prime interest rate was raised by the Fed to 22 percent for the first time in history. The appreciation caused a concern that the dollar was overvalued and that led to pressure to begin depreciation. More importantly, the dollar appreciation, as expected, worsened the United States trade balance and created massive trade deficits. In an attempt to solve this problem, the United States began depreciating the dollar in the foreign exchange markets. This aroused a serious interest by other countries and, as international concern grew, the EC and other major economic powers of the world attempted to coordinate their policies. In September of 1985, the "Group of Five" (G–5), which consisted of France, Germany, Japan, the United Kingdom, and the United States, announced a joint effort to lower the value of the dollar so as to improve international economic conditions.

However, some years after this meeting and after some large depreciations in the value of the dollar, the United States is still experiencing incredibly large trade deficits. For some reason, the policy of depreciation did not work as well as was hoped.

Despite the fact that no substantial improvement in the United States trade balance has yet occurred, it can be predicted that the trade deficit will fall in the near future. However, the main reason the balance of payments is improving only slightly is that any improvements in merchandise trade caused by the depreciating dollar are being offset by other factors.

One way in which the depreciations are offset is in examining those foreign currencies that are not in the group of ten considered in the trade-weighted index. Many of these currencies have appreciated against the dollar at rates less than the major currencies and some have even depreciated against the dollar. A good example of this is the four newly industrialized countries, or NICs. The currencies of South Korea, Taiwan, Hong Kong, and Singapore appreciated against the dollar after 1985 by far less, or not at all, than the ten major currencies appreciated against the dollar. This allows United States importers to buy less from the EC and other major countries and more from these NICs, whose import prices have not been seriously affected by currency movements. Imports would then not fall and exports would not rise as much as hoped and the trade balance would not improve enough. Empirically, United States export prices are rather insensitive to exchange rate fluctuations but West Germany's export prices appear to be much more sensitive.

Still another factor counteracting dollar depreciation is the fact that consumers have developed certain buying habits that are not easy to break. If United States consumers believe that EC and other foreign products are better or more reliable than domestic products, they may prefer them regardless of higher prices. In other words, if the price elasticity of imports is very low in the United States then a large increase in import prices would have minor influence on the quantity imported. If the United States cannot overcome this problem, as well as the other problems mentioned above, it is likely that large portions of the trade improvement expected from the dollar depreciation will be nullified.

When the G–5 nations met in September of 1985, the objective was to aid the United States trade deficit problem in two ways. The first was to allow the United States dollar to depreciate, which, as we saw, occurred. Secondly, the other four nations were to expand fiscally, since they had trade surpluses, so that their economies would expand and, thus, demand more imports, some of which would naturally be from the United States. However, during this time period there was a lack of the expected vigorous expansion from these other nations, primarily West Germany and Japan, which led to a less than expected improvement of the trade deficit. Moreover, excessive United States budgetary spending creates additional demand, part of which is channeled into foreign products.

The United States did its part by applying pressure to the surplus EC and other nations for more expansionary policies. However, not much was achieved. The ''statements of policy intentions'' released thereafter were really nothing more than a restatement of existing policies. In addition, the International Monetary Fund (IMF) supported this move and argued that recent trends give no grounds for a change in fiscal and monetary policy in the European countries and Japan. Inactions such as these obviously did nothing to help solve the problem at hand.

This lack of a willingness to coordinate policy by the European nations and Japan was a serious setback in efforts to solve the United States trade problem. For, although the dollar depreciation would aid the deficit somewhat, a boost was needed as well from these economies. An increase in their demand for imports would have allowed the United States to multiply the effect of the dollar depreciation not only by lowering relative prices but also by increasing exports outside of the concern for prices.

Time Lag in Exchange Rate Changes and Trade Imbalances

Another explanation as to why the United States currency depreciation did not help the trade deficit as much as expected lies in the time element. It is accepted that there is a lag between the time a currency is depreciated and the time that the trade balance is affected by it. In fact, it is expected that trade will first worsen as consumers adjust to price changes. This is because they would be paying higher prices for imports at first until they realize the price differential. This concept is represented by what is known as the J-curve, a graph which shows the relationship between time and the trade balance as a currency depreciates. It seems that what is currently being experienced by the United States trade balance is the effect of a delayed J-curve. However, the time lag is longer than it was normally believed to be. This implies that the depreciation will indeed have its desired effect but it will take a longer time than expected.

We get an idea of the massive appreciation, then depreciation of the dollar from Figure 7.1. This erratic behavior has led many observers to criticize the dollar as a world currency because of its instability. If indeed the United States is acting as a hegemonic economic power, instability of the dollar could eventually lead to an international monetary crisis similar to that of the interwar period. For these reasons, it becomes increasingly important for the other major EC economies and Japan to help support the United States in its policies to alleviate its massive trade problems.

Against the European Currency Unit (ECU), the British pound (£), and the Deutschemark (DM), used as examples, the dollar first appreciated and then fell, as shown in the graph by the upward sloping then downward sloping line. The connection to the trade balance, shown in the lower graph, allows us to examine the effects of the J-curve. The dollar first began its depreciation after 1984, but the trade balance did not improve until 1987. This three-year lag is quite substantial and lends support to the theory of the delayed J-curve.

Mutatis mutandis, a similar upward slope up to 1984, and then a downward slope afterwards, can be observed for the exchange rates of the dollar and the French franc, as well as the dollar and the Japanese yen and, to a lesser extent the Italian lira.

Figure 7.1
Relationship Between Dollar Movements in Exchange Markets and the U.S.
Trade Balance

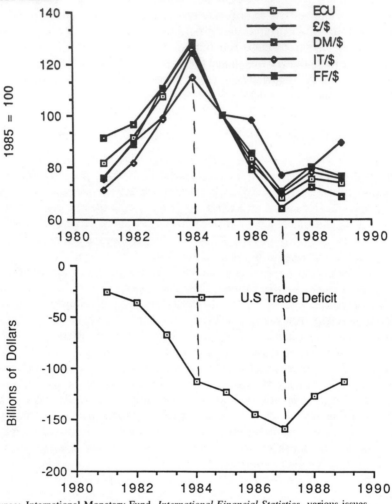

Source: International Monetary Fund, *International Financial Statistics*, various issues.

What is changing in the short run is prices of imports which are directly increased by the changing exchange rates. However, the volumes of exports and imports do not change in the short run when the exchange rates do. The reason for this is it is believed that price elasticities of demand for both exports and imports are relatively low in the short run, but they increase as people have time to adjust to the differences of price.

This is shown in the **Marshall-Lerner condition**, which is represented in the following equation:

$$\Delta T = X(N^* + N - 1)\Delta q/q$$

where ΔT is the change in the trade balance; X is exports; N^* and N are the price elasticities of demand for exports and imports, respectively; and $\Delta q/q$ is the percentage change in real exchange rates (e.g., $ vs DM). Thus $\Delta T = \$400$ $(0.8 + 0.6 - 1)0.5 = \$80$ billion.

If the sum of the two elasticities, N^* and N, is greater than one, then a depreciation helps the trade balance. If it is less than one, consumers don't react much to price changes and the trade balance worsens.

The J-curve theory assumes that in the short run, N^* plus N is less than one and thus not very responsive to price changes. However, in the long run, as consumers react to price changes, N^* plus N is expected to reach a level greater than one and thus the trade balance is aided by the currency depreciation.

The price pass-through, as it is known, may take a long time. There are two reasons for this. The first is that most United States imports, about 70 percent by IMF reports, are already denominated in the dollar before they get in the country. A change in exchange rates then has no effect on the prices of these items. This is an exclusive problem of the United States since the dollar is considered the world currency. The second reason for this phenomenon is that traders sign many long-term contracts in which the dollar prices of the transactions are fixed in advance. This too would serve to lengthen the time between the currency depreciation and the increase in import prices.

The trade deficit that has begun to shrink, even though not too much, has showed that the dollar depreciations have finally taken effect and that, after a relatively large lag, the trade balance has begun to move accordingly. The trend seems to be moving in the right direction and the related policies are working.

The experiences of the United States economy in the 1980s should be used as a learning process for the EC and other countries. Too rapid an appreciation can lead to crippling trade deficits. This type of problem then must be solved through coordinated policies of the major economic powers of the world, notably the EC, the United States, and Japan, so that possible confrontations be quelled.

Presently, large amounts of capital are diverted not only from the EC and Japan but also from developing countries. This is an inverse movement of that in the 1970s, when American banks lent or recycled OPEC's petrodollars and other savings to the third world countries. It seems that capital flows have become more important than trade flows in international transactions.

ADJUSTMENTS IN THE EC

The EC countries developed a monetary system with fixed exchange rates with respect to each other. All the currencies of the EC member nations are floating jointly against the dollar and other outside currencies. About half of the currencies are pegged to the dollar, while some others are pegged to the Special Drawing Rights (SDRs) or to a basket of currencies. The EC members agreed in 1972 to intervene and prevent wild fluctuations among their currencies and under certain circumstances, against the dollar ("snake in the tunnel"). However, in 1973, when the EC suspended dollar purchases, the tunnel was abandoned but the snake remained. After the turmoil of 1978, the EC introduced the European Monetary System (EMS) and the European Monetary Unit (EMU).

Although the EMS has not been completed as yet, it is expected to play a significant role in future international matters. Nevertheless, the use of a number of currencies as reserves ($173 billion in dollars and $149 in other currencies in 1980) can be a destabilizing element in the world monetary system. From that point of view, closer cooperation and currency harmonization among the industrial nations are necessary to avoid severe financial disturbances and worldwide economic declines. Inappropriate exchange rate policies usually lead to misaligned real exchange rates, that is, ones that differ from the long-run equilibrium.

Since March 1979, West Germany, Italy, Belgium, Luxembourg, Denmark, the Netherlands, and Ireland established the European Monetary System (EMS). In June 1989, Spain joined the EMS. The other three EC members, Britain, Greece, and Portugal, are expected to join it later. In order to stabilize the currencies and coordinate economic policies, the EMS commits member nations to limit fluctuations no more than 2.25 percent above or below the agreed exchange rates, except for the Italian lira and the Spanish peseta, which can rise or fall 6 percent. To keep values within the limits, the nine central banks are pledged to intervene and seek remedies through changes in domestic economic policies and even to realign exchange rates.

British reluctance to join the EMS, which lends greater uncertainty to business investment and sales, makes both Britain and the rest of Europe losers. However, member nations should cede major monetary powers to a pan-European institution and accept constraints on taxation and other budget powers. But for member nations running big budget deficits, such as Italy and Spain, or trade deficits, such as France, it would be difficult for the system to deal with a currency crisis after the complete elimination of controls. Free capital movement among the EC member countries as well as between them and the United States would present problems regarding policies of monetary stability. Also, expansionary economic policies in some EC members such as France and Italy may find it difficult to adhere to strict antiinflationary policies of other members such as Germany. Nevertheless, France abolished exchange controls from January 1, 1990, Italy from July 1, 1990, and Spain, Portugal, Greece, and Ireland from the end of 1992.

The European "Snake" allows the EC currencies to float jointly against the dollar. However, the floating, which was introduced in 1972 by the then six members of the EC, was limited to a total band of change of 2.25 percent, while the composition of the snake is subject to changes over time. In 1979, as a revival of the snake, the EC created the European Currency Unit (ECU), the value of which is based on a weighted average of the currencies of all members, with the German mark having more importance than the others. Also, the European Monetary Cooperation Fund (EMCF) was formed to provide assistance to the balance of payments of the member countries. The share of every member-nation to the Gross Domestic Product (GDP) of the EC determines mainly the weight of the national currencies or the ECU percentages.

The ECU was created by the EC to deal with international trade and finance, instead of having to deal with several separate and often volatile national currencies. It is based on a basket of the EC currencies, adjusted every five years with no intrinsic value, and is increasingly used as a real money with relatively stable exchange rates. In terms of dollars it is worth about $1.10. It is expected that the ECU would have a higher value after a barrier-free EC market is established. The ECU percentages to the weight of the national currencies (from June 19, 1989) are:

German mark	30.10
French franc	19.00
British pound	13.00
Italian lira	10.15
Dutch guilder	9.40
Belgian franc	7.60
Spanish peseta	5.30
Danish krone	2.45
Irish pound	1.10
Greek drachma	0.80
Portuguese escudo	0.80
Luxembourg franc	0.30
	100.00

To prevent money outflow, many EC nations keep currency controls. Individuals and companies cannot have bank accounts abroad or hold accounts in other currencies domestically. However, to help remove barriers in the EC, member-countries are eliminating currency controls. Thus, foreign exchange controls on companies were lifted currently by France, which has maintained them since 1968. Also, similar exchange controls on individuals are to be removed as part of a policy to create an economically united Europe. These measures are in conjunction with the EC policies of imposing a withholding tax to discourage movements of money abroad for tax evasion. As a result of eliminating currency controls, companies may lend money to nonresidents, and individuals will be able to have bank accounts abroad and in foreign currencies domestically. Substantial reduction in inflation by EC countries may be considered responsible for such free trade and exchange rate policies in the European Community. Thus, inflation in France is varying from 3 to 4 percent annually, still higher than the inflation rates of West Germany (2–3 percent) but lower than those of Britain and Spain (5–6 percent), as well as Greece (12–14 percent). Realignment of real exchange rates can be achieved through painful deflationary policies and currency devaluation.

Also, currency speculation between the United States and other nations plays an important role in dollar prices, investment decisions, and economic stability. At times, it forces central banks to interfere in the opposite direction to avoid unjustifiable effects on interest rates and other monetary policy tools, which, in turn, may trap stock markets, making them more bullish or bearish than otherwise, as well as to misdirect trade and investment among the countries involved.

With high short-term interest rates, the United States currency is in demand and becomes stronger. As long as this continues, interest in the dollar increases and its strength will be maintained and even increase. From time to time, the Group of Seven (Canada, Britain, France, Germany, Italy, Japan, and the United States) have meetings to coordinate financial and trade policies. In many cases, their central banks have been successful in slowing down the undue rise or fall of one or more of their currencies. Their coordinated interventions, though, have an effect on speculators and short-term investors, but not much on long-term trends.

Among the serious financial problems of the EC, and particularly of West Germany, are the monetary union with East Germany and the currency convertibility of the Eastern European countries. Although there are risks to currency adjustments on both sides of the aisle, the monetary union of the two Germanys will reduce unemployment and emigration from East Germany.

To absorb the excess money supply and avoid inflationary pressures, Eastern European nations can first sell state property to private companies and individuals. Then, through a reasonable exchange rate, weak East Bloc currencies can be exchanged with ECUs, German marks, dollars, and other hard currencies. For example, two East German marks were converted into one-half ECU or one West German mark, in July 1990, except for wages, pensions and savings up to 4,000 DMs for which the rate was one to one (compared to the six-to-one rate that prevailed previously in the black market). Such a convertibility of East Bloc currencies should establish a genuine relationship among prices, wages, and productivity. However, more generous exchange rates might be used for employee and worker earnings, pensions and long-term investment.

A similar meaningful link of United States dollars with West German marks and other Western European currencies occurred during the immediate post-World War II period. Also, old currencies of Western European nations were substituted with new ones to enhance people's confidence and reduce or stop inflationary spirals. In the case of West Germany, for example, 6.5 current marks were exchanged with 100 Reich marks in 1948.

The fact that Eastern European currencies are overvalued makes it difficult to adjust them to Western currencies because wages and prices should change according to the new exchange rates and the purchasing power of the related currencies. From that standpoint, a federal union or an association of the East Bloc states with the EC and an adjustment of individual currencies to the European Currency Unit (ECU) may be less painful and more effective than adjustments with separate currencies.

Furthermore, such a policy would reduce the fears that emanate from a strong united Germany in the center of Europe and the danger of outburst of a renewed German nationalism similar to that prevailing before the two world wars. Unlike before, a united Germany would be far more dependent on its neighbors, economically as well as politically. Already, Germany, along with the other EC members, is committed to an extensive surrender of sovereignty to the common causes of the EC. Therefore, within the framework of the EC institutions a united Germany would find it difficult to dominate Europe, especially after a common European Monetary System becomes effective. It would not be easy for Germany to dictate important policies in a diffused economic and political environment of a community of twelve and, eventually more, nations.

LINKS OF FISCAL AND FOREIGN TRADE POLICIES

Domestic and External Imbalances

Trade balances are of great importance to public policy for many governments, including those of the United States and the European Community. They are affected by budget deficits and other variables which, in turn, are influenced by domestic economic policies.

Government expenditures higher than tax revenues stimulate aggregate demand for domestic and foreign commodities and services. Sizable deficits, in turn, absorb substantial amounts of domestic savings, crowd out investment and attract foreign capital. With flexible exchange rates and growing international transactions, domestic fiscal policy greatly affects and is affected by foreign trade and capital movement among nations.

Although there is a strong criticism against trade deficits, demand for foreign products continues to be strong in the United States. And this takes place despite the fact that private and public sectors make substantial efforts to promote internal trade and induce their citizens to purchase domestic products. The increase of such trade deficits requires careful restrictions on the part of spending in order to reduce the gap between imports and exports.

Budget deficits increase demand for foreign products and increase trade deficits. The recent United States trade deficits, in turn, act as "locomotives" in pulling the European economies out of slow growth. On the contrary, reductions in trade deficits are the results of reduced budget deficits. This is in accordance with the well-established Keynesian macromodels—that fiscal contraction improves trade deficits and vice versa.[5]

Here an effort is made to compare trade balances between the United States and the EC and to determine the most important variables affecting them. Importance is given to the links of trade and budget deficits.

Economic policies to reduce trade deficits must be consistent with domestic targets. They should include fiscal policies that will diminish budgetary deficits, through changes in tax rates and government expenditures, and monetary policies to alter private saving and investment behavior, primarily through changes in interest rates and exchange rates. In addition, exogenous factors may affect internal fiscal deficits and external trade deficits. They include changes in the terms of trade, fluctuations in foreign demand, and sociopolitical disturbances. Nevertheless, there seems to be a close relationship, a "romance," between changes in domestic budget deficits and changes in trade deficits. This means that improvements in the balance of trade position are related to improvements in the government budget position.

The rapid expansion of foreign transactions suggests that the study of the effects of budget deficits on trade deficits should be linked to the international financing process. The prolonged United States trade deficits, which are related to budget deficits, create surpluses in other countries, such as Japan and Germany, part of which surprisingly enough comes back and finances United States budget deficits. Also, these countries with surpluses provide, directly or indirectly, credit to other countries which is usually used to increase demand for United States products or United States government securities. Thus, the United States is implementing some kind of globalization of demand-side economics, which is financed with a sort of credit card among nations.

The United States budget deficits absorb several billion dollars worth of foreign capital. The yens and marks used to buy United States government securities return back in the form of purchases of Japanese and German products. If the United States continues to rely on foreign capital to cover its budget deficits, the trade imbalance will remain. However, if stimulation abroad reduces the flow of foreign funds, interest rates may rise and recession will follow. Moreover, the money supply may be raised to accommodate the demand for credit, thereby risking inflation.

In recent years, an inverse trend can be observed between the United States and the EC, as the dollar has been depreciated in terms of other currencies, particularly German marks.[6] Therefore, we may witness an improvement in United States trade and a reverse movement of financial capital from the United States to the EC and other countries, as the international adjustment free trade mechanism requires. Also, the relatively lower EC interest rates are melting Europe's problems away and stimulating economic growth. As a result, EC domestic consumption and imports are expected to increase and thereby mitigate the problems of the United States trade deficits. On the other hand, the dollar is the currency upon which foreign transactions are based and facilitates the operations in the huge Eurodollar market.[7] As such, it affects the performance of international transactions as well as the domestic economic policies of other countries, particularly those of the EC. In addition, the climate of confidence of "safe-haven" and the favorable speculative expectations may feature the strengthening of the dollar and its appreciation in relation to the EC currencies in the years to come.

The previous United States economic policy, which was intended to deal with the problem of growth and inflation, has accomplished two things.

1. It attracted capital from other countries, which was partially used to finance the United States budget and trade deficits, and moderated domestic inflation.

2. It expanded the availability of loanable funds for United States investment, thereby counteracting the cyclical budget deficit effects.

United States budget deficits therefore have acted like a mega-Keynesian stimulus on a worldwide basis, as the EC and other countries stepped up their exports to the United States and increased their economic growth. It seems that the United States uses foreign saving to stimulate its economy and, in turn, to stimulate the economies of other countries, especially in Europe.

Budget deficits increased significantly in the European Economic Community, especially after 1970, while small trade surpluses appeared for all years after 1960, except 1979 and 1980. An important reason is that the EC countries trade among themselves and deficits in one country are compensated for by surpluses in another or other countries.

The interdependence of the EC national economies is such that virtually all the domestic economic policies and trends affect and are affected by conditions in other member countries. Among the various factors that generate such inter-actions are inflation and interest rate differentials, different rates of employment, variations in fiscal and monetary policies, and changes in regulations and re-strictions affecting international trade and capital flows. Although these variables that affect trade balances deserve separate consideration for each individual country, this section concentrates on the EC countries as a group.

For a number of years since 1960, trade surpluses in West Germany have balanced trade deficits in Britain, France and Italy. Thus, in 1983, France had 5.2 and Italy 2.9 billion dollar trade deficits respectively, while Germany had a 4.2 billion dollar surplus. On the other hand, budget deficits for the same year were 53.4 billion dollars for Italy, 21 for Britain, 17 for France, and 12 billion dollars for Germany. In 1987, France and Spain had less then a $1 billion trade surplus, Italy $6 billion, and West Germany $56 billion; and Britain and Greece had deficits of $6.7 billion and $3 billion, respectively (1986). Budget deficits for 1987 were $7.6 billion for France, $13.4 billion for West Germany, $10.2 billion for Britain (1986), and even higher for Italy.

The difference in the United States and the EC trade position is due partially to the fact that the American economy was expanding fast while that of the EC lagged behind in the previous years. Therefore, as mentioned previously, the United States trade deficit is acting as a stimulant to the European economies, leading to frequent large trade surpluses primarily in Germany and small average surpluses in the EC as a whole. However, the American economy is more flexible than the more protected European economies and its trade deficits are expected to decline when Europe achieves higher rates of economic growth.

On the other hand, there is a sharp contrast among EC countries, especially between France and Germany. France has pursued an expansionary policy, experiencing large budget deficits and, up to recent years, trade deficits. Given the structural rigidities and labor immobility in France, such Keynesian macropolicies easily ignite inflation. However, the cautious economic policy of Germany engenders export-led expansions, low rates of inflation, and comfortable trade surpluses. Currently, though, under the pressure of the EC directives, almost all EC countries experience relatively low rates of inflation.

The central result of the previous analysis is that budget deficits substantially affect trade deficits in the United States, while the statistical evidence indicates that there is no strong relation between these two variables for the EC. An important reason for this difference is that individual countries in the EC experience deficits or surpluses which balance each other. Also structural socio-economic and political differences among the countries considered may be additional reason for these discrepancies. Therefore, policy makers in the United States should implement different policies than those in the EC.

The budget and trade deficits of the United States, and to a lesser extent of some EC countries, are becoming an acute problem for their economies. However, eventual decreases in the United States interest rates are expected to reduce the budget deficits and eventually trade imbalances. Moreover, the stability or possibly the decline in oil prices would affect favorably the trade balances of the United States and more so of the oil-importing European nations and vice versa.

As long as the income elasticities of United States imports are higher than those in the EC, as they were in recent years, the United States trade balance is not expected to improve much. *Mutatis mutandis*, corrective fiscal and monetary policies for both the United States and the EC are needed for the improvement of the trade imbalances between them, especially for the United States.

Relationship Between Budget and Foreign Trade Deficits

In addition to the chronic federal budget deficit, there is the United States trade deficit that is equally alarming. Since 1893, and until 1970, that is, for 78 years in a row, the United States enjoyed a surplus in its merchandise trade with the rest of the world. However, since 1971, the United States has deficits in foreign trade, especially recently with Japan, Canada, Germany, Britain, France, Italy, and even with Brazil, Mexico, Singapore, and Korea.

America's budget deficits, and the historically high interest rates they have produced, are primarily blamed for the huge trade deficits. Yet the merchandise deficits remain large although interest rates have come down somewhat. Even when the dollar was weak the United States had foreign trade problems. Although some complaints that unfair trade practices of other nations may be justified, the globalization of the economy and severe international competition may be considered the main reasons for the American trade deficits. Other nations with cheaper resources, particularly labor, and disseminated and improved technologies, are producing cheaper products and are able to compete with similar American products.

The policy to combat "stagflation," and to offset the crowding out of domestic investment that cyclical budget deficits exercise in the economy, attracted capital from abroad. Such an inflow of foreign capital from the EC and other nations finances an excess of imports over exports and moderates domestic inflationary pressures. This leads to an enrich-thy-neighbor policy of revaluation, instead of a beggar-thy-neighbor policy of devaluation and engenders a global economic recovery. However, by attracting foreign saving to the United States, the international debt crisis is worsening as the debt servicing burden increases, and economic growth is declining.

Nevertheless, current greater private saving, to pay future taxes for debt servicing, may offset increased government borrowing and interest rates and investment may not be affected. This may be so if budget deficits are not large in relation to the rate of economic growth. On the other hand, higher taxes, required to pay the interest of a large debt, are distorting market effects and impose a "dead weight" burden on the economy. Moreover, the financing of budget deficits through capital imports, practiced largely by the United States in the 1980s, leads to the appreciation of the dollar and the pressure by special interest groups and politicians to deploy protectionist measures in favor of particular United States industries. Such measures include tariffs (motorcycles, cheese, textiles), trigger prices (steel), corporate bailouts (Chrysler, Lockheed), quotas (auto, textiles), government allocation of private credit, and other policies to protect certain industries from going off the cliff. Perceptively, the adoption of a prop-up-the-losers policy may lead to the erosion of United States competitiveness and to "a strategy for failure and lemon socialism."[8]

As noted before, budget deficits make the American economy increasingly dependent on EC and other foreign capital for investment. Most foreigners do not have to pay United States' or other nations' taxes on their investment, but Americans have to pay. A reduction in taxation that Americans are required to pay on investment income would reduce the cost of capital, particularly in industries that suffer from import competition. This would make the nation less dependent upon foreign investors and reduce the fears of protectionism stemming from a high level of imports because of the excessive demand and, at times, the overvaluation of the dollar. On the other hand, protectionism reduces the supply of the dollars for imports, as does the reduction of bank lending abroad. This, in turn, drives the value of the dollar further up and inflates the trade deficit.

A large amount of total foreign investment is in United States government liabilities, primarily bonds and other Treasury securities and growing amounts of companies' stocks and bonds. The return on them, together with all other investment, is tied to the interest rates on government securities. The high United States interest rates and the investment security lure EC and other foreign investors to sell their own currencies to buy dollars that may drive up the value of the dollar. This may result in a strong dollar, making American exports more expensive and imports cheaper, thereby increasing the United States current deficit, which grew to record figures in recent years.

As noted before, although foreign investment stimulates the American economy, there is the danger of sinking the economy into a severe recession when foreign funds flow out in large amounts. Moreover, domestic fiscal and monetary policies may be largely ineffective if foreign investors control large segments of the country's internal debt and assets of productive enterprises.

The rapidly growing United States public debt is mostly a paper wealth we owe ourselves. However, larger and larger proportions of the debt are financed by foreigners. According to the Commerce Department, from the total foreign-held assets in the United States about half belong to the Europeans, one-fifth to Canadians, one-fifth to the Japanese, and more than 10 percent to Latin Americans.

The huge fund flowing from the EC and other countries helped finance large United States budget deficits and domestic investment, keeping interest rates and inflation relatively low. Moreover, the Treasury made the inflow easier by dropping the 30 percent withholding tax on interest paid to foreign investors and allowing anonymous purchase of securities by foreigners. This leads to a soaring capital inflow. If this trend continues, economic and probably foreign policy gradually would be vulnerable to decisions made abroad. As Benjamin Franklin said: "He who goes a-borrowing goes a-sorrowing."

A gradual correction of budgetary imbalances and a smooth dollar landing would restore financial and economic stability in the American market as well as in the EC and international markets.

While budget deficits generate employment, trade deficits export jobs. The strong dollar abroad in the early 1980s undermined United States competitiveness in world markets, making imports a bargain and exports more expensive. The result has been the loss of more than three million jobs since 1980, especially in manufacturing. Already, steel imports count for about 25 percent of United States consumption, autos 23 percent, machine tools 42 percent, and shoes more than 75 percent.

To harmonize diverging national policies toward foreign investment and taxes, an international code of government behavior and business ethics may be needed, particularly between the EC and the United States. Common customs duties, common antitrust policies, transportation rates, benefits, and taxation may be included in such a harmonized code. Technological progress in our supersonic era makes the world smaller and the corporation bigger and very soon we may emphasize not independent fiscal and monetary policies, but unified international policies.

Excessive government expenditure and fiscal deficits play a significant role in balance of payment deficits and vice versa. When budget deficits are financed in inflationary ways, as frequently happens in a number of EC and other countries, demand for foreign products increases and balance of payment deficits rise. In many instances, reductions in current account deficits are the results of reduced

Figure 7.2
Relationship Between Budget Deficits and Trade Deficits (billion dollars)

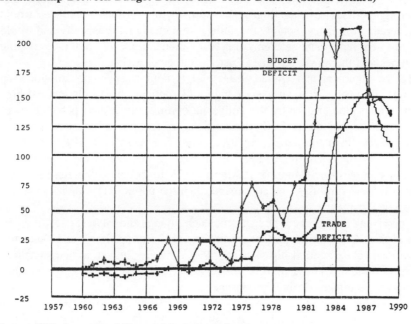

Source: IMF, *International Financial Statistics*, various issues.

fiscal deficits. On the other hand, when current account deficits rise, the main reasons are increases in government spending and budget deficits.

The United States gap between national savings and investment (or that between domestic income and expenditure) is related to the current account position. Therefore, balance of payment deficits can affect and be affected by policies which change net private sector savings and those which influence government deficits.

As Figure 7.2 indicates, foreign trade deficits follow the trend of the budget deficits. This is obvious after 1969, and especially after 1973, when both variables followed a close relationship. Appendix B shows a high correlation between United States budget deficits and trade deficits. If large trade deficits continue for long, the American economy will have to pay out large amounts of interest and dividends, instead of collecting them, as happened for many years in the past. Political power and international influence would be unfavorably affected by such a change in economic power and the dollar could be undermined, forcing undesirable fiscal and monetary policies which might have worldwide destabilizing effects.

To promote greater currency stability in the world, major western nations try to conclude a new monetary agreement which would give the International Monetary Fund (IMF) a significant role in coordinating related domestic policies.

Through a new International Open Market Committee, the IMF would set "target zones" for exchange rates and then encourage countries to adopt fiscal and monetary policies for their implementation. Such coordinated policies would stop certain currencies, notably the dollar, from changing drastically and would ease the debt repayment problems of debtor nations, especially of the developing countries and the newly reformed Eastern European nations.

To the argument that United States budget deficits spur consumption, sap savings and investments, and cause high trade deficits, high inflation and high interest rates, the answer by the Pollyanna optimists is that as percentages of the gross national product (GNP) these deficits are declining after 1983. Actually, they are less than the deficit of 1975 (about 5 percent of GNP). Therefore, changes in deficits are to be related to changes in the size of the economy for reliable comparisons. Moreover, if the overall government deficits, including state and local surpluses, are considered, then the public sector deficits are less by about 1 percent.

Concerning the effects of budget deficits on savings and interest rates, it seems that in the EC countries, particularly in England, France, Italy, and Denmark, there are no close relationships between these variables. In fact, as budget deficits increased, interest rates, adjusted for inflation, declined and vice versa, while savings rates remained roughly constant.

Budget deficits, from excessive government spending, increase consumption in domestic and foreign products. As exports are less than imports, trade deficits appear and, *ceteris paribus*, the debt of the country rises. Casandra pessimists or jeremiads predict that the twin deficits and the growing internal and external debts may lead the United States and the world to economic crisis.[9] Bear in mind, though, that a sizable portion of imports (15 to 30 percent) comes from foreign branches of American companies that sell more than $600 billion worth of goods overseas annually.[10]

Aid to Developing Countries

The sweeping changes to be effected in trade, labor, and capital, as a result of the EC integration and Eastern European reforms, will influence not only European and United States economic and political conditions but global relations and rearrangements with other countries, including the developing ones.

Although Japan became the largest donor and lender in the world (with $10 billion in foreign aid in 1988, compared to $9 billion by the United States), the EC as a group is the largest donor of official development assistance. Moreover, the European Commission often uses nongovernment organizations for assistance to third world nations, in addition to official EC support, in technical development, food, and supply of medicines.

As Table 7.1 demonstrates, the EC nations as a group provide the largest official development assistance to developing nations. However, the United States provided the largest aid until the early 1970s. After that time, the six

Table 7.1
Official Development Assistance from the EC Countries and the United States
(millions of U.S. dollars)

Country	Amount			Percent of Donor GNP		
	1965	1980	1988	1965	1980	1988
Belgium	102	595	592	0.60	0.50	0.39
Britain	472	1,854	2,615	0.47	0.35	0.32
Denmark	13	481	922	0.13	0.74	0.89
France	752	4,162	6,959	0.76	0.63	0.73
Germany, W.	456	3,567	4,700	0.40	0.44	0.39
Ireland	0	30	57	0.00	0.16	0.20
Italy	60	683	2,615	0.10	0.15	0.35
Netherlands	70	1,683	2,231	0.36	0.97	0.98
Total EC	1,925	13,002	21,191	0.45	0.46	0.53
U.S.A.	4,023	7,138	12,170	0.58	0.27	0.25

Note: For Italy 1987 instead of 1988. For the EC (total), percentages of GDP instead of GNP.
Source: World Bank, *World Development Report*; and OECD, *National Accounts*, various issues.

European Community nations, that is, without Britain, Denmark, and Ireland, which entered the EC in 1973, became the first donor group in the world and, together with the later member-nations, continue to be so at present.

Out of a total official development assistance (ODA) of $36.7 billion, or 0.35 percent of the related GNP, in 1986, the EC countries provided $16.1 billion, compared to $9.6 billion for the United States, $5.6 billion for Japan, and $3.6 billion for Saudi Arabia. In 1987, the EC provided about double ODA of that of the United States. The same thing can be observed for the aid as a percentage of GNP. For the EC it was 0.52 of its GNP in 1987, compared to 0.23 for the United States. France, West Germany, Italy, the Netherlands, Britain, Denmark, and Belgium, in a descending order of billions of United States nominal dollars, were the largest EC donors. However, as a percentage of GNP, the Netherlands, Denmark, France, and Belgium were the largest EC donors, followed by West Germany, Italy, Britain, and Ireland. The main recipient countries of aid from these EC nations were their previous colonies and present trade associates. On a per capita basis, the low-income countries, mainly of Africa and Asia (excluding China and India), were the main recipients of assistance from all sources ($19.6

billion in 1986), followed by the lower-middle-income ($14.5 billion) and the middle-income ($11.5 billion) countries.

As reported by the Export-Import Bank some donor countries offer foreign aid as a means to expand their exports. Such export-linked aid increased from $3.2 billion in 1982 to $15 billion in 1987, and is expected to rise even more in the future. However, there are complaints by the United States government that American industries, such as capital goods and telecommunications industries, are losing exports (about $1 billion annually) because other countries, primarily France, Germany, and Japan, are using aid to developing nations to promote their own exports. Low interest loans and grants are given to poor nations with a usual clause to spend part or all of the money for imports from the donor countries.

Nevertheless, as a result of the drastic reforms in Eastern Europe, developing countries in general feel neglected as attention for investment and aid shifted to the East Bloc countries. Already, some forty-two nations agreed to allow the newly created European Bank for Reconstruction and Development to provide loans not only to the private sector but also to the public sector (60 and 40 percent, respectively) of the Eastern European economies. Such loans to projects like roads, telecommunications, and other infrastructural facilities would help revive the economies of Hungary, Czechoslovakia, Poland, and other East Bloc countries. The European Community controls 51 percent of the bank, which was established in Paris on May 30, 1990, with an initial capital $12 billion. The United States controls 10 percent of the bank and Japan controls 8 percent.

8 Investment and Joint Ventures

FOREIGN INVESTMENT

Expansion and Problems

Because of the dollar's fall in value against other major currencies in recent years, a wave of foreign investment, primarily from the EC countries and Japan, entered the United State economy. Foreigners had already invested $1,768.2 billion in the United States by 1988 and more than $2 trillion currently. About $300 to $400 billion of that amount is in manufacturing companies. Also, about 20 percent of the $2.9 trillion United States national debt and 21 percent of American banking belong to the foreigners.

In 1985 American investment abroad was surpassed by foreign investment in the United States. For the first time in seventy-one years the United States became a net debtor country. Thereafter, the international investment position of the country continued to be negative and the United States net debt increased from $110.7 billion in 1985 to more than $700 billion currently. United States Treasury and other securities, direct investment, bank deposits, and corporate stocks and bonds are the main assets of foreign investment in the United States. It seems that the rising interest payments add to United States borrowing and press interest rates upward, making debt servicing more costly. If real interest rates exceed the GNP growth rate, debts will continue to rise (the debt trap).

Of growing importance is foreign ownership of United States companies that increased from $83 billion in 1980 to about $300 billion presently, while the United States foreign debt of about $700 billion represents about 25 percent of the value of all companies on the New York Stock Exchange. This proportion is likely to increase as the foreign debt increases and the process of financing budget and trade deficits, through selling long-term assets and businesses, will continue. Profits, dividends, and technology will be transferred abroad and the United States standard of living will be under pressure in the future. It is a process of short-term gains but long-term pains. EC and other foreign investments benefit the American economy in the short run but they may drain it in the long run.

It is likely that a more unified EC may reach a dominant position in manufacturing, finance, education, media, and related services. As United States visible liabilities on internal and external debts and camouflaged ones on saving banks are growing, the American preeminent role may shift in favor of the EC in the next century. Controls on telecommunications, electronics, financial institutions, and media, including book publishing, which is now practically foreign-owned, may be totally or partially exercised by the EC and other nations in the near future. From that point of view, there are arguments that United States restrictions or limitations that exist in defense industries, banks, data processing technology, TV, and other media be extended to other sensitive industries of national interest or, at least, reciprocal rights of ownership and mutual rules of acquisition be required.[1] Britain, France, Germany, Italy, and other nations exercise some government controls on foreign investment. If the same rules and regulations suggested for the United States apply to the EC and other partners there would be no fear or hysterical reactions to foreign investment and acquisitions.

The rush of foreign capital to buy American companies and property has been an important issue regarding the United States' dominance over the world economy. Some Americans are resentful about foreign investment and they feel that this trend would lead to an "America for Sale" procedure and the eventual decline of the country. Some forty-four of the top fifty firms were American in 1959 compared to only twenty in 1988. The unfortunate thing is that direct foreign investments are primarily directed to takeovers and often reduce employment instead of creating new jobs. It is estimated that only about 1 percent of new jobs is the contribution of foreigners. Dutch, British, and other European—and not many Japanese corporations—are the main owners of American companies and real estate. The adherence to the laissez-faire principle and the comparatively limited United States restrictions on foreign investment, as well as the recent depreciation of the dollar, are mainly responsible for the transfer of American companies and technology to foreign investors. Foreign companies' share of the United States workforce is about 45 percent in chemicals and 50 percent in building materials, while the big tire makers (General, Firestone, Armstrong, and Uniroyal Goodrich) are owned by West Germany, Japan, and the last two by Italy, respectively.[2]

The borderless capital market led to the explosion of cross-border direct and portfolio investment primarily between the EC and the United States. Thus, foreign direct investment in the United States increased from $54 billion at the beginning of the 1980s to $329 billion in 1988, while foreign portfolio investment increased from $53 billion to $345 billion, respectively. The financial Euromarket, centered mainly in London, facilitates the issuance of debt and equity all over the globe. This helps avoid the drying up of capital flows, thereby preventing worldwide depressions similar to that of the 1930s. Large merger and acquisition transactions (some $370 billion in 1988, of which about $200 billion were inside the United States) were partially financed by the Euromarket. American corporations are by no means out of the race and many more are expected to move into the EC financial markets.

Although net foreign investment is advantageous for the American economy in the short run, growing interest payments (especially from the purchases of United States government securities) swell internal and external deficits, dry up the economy from financial resources and crowd out productive investment. The greater the budget deficit, the lower the rate of domestic savings and the greater the need for foreign capital to cover the difference of excess consumption over production. Thus United States private savings are lower than 4 percent of GNP compared to more than 15 percent for other advanced economies, while foreign capital inflow is about $200 billion per year.

To insure American investment abroad, the Overseas Private Investment Corporation (OPIC) was established in 1969. It sells insurance against confiscations, revolutionary takeovers and other political risks, guarantees loans of United States banks, and makes direct loans mainly to developing nations. It backs more than 150 projects a year. Some recent loans guarantees include that for Bell South Corporation ($30 million), providing cellular communications services in Argentina, and that for American Telephone and Telegraph Company, building digital switches in Egypt ($35 million). Also, it provides political insurance for a dairy project of Land O'Lakes Inc. in Indonesia and the Philippine Capital Fund ($35 million), which is involved in debt-for-equity swaps. Although not much involved in the EC projects the OPIC became a successful institution with $1.2 billion capital and reserves and about $100 million earnings annually. Organized labor tries to block renewal of the OPIC charter by Congress on the grounds that it exports jobs. Expectations are that its operations will increase in the reformed economies of Eastern Europe.

Deficits and Foreign Investment

The twin deficits are causing high interest rates and sizable appreciation of European and other currencies. Foreign investors would prefer American commercial real estate (with yields of 7 to 10 percent) and United States Treasuries (with yields of 7.5 to 9 percent) instead of European and Japanese government bonds with low yields (4 to 6 percent). Moreover, the recent depreciation of the dollar by some 50 percent made American assets cheaper for the foreigners by an equiproportional amount. For the anxious European and the patient Japanese investor, ownership of American land, which is cheaper than in other countries, and other assets, is important from an economic and social point of view, while Americans gradually lose their economic independence.

Because Americans are living well by running up huge domestic and external debts, foreign creditors, mainly Japanese and Europeans, use their surplus and buy American assets. It is like an individual enjoying life by spending borrowed money, running up debt and selling off property. The main cause of the twin United States deficits is the unwise fiscal policy of reducing tax revenue, mainly through the Economic Recovery Tax Act of 1981 and the Tax Reform Act of 1986, without reducing as much spending. The idea was that tax cuts could encourage people to work more, save and invest more, and the growth in the economy would yield more tax revenue. However, these tax cuts did not produce the surge of working effort and the proportionate tax revenue. The result is a continuation of internal and external deficits and growing interest payments. In essence, this is an illusion of well-being based on borrowed money and borrowed time that leads to a gradual decay of influence and reduced standards of living, making American renters of the property they once owned. This is what happened, for example, with the recent Japanese purchase of 51 percent of the Rockefeller Group, owner of Rockefeller Center (for $864 million), CBS Records, Columbia Pictures, and many buildings in Los Angeles as well as a number of other companies.

In their inward-looking economic policy, American policy makers have not appreciated the strong linkages that exist between the domestic economy and the external world. The interdependence of internal and external economic conditions requires substantial changes in fiscal and monetary policies of the countries involved. Perhaps emphasis on research and development toward high-tech equipment and machinery should be given by the United States' policies for effective competition with West Germany and other EC countries, as well as with Japan. On the other hand, newly industrialized nations, such as South Korea, can excel at manufacturing consumer goods. It is suggested that in order to achieve the goal of high tech investment, a monetary policy of low interest rates and a greater tolerance of inflation via easy money should be pursued. From that standpoint, inflation in proper doses is not considered an economic drawback but a benefit for capital formation in advanced technology. As the argument goes, business profits not savings drive investment toward profitable ventures.[3] However, easy money may be inflationary and destructive to long-term productive investment. Moreover, inflationary psychology may make "proper doses of inflation" difficult to control.

The net United States domestic investment, about 6 percent of the GNP annually, is reduced by disinvestment abroad and presently accounts for only around 2 percent of the GNP per year. This net investment-to-GNP ratio is very low in comparison to that of the three previous decades, which varied from 9.4 in the 1950s, 9.7 in the 1960s, and 8.1 in the 1970s.[4]

A continuing foreign trade deficit that is not matched by domestic investment leads to sluggish productivity growth and undermines the international position of the country. A reduction in consumption and imports and an increase in investment in plants and equipment, research and development and education, and in export industries would put the achievement-oriented United States economy back to a strong competitive position.

In order to attract capital, the United States offers tax and other benefits to foreign investors. An important tax exemption was introduced in 1984 when the United States permitted overseas lenders to buy United States corporate bearer bonds and to receive not only tax-free interest payments, but anonymously as well. Whether advantageous or not, foreign investors enjoy benefits that Americans do not. United States taxpayers are obliged to add the interest they receive to their taxable income. It seems that EC and other countries which tax interest income may follow the United States policy, so that capital outflow will be curbed and foreign investment may be attracted. In such a case of reciprocity the United States tax incentives may not be effective.

Although the rate of return on capital for European business is less than that in the United States and Japan, investment productivity is expected to improve after the economic unification of Western Europe and more so with the closer cooperation with a democratized and economically reformed Eastern Europe.

For the first time in 30 years net foreign investment earnings for the United States presented a deficit in 1988. Even if there are improvements in the trade (commodities) balance, the balance of current accounts, which includes services (travel, tourism, investment earnings) in addition to commodities, may present deficits. As the United States foreign debt increases interest payments increase and, assuming other things being the same, the debt further increases. For the last two decades the United States has had annual deficits in the balance of trade. However, because of investment earnings, the current account balance had surpluses up to 1981. The growing internal debt (more than 3.0 trillion in 1990, compared to $1 trillion in 1981) is mainly responsible for the growing foreign debt, which has made the United States a debtor nation since 1985.

Services, which include foreign aid and Social Security payments to retired Americans abroad, had deficits for the first time (in 1988) since 1958. Foreign lending of about $200 billion a year allows the United States to run big annual trade deficits and keep a satisfactory level of investment. Consumption is about 4 percent above production, while around 22 percent of United States gross investment is financed by foreign funds. Already, the United States pays large amounts of interest on its international indebtedness, in addition to the obligations for the amortization of the debt. All these would mean further pressure on the American standard of living.

The United States xenophobia that foreigners may control vital industries and eventually colonize parts of the American economy may lead to severe restrictions to capital investment by non-United States citizens. Already, ownership of more than 25 percent of a company with assets of more than $20 billion by foreigners must be reported to the United States government. However, the formation of dummy corporations by foreign investors may circumvent such restrictions. On the other hand, Europeans had similar fears back in the 1950s regarding American investment. The feeling was that America was colonizing Europe through the almighty dollar. The result, though, was that United States investment helped Western European nations to rehabilitate and develop their economies. Conversely, British and Dutch investment largely financed the construction of railways in the United States about a century ago, which greatly helped the economic development of the country.

Nevertheless, restrictions on investment and trade in general reduce rather than strengthen economic growth and the welfare of the consumers. For example, United States consumers lost about $17 billion as a result of United States quotas on the imports of Japanese cars in 1981–1983. As the argument for protection goes, the country cannot allow foreign control in critical areas and industries, particularly defense industries. However, it is difficult to draw a line between defense and nondefense industries. For example, is the oil industry of vital or strategic importance to the defense of the country? What about the airlines or the computer industries, and so on?

In recent years, worldwide expansion of trade and investment, as well as the introduction of floating currency rates, necessitated a new consideration of antitrust laws. Up to now, their main purpose has been to promote primarily domestic competition. The increasing importance of global competition, though, suggests a change in antitrust treatment and regulatory developments. Thus, the United States Justice Department and the Federal Trade Commission look favorably on joint international ventures such as that of the General Motors Corporation of the United States and the Toyota Motor Corporation of Japan. Also, because of strong competition from Europe and Japan, a new look at steel and car industries is taken by the antitrust regulatory authorities in order to effect investment and technological development from the EC and other countries. Similar encouragement of joint ventures and cartelizations occurs in the EC nations, especially in France, as well as in the newly opened markets of Eastern European nations.

Supporters of legislative intervention argue that in order to ease the imbalance and reverse the trend of United States companies that move their facilities overseas and export jobs, the government should adopt protective measures and take steps to direct trade with other countries. This is so especially for manufacturing products, such as textiles and shoes (three-fourths of which are imported). To avoid further self-inflicting wounds, they suggest that the United States government set a fixed ratio between exports and imports, particularly on nations with a history of excessive trade surpluses. Also, limitations on the percentages of import increases are considered. However, there is the risk of retaliation by the EC and other trade partners.

There are charges by the United States that the Executive Commission of the EC introduced new rules requiring that the manufacturing of high technology computer chips take place in the community. Although Motorola Inc., a United States company, and NEC Corporation of Japan, along with other non-European companies, make chips in Europe, the EC imports more than $1 billion of chips from the United States and more than $500 million from Japan for a total EC market of $6.2 billion annually. American and Japanese producers consider the measure of excluding chips assembled in Europe from wafer diffusion (imprinting the pattern of the microcircuit on silicon wafers) elsewhere as protectionistic.

Also, the EC set minimum prices for memory chips (dynamic random access memories or D-RAMs) sold by Japan below cost (dumping), as the United States government did three years ago, to protect EC chip producers. On the other side of the Atlantic, the United States permitted the sale of the semiconductor subsidiary of Monsanto Company of Palo Alto, California, to Heuls A.G., a subsidiary of Veba A.G., a large chemical group in West Germany. Because Monsanto produces silicon wafers that are important to advanced semiconductors, there were discussions that such an acquisition may endanger national security as the country is losing a key technology to foreigners. However, the deal was approved by President George Bush on the grounds that the United States is in favor of reducing investment restrictions in international transactions.

As Figure 8.1 shows, Britain, West Germany, France, and the Netherlands are the main EC countries with business enterprises acquired or established in the United States. According to the United States Department of Commerce, there are about 1,000 United States enterprises acquired (around 600) and established (about 400) by foreigners every year. In 1988 alone, there were 646 acquisitions worth $60 billion and 366 establishments worth $5 billion. Outlays of foreign direct investors were $16.4 billion and the remaining $48.6 billion were investments in United States affiliates during the same year.

Comparatively speaking, there is a decline of affiliate employment, mainly in manufacturing, by the EC countries and a growth by Canada and Japan. Affiliates with ultimate beneficial owners (UBOs) in Britain and Canada accounted for 20 and 19 percent shares of total affiliate employment, respectively, compared to 12 percent for West Germany, 9 percent for the Netherlands and Japan each, and 7 percent for France. However, more than 50 percent of total affiliate employment in the United States was provided by the EC companies.[5]

Air and Rail Travel Industries

European deregulation of air travel, similar to that in the United States, is gradually increasing competition, especially regarding computer reservations systems. These systems lead to marketing alliances and mergers on a worldwide basis. European air carriers, such as British Airways, KLM, British Caledonia, Alitalia, and Air Portugal, are under the Galileo computer airline bookings system; and Air France, Iberia, Lufthansa, Air Inter, and Air Adria are under the Amadeus bookings system.

On the other hand, American air carriers use more advanced computer bookings systems than their European counterparts. They include the Sabre system, owned by American Airlines (with about 40 percent of the bookings share) and the Apollo System of United Airlines (with a 26 percent share). This last system

Figure 8.1
U.S. Affiliates of Foreign Companies: Employment Percent Distribution by Country and Industry

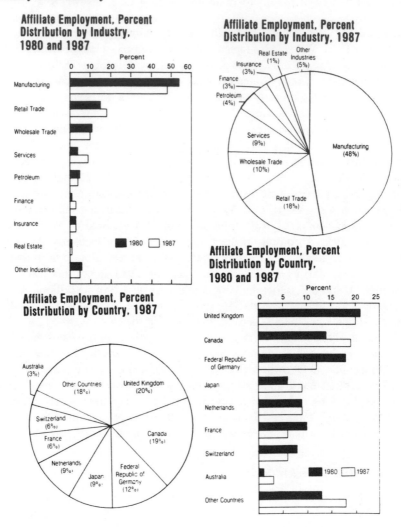

Source: U.S. Department of Commerce, Bureau of Economic Analysis.

was joined by five European airline companies recently. Systemone of Texas Air (15 percent), Pars of Northwest and TWA (15 percent), and Datas II of Delta (with 5 percent share) also joined this system. With the gradual deregulation of European air travel, ticketing restrictions and other curbs are reduced or eliminated. At the same time, American computer booking companies infiltrate the European markets and vice versa. Thus, five European airlines, led by British Airways, bought about half of Apollo in the recent past.

As to the aircraft trade, Britain's Air Europe ordered eighteen MD–11 jetliners from the American McDonnell Douglas Corporation, followed by France's Minerve and Italy's Alitalia with orders for ten jetliners each. Moreover, West Germany's LTU ordered three planes (767–300ER) from Boeing Corporation, another American aircraft producer. This was a successful deal mainly for McDonnell Douglas over its chief competitors, Boeing and Airbus Industry (the European consortium).

In addition to free internal trade among the EC member nations, improvement in transportation is also taking place gradually. Thus, the thirty-one-mile-long Calais tunnel, to connect Sangatte, France, with Dover, England, is under construction. The tunnel, which the French and British envisioned and started constructing more than 100 years ago (1875), was expected to seal a sincere alliance between the two countries. Although the digging was halted in 1882, when the British were afraid of an invasion by the French, the construction of the tunnel in the Calais Channel remained a dream thereafter.

It is expected that completion of this monumental project will take place in 1993. By that time the EC will, presumably, have completed its single internal market. There will be three parallel tunnels, two for trains and one for service. Once the project is completed, economic conditions on both sides will be improved. Trains will run from Glasgow to Hamburg, Vienna, Athens, Naples, and Madrid, while the French high-speed train known as the T.G.V. (Train de Grande Vitesse) will run from Paris to London. Also, a superhighway will connect Paris with the coastal area. The project, which has been undertaken by the Eurotunnel (British and French) consortium, promised to give economic stimulus to both sides of the Channel, especially in the depressed Pas-de-Calais region. Already tourism is flourishing in the towns of Sangatte and Calais in France and Dover, Cheriton, and Folkestone in England.

To help tie the large EC market together, a further improvement in the transportation network is needed. In order to facilitate trade transactions among the member-countries, the national rail system should be innovated and linked up to the pan-European railway network.[6] The Paris-London rail connection through the Channel Tunnel and the tying of Europe with high-speed trains, similar to those of France, could halve ground-travel times and speed the process of the EC integration. The Paris-Lyons fast trains, with speeds about 190 miles per hour, and with expectations of up to 250 miles per hour, proved to be a successful venture worth being imitated by other lines in France and other EC countries. The rail link of Paris-Brussels-Hamburg and then Munich-Vienna-Florence-Rome-Naples and back to Milan-Lyons-Barcelona-Madrid-Lisbon with fast trains would speed up movements of passengers and products and make the common market of Europe a real achievement. The financing of these lines can be made privately, as in the case of the Channel Tunnel, or through the state or EC subsidies.

The Eurotunnel Company is considering issuing bonds to finance part of the one billion pounds needed to construct the tunnel connecting France with Britain, which is interested in being connected with continental Europe.

The opening of the East Bloc markets requires immediate and effective connections to the transportation network of Western and Eastern Europe to facilitate trade and investment ventures. A pan-European rail system would speed transactions not only among EC member-nations but also between Western and Eastern European nations.

Growth of Business Enterprises

Rapid changes in business investment and financial services improve business conditions and help the expansion of domestic and multinational corporations. United States companies cross the Atlantic and establish or buy businesses in the European Community and vice versa. Large and small companies aggressively search for mergers and acquisitions into the domestic as well as the international markets.

Worldwide improvements in communications and the use of fax machines and the supersonic Concorde airplane intensify trans-Atlantic and international mergers and takeovers. With the expansion of new technology, Europe and America and eventually the rest of the world merge into a unified market. Business dealings that needed weeks and even months to facilitate some years ago, now may take less than an hour with the use of fax machines. Global markets require global or multinational companies and European executives feel that a dominant world position can be achieved through America, while United States businessmen think that such a position can be achieved in Europe. Western European, American, and Japanese companies move aggressively into each other's territory, as well as to the newly opened Eastern European areas.

Being helped by new technology and the pursuit of profit maximization, giant companies are created through mergers and acquisitions, synergies, and vertical and horizontal integration. Fewer new owners replace the old ones and the dissemination of truth, the exchange of ideas, and antagonistic sources of valuable information may be crippled, while the public interest may suffer and democratic institutions be damaged. This trend becomes more obvious with the expansion of multinational corporations and joint ventures and the development of global network organizations between the EC and the United States. Nevertheless, such organizations utilize human relationships and frequently advance media information in a competitive and democratic environment toward a more productive future.

The need for servicing multinational clients leads large accounting firms to merge. Thus, Deloitte, Haskins and Sells plans to merge with Touche Ross. Arthur Andersen and Company, the largest United States accounting firm, is expected to merge with Price-Waterhouse, another big firm. Moreover, Ernst and Whinney merge recently with Arthur Young. Both of them are international accounting firms and try to improve and expand services abroad, particularly in Western Europe.

According to Morgan Stanley Capital International, Inc., the largest companies on both sides of the Atlantic in 1989 were the following (value in billions of dollars).

United States	Market Value	European Community	Market Value
IBM	64.6	Royal/Dutch Shell	54.4
Exxon	54.9	British Telecom	24.3
General Electric	49.4	British Petroleum	24.1
AT & T	38.1	Unilever	16.6
Philip Morris	32.1	Glaxo Holdings	15.9
Merck	27.5	Assicurazioni Generali	14.8
duPont	26.1	Daimler-Benz	14.4
General Motors	25.2	B.A.T. Industries	13.5
Bellsouth	24.2	Imperial Chemical	13.4
Ford Motor	23.9	Siemens	13.4
Amoco	22.9	Nestlé (Swiss)	13.4
Coca Cola	21.5	Fiat	13.3

The rush of mergers and acquisitions in accounting and advertising firms is the result of growing business due to a "Europhoria" that is expected from the European integration. Large ad companies expect to serve large firms such as Grand Metropolitan and Philip Morris, as well as media moguls like Robert Maxwell and Rupert Murdoch. However, if acquisitions and takeovers by "hunters" continue, soon EC-United States advertising would be dominated by a few firms in an oligopolistic fashion.

With the removal of internal trade barriers and the integration of Europe, internationally minded investors from the United States, Japan, and other countries will try to broaden their bases and have a piece of the intra-European activity. Particular interest is expressed in the food and drinks industries, capital equipment, trade, transportation, and insurance.

Both the EC and the United States support their firms entering and increasing their activities into the territories of the other side, as well as into the Eastern European countries, through personal training, financial support, and market strategies.

The trend of closer business cooperation between the United States and the EC is expected to continue. It can be argued that there seems no better alternative or more efficient scenario in the arsenal of international economic policies. There may be short-term setbacks of free trade and movements toward protectionism from time to time. However, rapid developments in transportation and communications would bring about further liquidation of national and continental barriers of trade and investment.

The formation and advancement of the EC toward closer cooperation and integration aim, among other things, at enlarging European enterprises and mak-

ing them more competitive in relation to their United States and Japanese counterparts. From that standpoint, United States companies are expected to be forced
to move rapidly to a process of reorganization and modernization so that they
will be able to face the new challenge of international competition. Moreover,
a frenzied movement of mergers, acquisitions, and friendly or hostile takeovers
is expected to take place in the EC not only among European companies but
between United States and EC companies as the movement toward complete
economic and political integration of the European countries continues. Many
such mergers and acquisitions are reviewed in the following sections of this
chapter.

ACQUISITIONS OF EC FIRMS BY UNITED STATES
COMPANIES

To have a foot in the door and increase their share in a unified EC market,
American multinationals are aggressively opening more branches in Europe or
acquiring EC firms. This increases investment in the old continent and improves
economic conditions on both sides of the Atlantic.

Nevertheless, nationalistic politics remain strong in some EC member-nations,
as they are in a number of cases in the United States. Politicians in France, Italy,
and other EC countries intrude and present objections to acquisition deals over
management control of certain industries. Thus, deals of the United States' Ford
Motor Company with Italy's Fiat Scania A.B. Alfa Romeo and Britain's Rover
auto industry were faulted, but they seem to be successful with Saab-Scania
A.B., a troubled Swedish auto and truck company. Moreover, General Motors
Company of the United States has teamed up with Volvo. In any case, outside
of some strategic industries, such as auto companies and airline carriers, the
number of acquisitions of EC firms by United States corporations continues to
increase.

Intra-European harmonization policies are changing the complexion of United
States bilateral agreements with EC members, and American firms and affiliates
adjust their operations to new conditions before the door of opportunity is closed.
However, the countries of foreign-owned affiliates should provide reciprocal
treatment to EC service and other companies. From that point of view, related
United States laws, such as the Glass-Steagall Act, which prohibits banks to sell
insurance, should change and adjust to those of the European Community. On
both sides of the Atlantic, changes in trade-services rules should be made in the
context of the Uruguay Round under the umbrella of the GATT, so that international harmonization standards prevail for all nations concerned.

From the standpoint of investment, it seems that American corporate executives and investors are more enthusiastic and aggressive in their expansionary
policies than their European counterparts. A number of United States companies
enter joint ventures with European firms. Other United States firms establish
subsidiaries or offices in the EC member-nations, as well as in East Bloc nations,

while some others try to enhance their European positions through mergers and acquisitions. Their aim is to take advantage of the barrier-free market of the EC, regardless if integration plans are, at times, bogged down in debates over tax harmonization, exchange rates coordination, and other common regulations. The feeling is that there is a no-lose situation in preparing for Europe's attractive market. That is why American top management is soliciting broad-brush advice from its overseas counterparts.

The rush of Japanese investment in Europe is an additional reason forcing American corporations to invest in the EC. Already, the United States' direct investment in the EC increased from about $70 billion in 1984 to more than $120 billion at present. Britain absorbs the largest proportion of such investment (about 37 percent), followed by West Germany (20 percent), France (10 percent), and the rest of the EC countries with lower percentages. According to Translink's *European Deal Review*, there were 185 United States acquisitions in Europe in 1989. About two-thirds of them were enacted during the second half of the year. The price that 40 percent of them reported was about $15 billion, $11 billion of which was in Britain (including Ford Motor's acquisition of Jaguar for $2.27 billion). Out of $50 billion worth of worldwide deals that year, about half were in Britain. During the year 1989, other acquisitions were $10.65 billion by France, $7.32 billion by West Germany, $6.1 billion by Britain, and $1.85 billion by Italy. However, there is skepticism that American firms well established in Europe may support protectionism against Japan and even the United States. Such efforts may include limits of imports not only in the EC but eventually in the reformed Eastern European countries which are expected to conclude association agreements with the EC.

From the standpoint of investment, it seems that America discovers the Old World in its new path of integration. Many United States companies have already moved into the EC and exploit the new opportunities. A number of executives rush to learn French, German, Spanish, and other EC languages and examine the ways to conduct business more effectively. Europe is considered as one of America's hottest places of investment and future operations are expected to increase dramatically.

An effective way to reduce and even eliminate barriers not only between the United States and the EC but among many other countries in the world, including the Eastern European countries, is through the rapidly growing cable networks. Already CNN (the Cable News Network) of the United States airs in 83 nations, including Britain, Greece, Italy, and soon in West Germany and other EC countries, as well as in Eastern Bloc nations, such as Hungary and Poland. As can be observed from visits to various European nations, such cable networks provide a very efficient means of cross-cultural influencing and liquidation of various barriers among nations. However, there are major hurdles in the process of expansion, such as lack of a common language and a homogeneous market, high costs for satellite time, obstacles from state-owned TV operations, and shortages of homes with cable hookup.

Other United States cable operators include: American Television and Communications, a subsidiary of Time Warner, concentrating its efforts in Britain, France, and Ireland; Cox Cable Communications, which owns half of Denmark's largest cable company; and Pacific Telesis, U.S. West, and United Artists Entertainment, all with cable franchises mainly in Britain, France, and Ireland.

Paramount Pictures Corporation, MCA Inc., and MGM/UA Communications Co., all American movie firms, set up a joint distribution subsidiary, United International Pictures, to avoid administrative duplications in Europe. However, the Treaty of Rome, which founded the EC, outlaws agreements among enterprises that restrict or distort competition in the community, but exceptions can be made as long as they benefit the consumers. Thus, the European Community's executive body approved this venture by these three major United States movie companies after they complied with EC antitrust rules.

The Omnicom Group, the American parent company of DDB Needham and BBDO Worldwide, will merge BMP Davidson Pearce, a Boase agency in London, with Needham's office in London into a new advertising company named BMP/DDB Needham. This friendly takeover was announced after Boulet Dru Dupuy Petit, a French advertising agency, dropped its bid for Boase's agency in London. Boase is the parent of Ammirati and Puris, a marketing research company in New York.

To overhaul its antiquated telephone network, Italy plans to spend about $30 billion on telephone equipment. To achieve that goal, Italtel S.p.A., the Italian state-owned telecommunications company, formed a partnership with the American Telephone and Telegraph Company (AT&T), which would have a large portion of Italtel's new equipment. This was quite an achievement for the AT&T that had difficulties in putting a foot in Europe, facing severe competition from Siemens A.G. of West Germany, Alcatel N.V. of the Netherlands and Ericsson Telefon of Sweden. The equal partnership of AT&T would improve technological development and joint marketing in selling switches and other Italtel products outside Italy, particularly in other EC countries.

In order to globalize its operations, Ford Motor Company of the United States is investing heavily in new plants in Western Europe, mainly in Spain and Portugal. Such investments concern the production of sophisticated electronic engine management systems, car audio equipment, on-board computers to manage engine performance, fuel economy and emissions control, and other auto-related products.[7] Ford also is considering entering into a joint venture with Mazda Motor Corporation to produce vehicles in Europe, mainly compact cars in West Germany. It owns about 25 percent of Mazda, which builds the Ford Probe at a Michigan plant.

In competition with General Motors Corporation (G.M.), the Ford Motor Company acquired the Jaguar P.L.C. of Britain for $2.38 billion. It plans to use its advanced technology to modernize the luxury, gas-guzzling Jaguar and to promote its top-notch European products through Jaguar's network without competing directly with it. Ford also plans to buy a major share of Saab-Scania, a

Swedish automotive and aerospace company. This linkup would enhance Ford's position in Europe regarding cars for young professionals. Smaller moves during the past few years include Ford buying 75 percent of Aston Martin Lagonda; G.M. linking up with Group Lotus; and Chrysler buying Maserati and Lamborghini, and linking up with Fiat S.p.A. of Italy.

To provide access to the European market, the United States' Chrysler Corporation announced a joint venture with Renault, the French auto maker, to build a sports utility vehicle in Europe. This youth-oriented small vehicle (J.J.), to be built either in Spain or Portugal, will compete with the Suzuki and Samurai vehicles of Japan and the Geo-Tracker of G.M. In this venture, advanced manufacturing technology would be used to reduce complexity and weight and save cost, so that competitiveness would be raised. The venture is expected to increase the sales of Jeeps and passenger cars in Europe's tough and demanding market, which absorbs about 35,000 Chrysler cars per year. West Germany, Austria, Switzerland, and France are the main customers for these cars, which are guaranteed for 110,000 kilometers or three years. Chrysler also agreed with an Austrian firm to produce mini-vans for the European markets.

Avis Europe P.L.C., which became a separate unit after its United States parent (Avis Inc.) was bought by investors and managers in 1986, agreed to be acquired by a consortium which includes General Motors (G.M.) Corporation and Avis Inc. It has 76,000 vehicles operating in Europe, the Middle East, and Africa with annual revenues of about $1 billion. The deal is considered as a step to reunite Avis Europe with its parent Avis Inc. and an effort to increase the number of G.M. cars sold in Europe.

In contrast to the European banks and large corporations, American big banks and companies are in a good position to serve a continental market. General Motors, Unisys, Digital Equipment, Ford, IBM, Citicorp, and American Express are some of the American companies already operating in all or in most EC countries; and Volkswagen, Peugeot, Renault, Fiat, and many other large European companies operate primarily in their own national markets.

Although computers and office equipment production in the EC grows rapidly (with about $40 billion annually), American computer companies sell more computers in every EC country than their European counterparts. IBM, with about $20 billion sales in Europe per year, Digital Equipment, Unisys, and Hewlett-Packard, with European sales from $2 to $4 billion annually each, are among the most successful and growing American companies in the EC. Motivated by the fear of the Japanese domination of semiconductor markets, IBM joined Siemens A.G. of West Germany to develop memory chips capable of storing 64 million bits of information or the equivalent of about ten large novels, in a fingernail sliver of silicon. With this trans-Atlantic collaboration, IBM participates in the operations of Project Jessi Consortium, which includes Siemens, Philips N.V., and Thomson CSF.

Compaq Computer Corporation, a Houston-based company, is a fast-growing major American enterprise in Europe that makes business computers. The surging

European demand and the use of modern marketing techniques are responsible for the success of Compaq, as evidenced by their surpassing Olivetti and Apple and trailing only IBM in supplying business computers to Europe. Compaq and other United States computer companies still have a technological edge over their European counterparts and are successful in promoting faster and more flexible computers by setting up their own subsidiaries managed by European nationals instead of using distributors.[8]

Among the top advisers to European mergers and acquisitions are: Morgan Stanley; Wasserstein, Perella; Merril Lynch; Lazard Frères; Dillon, Read; Kohlberg Kravis Roberts; First Boston/C.S.F.B./C.S.; and Shearson Lehman Hutton. They are involved in national and international mergers, equity and security exchanges, asset management, and arbitrage activities.

Kidder Peabody, a United States investment bank owned mainly by the American General Electric group, positioned a special team with S.G. Warburg, a London-based bank, for advising companies interested in mergers and acquisitions. Although the main function of this team is to advise British and other companies on friendly acquisitions of United States firms, hostile takeovers and mergers of any firms may be considered.

Moreover, the Morgan Stanley Group Inc., Solomon Brothers Inc., and other American investment banks expanded their operations in Paris, Madrid, Milan, Frankfurt, and other EC cities to help mergers and acquisitions and other financial dealings throughout Europe. Also, Citicorp, with some 18,000 employees in Europe, introduced credit cards in Belgium, West Germany, and Greece, and is acquiring banks all over Europe.

In 1988, the WPP Group bought Anspan Grossman Portugal, a large corporate identity firm, for $36 million, and together with Dentsee, a big Japanese ad agency, are considering the acquisition of Landor Associates, an international corporate identity consulting firm. Another competitor, Young and Rubicam, is also attempting to acquire Landor Associates. Landor helped change Allegheny Airlines to US Air, the American Can Corporation into the Primerica Corporation, and advised the merging of Burroughs Corporation and Sperry Corporation into Unisys. Also, it helped redesign and restructure British Airways. Another merger of two accounting and consulting firms, Arthur Andersen and Price-Waterhouse, is not just a United States issue but an international issue.

RJR Nabisco Inc., with headquarters in New York, sold five of its food businesses in Europe to BSN, a large food company in Paris, for $2.5 billion. RJR Nabisco was taken over privately in a large $24.53 billion buyout in February 1989. The sale was made to cut its debt of $5.5 billion.[9]

Moreover, leveraged buyouts are considered by the Great Atlantic and Pacific Tea Company (A&P), a leading American supermarket chain, and Kohlberg Kravis Roberts and Company, an active investment banker, to acquire Gateway Corporation, a British retail food chain. They compete with Wasserstein, Parella and Company of Britain, which offers $3.5 billion, and the Tengelmann Group of West Germany.

Some additional mergers and acquisitions across the Atlantic include: the buying of the Howson-Aligraphy, the British supplier of lithographic plates by E. I. duPont de Nemours and Company for some $400 million; and K-III Holdings, Inc., an investment company associated with Kohlberg Kravis Roberts and Company, which acquired Macmillan Book Clubs and Gryphon Editions of Macmillan Inc., for $143 million.

Also KLP, an international sales promotion firm, acquired agencies and affiliates in some fourteen countries. Its holdings in the United States include Comart-KLP with clients Kraft General Foods, Field Research Inc., and other research and development companies. Serious efforts are made by this firm to reinforce its position into the EC, especially in Britain, France, and West Germany, and the East Bloc countries to put teeth into its pan-European marketing. Random House, an expanding publishing firm, will acquire Century Hutchinson Ltd., another publishing firm founded in London in 1887, at about $100 million. An arrangement with Century Hutchinson Ltd. would have given 20 percent ownership to Little, Brown and Company, a unit of Time Warner Inc., while Simon & Schuster, a unit of Paramount Communications, has offered to buy Century Hutchinson.

Two European companies, Philips N.V. of the Netherlands and Thomson CFS of France, formed a consortium with the National Broadcasting Company (NBC), owned by the United States General Electric Company, to develop a new TV system that would produce detailed, high resolution pictures similar to those in movies. This joint venture or consolidation was considered better than the existing fragmentation to meet the Japanese challenge in future competition in television technology.

To establish a solid European base, Pepsico Inc. bought two British firms, Walker Crisps and Smiths Crisps, which were acquired from BSN, a French firm. BSN had purchased these two and three other companies recently from RJR Nabisco Inc. Moreover, Pepsico, a worldwide corporation dealing with snack foods, Kentucky Fried Chicken and Pizza Hut Restaurants, as well as Pepsi and other soft drinks, has snack-food operations already in Italy, Spain, Greece, and Portugal. With these new purchases, and probably others in the future, it is expected that Pepsico would strengthen its position in Europe.

The subsidiaries of the Pepsi Cola Company in Greece (in Marousi, Loutraki, Solonika) introduced an investment program of $90 million for improvement and modernization of production and distribution. The investment program, which will be extended for twelve years, will introduce the production of metallic cans, which are imported from Holland, and plastic bottles, as well as new advertising campaigns not only for Greece but for Bulgaria, Yugoslavia, and other Balkan countries.

The Coca-Cola Company, based in Atlanta, Georgia, acquired Société Parisienne de Boissons Gazeuses of France for $140 million so as to market Coke in France. Also, it is building a large canning factory in Dunkirk, France.

Sea Containers, Ltd., a Bermuda-based cargo and port operations firm with interests in containers and British ferries, asked the European Commission to block a hostile takeover bid by Temple Holdings, Ltd., arguing that such a takeover would restrict competition and violate the Community's laws. Sea Containers charged that Stena A.B. (a Swedish ferry operator), which, together with Tiphook P.L.C. (a British cargo company) controls Temple, dominates ferry services between Britain and Ireland and the English Channel, as well as in other parts of northern Europe, and aims at monopolizing the market. These complaints were released in a filing with the United States Securities and Exchange Commission recently.

Wentworth International Group, a United States polythene firm and bag maker, acquired Printway Company, a cardboard carton maker, and retains its commitment towards expansion in Europe.

Isosceles PLC, a group of British investors, had fought fiercely for control of the Gateway Corporation of Britain, which is a large food retailer. Its campaign has been boosted as Goldman Sachs, the United States investment bank, made a grey (unofficial and indicative) market in its shares. Isosceles is in competition with Newgateway P.L.C. for the acquisition of Gateway for $3.3 billion. Newgateway is a vehicle set up by Wasserstein Perella, a United States bank, and the Great Atlantic and Pacific Tea Co., a West Germany-controlled United States supermarket chain.

The General Electric Company of the United States is in the process of forming joint ventures in Britain for appliances and electronics and building plastic factories in Spain, in addition to the acquisition of a large medical equipment company in France.

The Whirlpool Corporation formed a joint venture with Philips N.V. of Holland to enlarge its appliance and electronics markets in Europe.

DuPont and Co., a large United States chemical company, will build a new European plant. Likewise, Archer-Daniels-Midland Co. will construct a $70 million plant at Europort in the Netherlands to produce soybean products.

UOP Inc., a joint venture between Union Carbide and Allied Signal Company, entered into a venture with Shell Chemical Company involving polypropylene and other products.

AM International Inc., a Chicago maker of supplies for the graphics industry, agreed to acquire Wohlenberg K.G., a graphics equipment and machine tools company in West Germany. Scott Paper Co. of Philadelphia acquired 51 percent of the sanitary-tissue business of Feldmuehle A.G. of Germany for $125 million, and International Paper Company of New York bought additional shares of Zanders Feinpapiere A.G. of Germany to raise its total holdings in Zanders to 80 percent.

Also, Donald Trump, the New York developer, agreed to acquire a 20 percent interest in the Wilshire Center PartnerShip of Power Corporation, P.L.C., Ireland.

The International Paper Company bought a French paper maker; and Sun

Microsystems Inc. of California opened a technical center in West Germany and is building a factory in Scotland.

This fever of joint ventures, mergers, and acquisitions is expected to continue in the future as the EC and all European nations move toward closer economic cooperation and integration. For investment in the East Bloc nations, see chapter 9.

ACQUISITION OF U.S. FIRMS BY EC COMPANIES

Not only American firms establish subsidiaries in the EC, but Western European companies move also into the United States and other markets. Fat with cash and credit, EC companies initially search for acquisitions within Europe, and afterwards move to the United States and the rest of the world.

Among the largest EC acquisitions of United States corporations during the last decade are: the Standard Oil Co. by British Petroleum Co.; Pillsbury Co. by Grand Metropolitan P.L.C. (of Britain); Farmers Group by BAT Industries (of Britain); Shell Oil Co. by Royal Dutch/Shell Group (of the Netherlands); Chesebrough-Ponds Inc. by Unilever N.V. (of the Netherlands); Texasgulf Inc. by Société Nationale Elf Aquitaine (of France); Celanese Corporation by Hoechst A.G. (of West Germany).[10]

Hanson PLC, a British conglomerate, has a number of operations on each side of the Atlantic. It produces a number of products from greeting cards, bricks, tobacco, and fertilizer in Britain to fish processing, whirlpool baths (Jacuzzi), building products, chemicals, and Smith Corona typewriters in the United States. It has at its disposal some $20 billion in cash and is searching for big takeovers, especially when LBOs run into troubles. In 1987, it bought Kidde, a United States conglomerate, for $1.7 billion. Usually, Hanson is using debt, secured against the assets of the companies bought, and not junk bonds, to buy new companies. Its annual profits are estimated at $1.5 billion, about half of which is from the United States.[11]

Again in July 1989, Hanson PLC acquired Consolidated Gold Fields PLC, the world's second largest gold producer, after the unsuccessful offer by Minorco S.A., with $5.5 billion. This was the largest takeover in British history. Gold Fields, which opposed a hostile takeover by Minorco and won a United States court suit prohibiting this takeover on the grounds of lessening competition, owns 49 percent of the Newmont Mining Company, the largest gold producer in America.

Hanson Industries, the British conglomerate's American arm, is also buying shares of other companies for investment purposes and primarily for takeovers of other firms, such as Cummins Engine Company of Indiana, SCM Corporation of California, and Kidde, Inc., of New Jersey. On the other side of the Atlantic, Hanson P.L.C. invested $4.5 billion for the Imperial Group, the British tobacco and food giant, and Midland Bank, Britain's third largest bank, and is expected to invest in other European companies. At times it buys shares and sells them later for a profit, as happened with Milton Bradley, Gulf Resources, Avon Mills, and Dan River, or invests in other companies that are under attack by other takeover aggressors.

Faced with British labor unions and weakened British management, Hanson P.L.C. and other companies have moved investment primarily into the United States fertile markets. With European integration, expectations are that more investment will be made into the European Community. Similar mutual movements can be observed in the law profession, as lawyers are eager to follow the rapidly growing financial and investment dealings of their clients on both sides of the Atlantic. For instance, Italian lawyers played an important role in the partial financing of Kohlberg's acquisition of Duracell in 1988.

Sir James M. Goldsmith, the buccaneering Anglo-French financier, after a decade of raiding and breaking United States conglomerates, launched a $21.3 billion bid for London-based BAT Industries P.L.C., the owner of Saks Fifth Avenue, Farmers Group Insurance, Kool and Barclay Cigarettes, Marshal Field, Horten, and other firms in the United States, Europe, and other countries. Some $17 billion was made up of debt and distributed by Drexel Burnham Lambert Inc. and Bankers Trust Co. The BAT deal is forcing European companies to rethink their survival strategies and their independence from hostile takeovers. Moreover, regulators worry that EC companies will be too debt-laden to compete in the EC integrated market and that corporate raiders may squeeze companies for short-term profits and not for investments for a more competitive standing.

In the BAT deal, joining in were Banque Paribas and Rothchild, and Gie Banque of France, General Electric Co. P.L.C. of Britain, Pargesa of Switzerland, and the Agnelli family of Italy.

Recently, WPP Group P.L.C., a large British advertising firm, bought the Thompson Company and the Ogilvy Group, two famous American advertising firms. Its operations have been expanded to public relations, market research, sales promotion, graphic design, business entertainment, and audio-visual communications. Through friendly and hostile takeovers, WPP has invaded America's Madison Avenue, which is gradually losing its long-unchallenged global advertising domination. Together with Saatchi and Saatchi P.L.C., another British advertising firm, they control about $30 billion or about 10 percent of the world's spending on marketing.

Harrisons and Crosfield Company, which operates the Harcros building business in Britain, shifted its interests away from commodity trading and plantations to chemicals, timber, and builders of merchant markets. In its effort to expand, it bought Moores Business Forms from Grossmans, Inc., which has about 59 outlets primarily in the states of Maryland, Ohio, Pennsylvania, and Virginia. Harrisons and Crosfield, which also has interests in Australia, first moved into the United States in 1988 when it acquired Woodburys Company, a timber and building supplies firm with operations in New York and Vermont. A new holding company, Harcros Lumber and Building Supplies, was formed for the enlarged United States market.[12]

Laird Group, a British engineering firm, is in the process of raising money to acquire 65 percent of Panel Prints, a United States printing company, for some $25 million. It also acquired 35 percent of the same company in January of 1989.

McCaw Cellular Communications, a large United States cellular telephone company, 20 percent owned by British Telecom, offered $110 per share, which was less than an earlier offer of $120, in an effort to acquire 90 percent of Lin Broadcasting. The new amount, which totalled $5.35 billion, was reduced because Lin failed to buy its joint venture partner in New York City and Philadelphia.

To cope with the competitive market of the EC and the growing global route networks, European carriers prefer more links with American carriers. That is why British Airways, the third in the North Atlantic market behind Pan Am and TWA, plans to buy shares in other United States air carriers. The limit permitted under regulations of the United States Transportation Department for foreign ownership of American airlines is 25 percent. Already, British Airways, a profitable carrier since its privatization in 1987, is a partial owner of Apollo, a computer reservation system of United Airlines that facilitates customers for both carriers. Also, KLM Royal Dutch Airlines acquired recently a large stake of Northwest Airlines, while the Scandinavian Airlines Systems acquired close to 10 percent of Texas Air Corporation. Swissair and Delta Air Lines have a joint marketing agreement and decided to buy 5 percent stakes in each other, while Australia's Ansett owns 20 percent of America West. Nevertheless, such transactions and takeovers of large United States airlines raised the concern of the United States Department of Transportation to reduce or stop too much control by foreign interests.

Cadbury Schweppes P.L.C., a British soft-drink company, agreed to buy Crush International, a beverage branch of the Procter and Gamble Company, a Cincinnati-based firm, for $220 million. With this acquisition, Cadbury expands business not only to North America and Europe, but to the Middle East, Latin America, and Africa. Thus the share of the company in the United States soft-drink market is estimated at 5 percent and that in Canada at 15 percent.

One of the fastest growing companies in telecommunications is British Telecommunications P.L.C. (BT). In 1986, it acquired ITT Dialcom, Inc., a leading United States electronic mail service, for $35 million, and 51 percent of Mitel Corporation, a Canadian supplier of phone equipment, for $251 million. In 1988, it bought 80 percent of Metrocast, a United States national paging system, for $28 million. In 1989, it got 22 percent of McCaw Cellular Communications, a United States mobile phone operator, for $1.5 billion, and Tymnet and other McDonnell Douglas data communications operations for $355 million. Furthermore, BT is expected to move aggressively into West Germany and other EC countries as well as into the United States and other countries.

Marks and Spenser, Britain's largest retailer, bought Brooks Brothers, the oldest American clothing retailer, for $750 million in May 1988. Further expansion of this firm, with 550 stores worldwide and $7.8 billion annual sales, is planned with new stores in Paris, London, and Dusseldorf, West Germany, as well as in the United States. The focus would be on women's classic fashions, mainly flannel skirts, tailored shirts, and blazers.

Siebe P.L.C., a British engineering firm, agreed in June 1990 to acquire Foxboro Company, a Massachusetts industrial controls firm, for $655 million.

Ladbroke Group P.L.C., a London operator of resorts and hotels, is interested in managing contracts for some American hotels of the Hilton Hotels Corporation in Beverly Hills, California.

Bass P.L.C., a British brewer with many pubs and other food and drink interests in Europe and elsewhere, agreed with the Holiday Corporation to buy its Holiday Inn hotel chain, paying $125 million to stockholders and assuming about $2.1 billion of debt. Previously, Holiday Corporation borrowed heavily to pay the stockholders in order to avert a takeover by Donald Trump, the New York developer. This deal with Bass would help Holiday to pay back part of its debt. Bass will pick up 55 Holiday Inn hotels and franchises and other agreements covering some 1,400 more hotels in North America.

A British glass maker sold 20 percent of its American subsidiaries to Nippon of Japan for $410 million.

Grand Metropolitan, a British food and drinks firm, recently acquired Pillsbury, the owner of Green Giant Vegetables and Burger King, and purchased Mont La Salle, a large vineyard in California.

Suter P.L.C., a British holding company, acquired a 6 percent stake in Sudbury Inc., a Cleveland manufacturer, for investment purposes. It appears that, because of favorable tax and accounting rules, there is a wave of British acquisitions of American companies, particularly in advertising and other service industries.

In its effort to achieve a slow but steady expansion, Courtaulds, a British chemical and textiles group, agreed to buy Products Research and Chemical Corporation, a United States polymer systems and sealants firm for $260 million. In the late 1960s Courtaulds bought International Paint Company and in 1989 acquired Wheeling Stamping, a plastic tubes producer in West Virginia.

Blue Circle Industries of London, through its United States subsidiary Blue Circle Holdings Inc., acquired Georgia Marble Aggregates Corporation for $148.5 million in cash. Georgia Marble operates seven quarries in the United States.

ABS Holding Corporation, a United States check-printing company, agreed to be acquired by MB Group P.L.C. of Reading in Britain for $300 million. ABS (American Bank Stationery) was sold, in 1986, to Gibbons, Green, Van Amergongen, a merchant banking firm, and ABS management acquired American Standard Inc. Moreover, MB already owns Clarke Checks Inc., another check-printing firm.

BBDO Worldwide, a United States-based firm, created links with advertising agencies in Europe as well as in Asia and elsewhere. Thus, it signed an agreement with Doherty Advertising Ltd., an Irish agency, and acquired a minority interest in Jenssen and Borkenhagen A.S. of Norway and similar agencies in Taiwan and Pakistan.

Unilever Group, the British-Dutch giant of consumer goods, agreed to buy Fabergè Inc. and Elizabeth Arden cosmetics firms of the United States for $1.55 billion. The deal is the biggest transatlantic takeover of this sort by European firms and makes Unilever a close rival of Avon Products Inc. of the United States, L'Oréal of France, and Shisieido Co. of Japan. In July 1989, Unilever made a $376.2 million friendly offer for Minnetonka Corporation of the United States and in 1987 it took over Chesebrough-Ponds Inc. of the United States for $3.1 billion. Also, it has embarked on acquisitions of smaller cosmetics and toiletries firms in Europe, such as two units of Schering-Plaugh Corporation, one in West Germany and one in Britain.[13]

Mark IV Industries Inc., a New York company, agreed to sell its Blackstone Corporation subsidiary to Valeo S.A., the second largest auto parts firm in Paris. In its aggressive takeover policy, it plans to use the money for additional acquisitions. In 1989, it also acquired Armtek for $575 million and agreed to sell its rubber subsidiary.

Axa Midi Assurances of France filed applications in nine United States states to acquire Farmers Group Inc. Hoylake Group agreed to sell Farmers Group to Axa if the hostile takeover of BAT industries, the parent of Farmers Group, is concluded.

Pechinery, a French aluminum company, bought the American Can Company from Triangle Industries, Inc. and, as a result, became the number one packaging company. Similarly, Lafarge Coppée, a French cement firm, bought Cementia, a Swiss holding company, and became the second largest cement company in the world. Other similar moves are expected from Groupe Bull, a French state-controlled computer company, and many other EC firms. From that standpoint, corporate Europe may soon become equivalent to corporate America on an international level.

Carrefour S.A., a French chain of hypermarkets with more than $12 billion sales annually, moved with aggressive marketing into Philadelphia, Cincinnati, and other places in the United States. Carrefour, which means crossroads in French, also has a 22 percent share in the Costco Wholesale Corporation with a number of warehouse discount stores on the West Coast. In addition, it has a number of stores in Spain, Brazil, and Argentina. The company expects rapid growth through product diversification and international expansion in the EC and other countries.

Compagnie de Saint-Gobain, a French conglomerate, agreed to acquire Norton Company, an engineering materials firm in Massachusetts, for $1.9 billion in cash.

Hachette S.A., a big French publishing firm, acquired Grolier Inc., a publishing company in Connecticut, for $450 million, in 1988. Moreover, the United States government decided to permit the acquisition of three divisions of Fairchild Industries, dealing with communications and electronics control systems and space, by Marta S.A. of France. The decision was based on the results of an investigation by the Committee on Foreign Investment in the United States concerning foreign ownership.

Owners and executives of Fiat, Olivetti, Feruzze, Fininvest, and the Gartini Group of Italy are expanding their operations not only in Europe but in the United States as well. Thus, Fiat, in cooperation with Chrysler Motors Company, is promoting its luxury car, the Alfa Romeo, into the United States market.

A group of foreign investors, including Friendly Partners C.V. in Amsterdam and Vik and Partners Ltd. on the Isle of Man, is in the process of selling its 23 percent stake of the Italy Fund's 6.3 million common shares outstanding with a price of $8.4 per share on the New York Stock Exchange.

Pirelli S.p.A., a large Italian tire company, acquired the Armtek Corporation tire operations in 1988 for $190 million and plans to buy Goodyear Tire and Rubber Company of the United States.

Finmeccanica Società Finanziaria per Aziona, a high technology holding company of Italy, agreed to buy the Bailey Controls operations of a Babcock and Wilcox unit which belongs to McDermott International Inc. for $295 million. Bailey supplies diagnostic and computer systems to chemical, paper, and electric utility industries.

Bennetton Group S.p.A of Italy formed a joint venture with Sports Inc. of the United States and Marubeni Corporation of Japan to produce and market shoes for women all over the world.

The Banca Nationale del Lavoro, the largest state-owned bank of Italy, has a branch in the United States (Atlanta) that had issued unauthorized export credits to Iraq worth $2.6 billion. A significant part of credits involve American grain exports guaranteed by the United States Commodity Credit Corporation.

Henkel, a West German firm, acquired the Emery division of America's Quantum Chemical for $480 million, which is one of more than forty of its acquisitions made in the last three years.

In order to strengthen its position in American and International markets Siemens A.G. of Germany agreed with IBM of the United States to develop advanced computer memory chips for the mid–1990s.

On the other hand, Vendex, the largest retail firm in the Netherlands, invested some $24 million in the United States' Dillard Department Stores, which expanded from 44 to 150 stores and has an estimated value now of $570 million. Dillard, the nations' largest family-owned retail firm, wants to buy back Vendex's stake of 41 percent out of fear that it may lose its majority position to this Dutch company, which already owns 50 percent of B. Daltons, the United States book chain and computer programming retailer. Similar fears are expressed by other American managements that foreign investment in the fertile market of the United States may lead to takeovers.

A Belgian supermarket, GIB, was permitted by American authorities to buy the remaining 42.7 percent of the share of its United States subsidiary known as Scoty. There are some 160 Scoty stores in Florida alone, among their chain stores in other places, with tools, construction material, woodwork, and other products.

The Algemain Bank of the Netherlands acquired the Cancorp of Chicago worth $420 million.

L.M. Ericsson A.B., a large Swedish telecommunications firm with units in Spain, Denmark, and other European nations, agreed with General Electric Company, a giant United States firm with many manufacturing and distribution units in North America, to form a joint venture called Ericsson-G.E. Mobile Communications, in which Ericsson will hold a 60 percent stake. With this deal, both companies would have access to the huge markets of Europe and North America in digital cellular technology and communication systems. Even Eastern European enterprises started buying American companies. Thus, Polygraph Export-Import, a state-owned firm of East Germany, acquired Royal Zenith Inc. of Long Island, New York, and renamed it Planeta North America, Inc. Two West German banks provided partial credit for that deal, which would increase Polygraph's supplies of printing machines and related equipment into the United States. With the fall of the Berlin wall and the drastic economic and political reforms in East Germany and other Eastern European countries, mutual investment ventures are expected to increase.

To slow the pace of mergers and buyouts and to put a damper on stock prices, the United States Congress considers legislation to eliminate the corporate tax deduction for noncash interest payments on junk bonds, which sometimes are termed as fake "wampum." (Wampum was used as trading currency years ago by American Indians.) Also, the United States Congress granted a three year takeover protection to Conrail, a railroad company, and is considering other restrictions on hostile takeovers.

On the other hand, Congress considers repealing the Glass-Steagall Act of 1933 that prevents banks from owning securities companies as concern grows over greater European and Japanese competition.

MERGERS AND ACQUISITIONS WITHIN THE EC

As global competition stiffens, corporate Europe is tuning up through restructuring and takeovers to be able to compete mainly with the United States and Japan. British, French, Italian, and West German companies are issuing new equity or debt to carry out ambitious acquisition plans similar to those in the United States.

The EC's large companies account for 17 percent of the top 1,000 firms in the world, with a market capitalization value of about $1 trillion. By comparison, Japan's large companies represent 47 percent of these firms and the remaining 36 percent belong to the United States. However, the waves of deregulation and privatization in Europe will intensify mergers and acquisitions and the number of giant companies in Europe is expected to rise significantly.

The merger mania, which has prevailed in the United States for some years, struck Europe as well. The number of mergers and acquisitions by EC companies has been increasing dramatically year after year. The removal of internal barriers and the growing competition from American and Japanese firms encourage European companies to merge with or acquire other companies in order to keep and increase their competitive edge against their external counterparts.

There were some 1,200 mergers and acquisitions of major companies in Europe and more than 1,100 acquisitions involving small- and middle-sized companies in West Germany in 1988 alone. Although West Germany runs the largest trade surplus ($88 billion in 1988), it has only about thirty entrants in the global 1,000 large companies. This is mainly because of the plethora of small- and mid-sized but efficient companies it has. As American companies invest heavily in Europe, EC corporations, from London and Madrid to Rome and Athens, use the growth-by-acquisitions strategy, instead of investing in new plants the old-fashioned way.

According to *Acquisitions Monthly*, in Britain alone there were 295 management buyouts worth about $7 billion in 1988, compared to 2,262 mergers and acquisitions worth $250 billion in the United States and 5,534 deals worth $376 billion worldwide. Almost an equal amount can be observed in 1989. As reported in the journal *Manda*, there were 600 mergers worth $16.6 billion in the EC during the first semester of 1989 alone, and the merger mania continues with more intensity, particularly in Britain. Therefore, more cross-border mergers and acquisitions are expected in EC companies in the near future as a follow up to similar American activities for purposes of competition with giant United States and Japanese companies.[14]

It seems that the spillover effect in Europe from big leveraged buyouts (LBOs) is growing. Such buyouts embrace telecommunications, power generation, consumer electronics, military contracts, and many other products and activities. To support friendly or hostile takeovers and LBOs in general, American-style debt financing has been introduced. Not only bank loans but "junk bonds" are used to fuel big corporate takeovers.

Yet EC member nations have their own laws and regulations regarding protection of competition against monopolization of the market and unfair price fixing and quantity restrictions. To supervise the implementation of these laws, they have special institutions or public commissions, such as the Monopolies and Mergers Commission of Britain, that do not permit takeovers and mergers as long as they reduce competition and lead to monopolistic practices.

Although there is no specific control provision in the Treaty of Rome, Articles 85 and 86 of the Treaty, which deal with competition, can be applied to mergers and acquisitions, in addition to national competition laws of EC member states.

More than fifty directives have been issued by the EC that affect internal services industries. They include: financial services (banking, securities, insurance, investment consultancy); transport services (air, shipping, roads); information services (computer programs, broadcasting, advertising); tourism, educational and professional services (training, research, medical practice, engineering, accounting). Other directives deal with government procurement services, which account for about $200 billion in the EC (including public works), residence permits, and mutual recognition of college diplomas.

Under the pressure of large United States and Japanese companies, the EC policy makers try to develop a common policy of cross-border takeovers and have member-nations surrender much of their power on industrial policy. Although Britain and West Germany argue that such power may be abused by the EC commissioners to the detriment of competition in related industries, France and other EC members prefer to have the commissioners' approval of large mergers and to have them consider incursions from the United States and Japan. Such policies are related to present trends of deregulation and privatization in the EC industries, particularly in aviation, where many airlines now operate mainly under the public sector.

To catch up with American and Japanese technology, Europeans are forming cooperative ventures and consortiums to build planes, missiles, advanced computers, new television systems, and other competitive products. Thus, a four-nation consortium of the EC developed Airbus Industries, the second largest aircraft company in the world after Boeing. Also, three semiconductor firms (Siemens of West Germany, Philips of Holland, and SGS-Thomson, a French-Italian company) launched a $5 billion program to build the most advanced computer chip in the world with 64 megabits of capacity, compared to the 4-megabit chips of the United States and Japan. Because antitrust laws in Europe are looser than in the United States, cooperation in research and other ventures is more effective in avoiding duplication by individual national projects.

Through effective management, acquisitions, and creations of new enterprises throughout the EC, European company owners and successful managers or "Euro-capitalists" speed up business expansion not only in the EC but in Eastern Europe as well. They are more successful in promoting economic development and making European integration a reality. They achieve better results than those that politicians tried to achieve for decades. Competition from big firms in the United States and Japan push Euro-capitalists into innovation, business organization, and modernization.

As the EC gradually removes trade and investment barriers, French companies and banks adjust themselves to new competitive conditions through joint ventures, mergers, and other corporate arrangements. Thus, there are efforts to rearrange and modernize the Société Générale, France's largest non-state bank, with $150 billion assets, through selling a portion of the shares to three investment groups including two state-owned companies. Although there are allegations of insider trading, this bank, which was privatized in 1987, is expected to improve and expand operations not only in France but also in other EC countries.

In the EC, British Airlines, which was privatized in 1987, and KLM Royal Dutch Airlines, which is 38 percent owned by the Dutch government, would each buy 20 percent of the shares of Sabena Airlines, which is 54 percent owned by the Belgian government. After clearance by EC antitrust regulations, this consolidation of major European airlines would be the largest cross-border alliance in the airline industry on the old continent.

It is recognized that through cooperation the EC computer industries may advance and survive competition from their United States and Japanese counterparts. Although a joint venture of French, German, and Dutch computer companies did not succeed in the 1970s, expectations are that, under the common EC's Esprit program of a single European market, they will reorganize and be more competitive in the future.

Through standardization and systems integration, the new computers (mainly of the Unix operating system) would allow software from different firms to run on them. According to the Yankee Group, a company of American computer analysts, European firms of medium-sized computers would be able to withstand competition by non-EC firms, especially in data and telecommunication systems.

To overcome the antimonopoly regulations of the British government, General Electric Company P.L.C. of Britain and Siemen A.G. of West Germany revised their bid for a hostile takeover of Plessey Company of Britain. Under the new bid, a number of Plessey military and telecommunications businesses would be owned by one bidder, not by both the above bidders jointly. Also, Daimler-Benz of Germany has acquired Freightliner; and Renault of France has 45 percent ownership of Mack Trucks.

Groupe Bull, the largest computer manufacturer of France, in addition to its expansion in Europe, agreed to buy Zenith Electronics Corporation, one of the largest producers of battery-powered laptop computers in the United States, for $635 million. Zenith, with a debt of $476 million, wants to concentrate on high definition television and other electronics technologies. Groupe Bull, which is owned by the French government, wants to expand globally and be able to compete with I.B.M., Apple, Compaq, Toshiba, Tandy and NEC, and other American and Japanese companies. This acquisition will increase Bull's sales to more than $7 billion a year, with about $2 billion sales in the United States.

In addition to the acquisition of the British Rowntree P.L.C. and the Italian Buitoni S.p.A. (pasta makers) by Nestlé, Rhône-Poulenc, a French pharmaceutical firm, acquired Nattermann, another pharmaceutical firm, of Germany. This is one of six other acquisitions in Europe and another six in the United States (including Stauffer Chemical) over the last two years.

The Thomson Group in France acquired Telefunken, the German electronics powerhouse, in 1983, and Mostek, an American semiconductor firm, in 1987. Also, Thomson Group bought Thorn-EMI of Britain and formed a semiconductor joint venture with S.G.S. Microelectronica S.p.A. of Italy.

Scheider S.A., a French construction and electronics company, acquired Télémecanique Electrique S.A., a French electronics firm. Also, the German Rheinisch-Westfoelisches Elektrizitaetswerk A.G. bought Deutsche Texaco A.G. (a German subsidiary of Texaco).

Although there may be cultural and ideological conflicts among EC members regarding permission for mergers and acquisitions, particularly between the Anglo-Saxon and the German traditions, friendly or hostile takeovers are spreading all over Europe, not only by European corporations but by others as well. This trend is supported by European banks, such as the Banque Paribas and Banque Indosuez in Paris and Mediobanca in Milan, as well as American banks, such as Morgan Stanley. Moreover, banks themselves, such as the Banco Central and the Banco Español de Credito (the largest banks in Spain), practice acquisitions and mergers or have large holdings in industrial companies, especially in Germany. To avoid conflicts with national antitrust laws, the EC is moving to introduce common regulations on disclosures of shareholdings above certain percentages as member-nations have, except Italy, Spain, and Greece. Moreover, in their efforts toward democratization and industry privatization, Eastern Bloc countries introduce similar regulations.

An aggressive acquirer is the British Petroleum Company (B.P.), the world's third largest oil firm. In its efforts to expand production and retail outlets in Europe and refining and marketing outlets in the United States, it bought Britoil in 1988 for expansion in its North Sea holdings, and the rest of the Cleveland-based Standard Oil Company. Also, there are expectations that B.P. would try to acquire a number of chemical companies in East Asia, Japan, and other regions.

However, a serious problem appeared between France's Ministry of Agriculture and Japan's Takashimaya Company when the latter tried to buy Burgundy Vineyard, which is prestigious and is related to France's cultural heritage. A bottle of this red wine (Romancée-Conti) has a price of about $500. The Finance Ministry of France, though, has the right to block any purchase of more than 20 percent of a French company by a non-EC firm. That is why efforts are made to have a French company buy it instead of having a foreign one acquire such a prestigious vineyard.

The Irish Distillers Group P.L.C., a near monopoly on Ireland's whisky market, was considering a friendly takeover by Pernod-Ricard S.A., a famous French wine company. Grand Metropolitan P.L.C., a large British hotel and liquor company, was also in competition for the takeover of Irish Distillers. However, the European Commission, which is the executive branch of the EC, blocked this effort as monopolistic as it aims to fix the market price of the Irish Distillers' products.

In the tourist sector, the European integration is encouraging tour operators to expand across borders, leading to mergers and acquisitions in that industry. Thus, TUI, the biggest West Germany package-tour operator, acquired 40 percent of ARKE, the largest tour company in the Netherlands. Earlier, it had acquired control of Robinson Club, another German tour company, and it has interests in Touropa, a French tour agency. In France, Club Aquarious teamed up with Go Voyages, which Havas merged with Wagons Lits Tourisme. They plan to build vacation villages to compete with Club Med, Inc., which pioneered the industry back in 1960. Because of troubles at its 74 percent-owned United States subsidiary, Club Med turned to expansion in Europe and acquired a 34 percent stake in Nouvelles Frontières Touraventure to build new villages and to start a joint airline venture perhaps with Britain's Air Europe. In any case, competition among large tour operators may lead to price wars in Europe and across the Atlantic to the benefit of EC and United States vacationers. Such competition has been intensified with the opening of the fertile Eastern European tourist markets.

There are some 25 million "package holidays" with about 100 to 150 million tourists in the EC countries annually and the numbers are growing steadily year after year. To improve tourist services and to increase revenue, the EC put certain rules regarding advertisement brochures for transportation, prices, food, entertainment, and other services.

Intra-European mergers and business concentrations are rather encouraged by the EC for industries that are expected to be competitive against similar United States and Japanese industries. At the same time, existing small- and middle-size firms are supported by the EC through subsidies and loans primarily from the European Investment Bank. Thus, more than 1,350 tourist firms were supported by the EC since 1984 and many construction, metallurgical, food, textile, and other enterprises were given favorable loans for expansion, especially in the less developed regions of Europe, such as Greece (where about 500 firms were supported financially), Portugal, and Spain. Emphasis is placed on transportation, energy, communications, and other infrastructural investments that are expected to facilitate EC trade and development.

It would seem that the waves of mergers and consolidations and friendly or hostile takeovers observed in the United States are entering the European Common Market. Thus, Daimler-Benz A.G. acquired Messer-Schmitt-Bölkow-Blohm G.m.b.H., both in West Germany. This acquisition and the restructuring of Daimler-Benz transformed it from the maker of Mercedes cars and trucks into a high technology aerospace and armaments conglomerate with annual sales of more than $40 billion in competition with Aerospace P.L.C. of Europe and United Technologies and Boeing of the United States.

Compagnie Financière de Suez of France is considering a takeover bid for Gie Industrielle, a French holding company, for $2.48 billion. Minority stakes of Gie Industrielle and its main asset, a 40 percent stake in insurer Groupe Victoire, are considered by Ferruzzi Finanziaria S.p.A of Italy. Groupe Victoire had already acquired Colonia Versicherung A.G., the second largest insurer company of West Germany in July 1989. There are questions though, on how Financière de Suez will finance the transaction. Other companies such as Gie Financière de Paribas, Gie de Navigation Mixte and Gie du Midi may ally with Gie Industrielle against Suez for possible cancelation of the takeover bid. However, Suez, the Paris-based banking group that financed construction of the Suez Canal in 1858 (which was nationalized by Egypt in 1956), won control of Groupe Victoire for $4 billion in September 1989.

French firms became aggressive in acquiring companies in other EC countries.

Thus, Abielle Groupe acquired 50 percent of Prudential Holding S.p.A. from Edizione Holding S.p.A. of Italy; RSCG Group S.A. agreed to buy KLP Group P.L.C. of Britain; and Thomson S.A. entered joint ventures with the British Aerospace P.L.C. and Philips N.V. of Holland.

Electra Investment Trust, a big and successful investment company, would join with other international institutions to form a fund in order to invest in joint ventures and management buyouts, mainly in Europe. The new company to be formed, Kingsway Managers Holdings Ltd., 20 percent owned by Electra, would reward executives according to their performance, making them partners of this management company.

Peugeot Company, the biggest French auto company, expressed interest in acquiring the Porsche Company of Germany. Such an expansion would make Peugeot a well-known European auto firm able to compete with its American and Japanese counterparts on a worldwide scale.

Renault, a French state-owned auto firm (partially privatized currently), and Volvo of Sweden each agreed to own large shares of the other (45 percent of the truck operation of the other) to create the world's largest truck maker and a strong car competitor to the United States Ford Motor Company that recently acquired Jaguar P.L.C. of Britain. The cooperation of Volvo with Enasa, an equivalent Spanish firm, and Renault brings it inside the EC to promote production of trucks and cars in Europe. Also Costab lanca Group, a Spanish oil company, was acquired by Unilever, a British-Dutch firm, for $120 million.

Britoil, Harris Queensway, and Ross Youngs of Britain were acquired by British Petroleum, Lowndes Ventures, and United Biscuits, respectively, all of Britain. Moreover, G.H. Mumm of France acquired Martell of France, and Royal Dutch/Shell of the Netherlands acquired Tenneco of Colombia. Ritz, a British firm, acquired, in turn, British Petroleum Company for $4.3 billion, while Compagnie Bancaire, the French group of economic services, acquired Hyberclyde Investment, a British company, with a price of $155 million (about one billion francs).

Pitsos Company of Greece, which belongs to the Siemens-Bosch Company of West Germany, is scheduled to merge with the Elinta company of Greece. They both produce refrigerators, kitchen ovens, and washing machines mainly for Greece and, to a limited extent, for the Middle East. If Siemens-Bosch Company acquires Elinta, which produces Izola and Eskimo products (180,000 pieces annually), and represents Kelvinator Leonard, and Luxor companies, it will control about 60 percent of the Greek market. The relatively low labor cost in Greece will make Siemens-Bosch products competitive not only for the domestic market but for the export market as well.

BSN, a French holding company, agreed to buy Henninger Hellas, a beer company in Greece. BSN produces and distributes such products as Evian mineral water, Danon dairy products, and Kronenburg beer and acquired the trademark of Henniger of West Germany for Greece. Expectations are that the beer market would be important in touristic Greece. The strategy of BSN is to expand and control important trade in other European countries as happened also with the Maes Company of Belgium, Peroni of Italy, and Mahou of Spain. Hoechst A.G., a chemical group in Frankfurt, agreed to acquire Fribos Sinteticos S.A. of Portugal.

In order to control big mergers, the EC empowered the European Commission to review mergers within the EC for firms, including those of the United States and other nations, having revenues more than five billion ECUs ($5.85 billion). Companies with less revenue would be reviewed by individual member nations. However, regardless of the new controls and regulations, mergers and acquisitions and joint ventures are expected to increase in Western as well as in Eastern Europe. To facilitate large takeovers, and encouraged by the end of trade barriers in 1992, big financial firms such as Wasserstein, Parella Group Inc. and Drexel Burnham Lambert Inc. (still operating in Europe but collapsed in the United States) established investment funds in Europe. Also other American firms in coordination with similar financial corporations, such as Banque Paribas of France, Commerz-Bank of Germany, Amro Bank of the Netherlands, and other investment firms from Italy, Spain and Japan, created huge funds for industrial restructuring and buyouts in Europe.

9   Effects of Changes in Eastern Europe

REFORMS TOWARD WESTERN MARKET ECONOMIES

Problems of Efficiency

The rapid democratization and openness of Eastern European countries revealed that Comecon or the Council of Mutual Economic Assistance (CMEA), which includes the Warsaw Pact countries (Bulgaria, Czechoslovakia, East Germany, Hungary, Poland, Rumania, and the Soviet Union), plus Cuba, Mongolia, and Vietnam, lacks dynamism. This economic group, initially established in 1949, is a monolithic bloc characterized by managerial rigidity, backward technology, low productivity, and currency inconvertibility. Member nations such as Czechoslovakia, Hungary, and Poland criticized it as obsolete and undemocratic with the Soviet Union (the big brother) in a dominating position and the small brothers as the satellites.

Both the smaller members and the Soviet Union complain about the low performance of Comecon, compared to the EC, and want substantial changes and reorganization toward more flexibility and free market operations. The smaller members think that the Soviet Union exploited them for a few decades during the post-World War II period and that it still exercises control upon them. On the other hand, the Soviet Union wants to stop subsidization of their economies through the supply of oil and gas at low prices in return for inferior products. They all prefer to scrap binding agreements and want more trade with western nations than with the Soviet Union and other Comecon member-nations.

On January 1990, the Comecon leaders had a conference in Sofia, Bulgaria, to consider new policies because of the dramatic political and economic changes in their countries. What the four-decade-old East economic bloc achieved was to isolate the countries involved from the market discipline of international competition and to deprive them from modern technology and entrepreneurial know-how. That is why the participants at the Sofia conference decided for a thorough overhaul of Comecon, short of dismantling it.

From the 1940s to the 1970s, the Soviet Union exploited the smaller members of Comecon (the satellites) by selling at higher and buying at lower prices than those in the international markets. But after the oil price increases in 1973, and later, things turned around as Soviet oil and gas were exported to the satellites at prices lower than those of world markets. Therefore, the Soviet Union was and still is subsidizing the other East Bloc countries and wants to end this policy by using dollars or other convertible currencies in calculating export-import prices. This means that Hungary, Poland, Rumania and, to a lesser extent, Czechoslovakia, Bulgaria, and East Germany would end up having huge trade deficits, instead of surplus, with the Soviet Union. Soviet oil exports to Eastern Europe are estimated at 1.5 million barrels per day, out of a total production of 12 million barrels, compared to 7.5 million for the United States, 5 million for Saudi Arabia, and 60 million barrels a day for the world.

In all communist countries, socialism was practiced as a command economy with state ownership of the means of production and bureaucratic planning. For some seventy years in the Soviet Union and forty-plus years in the other East Bloc countries, the free market mechanism seemed to have been lost. It has, however, been discovered by these nations in recent months as a more effective tool of economic growth and political freedom. While good cooperation and long-term development have been achieved during the first two decades of the post-World War II period, it was not nearly as much as in the EC countries and at a much higher cost to the citizens.

Gradually the need for capital and modern technology forced greater cooperation of the East Bloc or Comecon-planned economies with the EC and the West in general. From that point of view, more dramatic changes can be expected with the economic relations of the Comecon countries and the EC neighboring countries, particularly West Germany. In financing more trade and joint ventures among the two economic groups of Western and Eastern Europe, as well as the United States, the World Bank, the International Monetary Fund (IMF), and the International Bank for Economic Cooperation (IBEC) can play an important role. Perhaps a more effective way is the recent establishment of the European Bank for Reconstruction and Development, with some $12 billion capital shares held by the EC, the United States, and Japan, to offer loans and other services to the East Bloc countries that are under democratic and free market reforms.[1]

In spite of their controlled economies, centrally planned countries of the East Bloc have problems similar to those experienced by the EC and other market economies, and are not fully immune to stagflation emanating from abroad. As the worldwide economic slowdown catches up with them, the rates of economic expansion are slowing and shortages of manufactured goods and food are becoming more acute. East European countries, except perhaps Russia and Rumania, are weighed down by a heavy burden of foreign debt, and it is difficult to continue borrowing. Although they utilize central planning and more controls than the EC countries, they are not better able to resist current economic trends.

To stimulate incentives and increase productivity, these countries move rapidly toward relaxing the cumbersome centralized planning, assigning a greater role to market forces, and contemplating self-management and decentralization in decision making. In their effort to reduce bureaucracy and maximize effectiveness, they take a less doctrinaire approach to economic policy, relaxing many of the ideological shackles that bind them. However, economic changes are so tied up with political issues that much depends on what the political leadership decides. The pressure for reforms, though, is so high that there are cases in which room has been created for private entrepreneurs and variation in wages according to productivity. This form of "new economic mechanism," which was first introduced by Hungary in 1968 and has rapidly spread to other East Bloc countries, including the Soviet Union, allows bands of skilled workers to sell their services to state-owned enterprises. Also, it permits farmers to retain substantial private plots which can be sold or passed on to their children, although most farmland is owned by cooperatives and profits are divided among the members. Moreover, factories are not ordered to achieve given production targets and sell their products at prices fixed by the planners, and they have more control over what to produce and how much to charge. This policy encourages them to secure cheap supplies and sell their products at the highest possible prices.

As mentioned earlier, Comecon has not advanced as much as the EC, mainly because of much duplication in industrial production among the member states. At present, efforts are being made to emphasize specialization, so that production in one state complements production in other states. This is a situation achieved, to some extent, by the EC through tariff reduction and expansion of multinational corporations. The chief partner of Comecon, that is, the Soviet Union, seeks less bilateral trading among member states. However, the gradual abandonment of Russian subsidies to other Comecon countries presents problems, primarily because of high Soviet energy prices, which are close to those of OPEC (the Organization of Petroleum Exporting Countries).

At the present stage of development, East Bloc countries seem to have parallel economies, producing largely competitive goods. This suggests that opportunities for substantial trade expansion between them are limited. However, the United States' and especially the EC's trade with Eastern European countries is expected to grow because of different orientations and specializations, and because of the new economic conditions to be created as a result of gradual adjustment and closer cooperation between them.

The construction of the natural gas pipeline, which is being built primarily by Western European companies to link Siberia to Western Europe, is expected to reach many European nations. Although such a link would increase the influence of the Soviet Union upon the economies of the other countries involved, low gas prices would relieve part of their energy and balance of trade burdens.

Many state enterprises in Eastern Europe are up for sale but, with no private banks or bond and stock markets, it is difficult for managers, employees, and foreigners to buy them. The hope is that foreign investments would pour in and buy such enterprises or establish their own, thereby providing jobs and stimulating East Bloc economies. Moreover, loans and other assistance are expected from the EC countries, the United States, the International Monetary Fund (IMF), and the World Bank. In the meantime, layoffs, subsidy cuts, and even foreclosures of inefficient enterprises occur, especially in Poland.

Already, the United States Congress has approved $852 million in assistance for Poland, while the IMF is planning to lend Poland $700 million and the World Bank another $1.67 billion. Furthermore, if austerity measures are taken pertaining to wage restraints, reduction in government spending, and price adjustments to the supply and demand mechanisms, then commercial EC and United States banks would extend loans to Poland and other East Bloc countries. In such a case, the Polish zloty and other East Bloc currencies may be convertible into EC, United States, and other hard currencies.

Economic Reforms in the Soviet Union and Other East Bloc Countries

The new economic and political changes in the Soviet Union and the Eastern European nations create a new cooperative environment for Western and Eastern Europe. Two key words which signify the dramatic transformation of the Soviet system are *glasnost* and *perestroika*. The first word means "openness" regarding public expression. The second word means the restructuring of the economy, in the sense of changing the organization of the economy toward a more competitive process with more incentives of work and higher productivity.

Openness is related to more freedom of expression, greater latitudes in news media, distribution of once-banned books (particularly under the harsh reign of Joseph Stalin), and easier emigration rules for Soviet minorities and ethnic groups. Restructuring of the economy refers to the introduction of reforms, decentralization of decision making, and adjustment to the realities of the marketplace, which means a gradual shift from centralized planning. Such reforms, which are more drastic than those introduced by Nikita Khrushchev in the late 1950s, are needed to revive and modernize the Soviet economy.

The recent revolutionary changes in Eastern Europe created new conditions for the EC and the United States. Forty-plus years of Soviet domination of Eastern Europe and protective but intrusive United States presence in Western Europe had not obliterated the notion of a common heritage and destiny of all of Europe. As Mikhail Gorbachev told the twenty-three nation council in Strasbourg on July 6, 1989, "The philosophy of the 'Common European Home' concept rules out the probability of an armed clash. . . . " George Bush, the President of the United States, reiterated his wish for a "Europe—Whole and Free."[2]

Moreover, at the December 1989 summit in Strasbourg, the EC was favorable toward an associate status of East Bloc countries and endorsed the reunification of Germany. As Europe moves forward toward a new self-reliant destiny, the role of the United States changes from the standpoint of commitment and leadership. However, Europe lacks a constructive pan-European ideology and leadership and the American presence may be needed for some time to come.

Recent agricultural and other reforms in the Soviet Union and other Eastern European countries bring their planning system closer to the market system of the EC and open the way toward more cooperation. However, bureaucratic controls for more than half a century, inefficient management, and inflexibility in prices present serious difficulties in the process of economic reconstruction.

The electrifying reforms toward returning the land to families, by making long-term leases to collective farms, have not produced satisfactory results so far. Therefore, budget deficits, running about 10 percent of the gross material product annually, are expected to continue due to high agricultural subsidies that account for about 20 percent of the Soviet budget.

The reforms allow bands of workers to lease farms or shops and run them like private subcontractors in a competitive fashion. Not only can peasants lease farms but can also buy, sell, or sublet them, while cooperatives can employ private labor. Moreover, more autonomy has been given to individual republics and provinces regarding taxes, environmental protection, and other matters. Furthermore, Soviet entrepreneurs travel to the EC and other nations to learn new management techniques and to attract foreign investment. Nonetheless, all these reforms have not produced satisfactory results in agricultural production (only about 200 metric tons a year). This necessitates about an increase of about 40 metric tons in annual imports currently compared to 5–10 metric tons in the 1960s.

In order to close the technological gap with other advanced countries, Russia is interested in developing closer relations with the EC as well as the United States and Japan. To the surprise of his Western counterparts, Mikhail Gorbachev, the Soviet leader, is promoting such drastic reforms and changes that in some cases Western leaders booby-trapped themselves. More dramatic reforms started in the other nations of Eastern Europe, while German officials moved rapidly toward the unification of West and East Germany.

On the other hand, the increasing preoccupation of the United States with Latin America and the Middle East results in fundamental changes in economic and security matters that were established after World War II. France, West Germany, and the other EC member nations, and eventually all of Europe are considering plans for their own defense strategy. This became more obvious with the removal of United States medium-range missiles, the expected reduction and the eventual removal of United States ground forces, as well as the weakening of America's atomic umbrella, which protects the NATO (North Atlantic Treaty Organization) allies.

From another point of view, there is suspicion and, at times, border conflicts and ideological disputes between Russia, the world's largest inland country, and China, the world's most populous country. The Sino-Soviet hostility, with roots in the Tartar-Mongol occupation of Russia for some 300 years, may force the Soviet Union to a friendship and a closer relationship with Western Europe. China's population of more than one billion people looks at neighboring Russia— with its vast land, large parts of which were ceded to Czar Alexander II by Manchu emperors about a century ago—as the Chinese claim. The demographic fear and the disputes with China may force the Soviet Union to pursue a Russo-European accommodation and closer economic and even political ties with the EC.[3]

After the decision of the Communist Party Central Committee in June 1987 to introduce reforms and to decentralize the Russian economy, gradual changes started taking place, but at a slow pace. More radical economic and political reforms were accepted by the National Conference of the Communist Party from June 28 to July 1, 1988. The 4,991 delegates of the party's first National Conference in forty-seven years decided to increase efforts towards social and economic restructuring (*perestroika*) and political and sociocultural openness (*glasnost*). Two major reforms introduced in the conference were to shift authority from local Communist Party bureaucrats to local government councils and establish a more powerful president, by indirect election. The tenure of all elected officials, including the chairman of the party or the president, would be for five years, with a limit of ten years at most. As Mikhail Gorbachev said, "We are introducing a pluralism of opinions, rejecting the intellectual monopoly . . . a new human image of socialism as the goal of *perestroika*."

Danube Basin or Balkan Common Markets?

The establishment of a Danube basin common market, including the old Hapsburg countries, as a buffer against a reunited strong Germany seems impractical in present-day Europe. Such a group, which may include Austria, Hungary, Czechoslovakia, Rumania, and Yugoslavia, may be useful to the security interests of the United States, the Soviet Union, and a rejuvenated Germany for some time to come. However, an economic association and eventual integration with the EC is more effective and beneficial to all European countries, instead of departmentalizing the old continent in different fortress groups.

A similar intrabloc common market may be considered by the Balkan countries (Albania, Bulgaria, Greece, Rumania, Turkey, and Yugoslavia). Nevertheless, intra-Balkan trade may impose costs upon the countries involved insofar as it means trade diversion. The beneficial effects of intrabloc trade on the balance of payments, industrialization, and economic growth may not exceed the detrimental effects of trade diversion of a Balkan common market. This may be so because the Balkan countries produce mainly competitive primary products, not so much complementary products, and a formation of a common market may make them poorer instead. Again, a closer cooperation with the EC may be more beneficial, although painful, for a transitional period of adjustment. Otherwise, Greece is already a full member and Turkey an associated member of the EC, and Yugoslavia has signed a number of trade agreements with the European Community.

EFFECTS OF GERMAN UNIFICATION

The dramatic changes in Eastern Europe and particularly in East Germany present a great challenge to the EC and United States policy makers and entrepreneurs. The outflow of large numbers of East Germans to West Germany indicated the strong desire of the Germans for reunification. Although Germany was united only from 1870 to 1945, the argument of the German traditionalists is that the envy of its European neighbors was responsible for the division of Germany before and after that period.

The German question is not only affecting East-West relations but relations within the Western world as well. Both the EC and the United States are interested in creating a united Germany that will be an important economic entity and will influence the trend toward a united Europe, an argument supported mainly by the Europeanists. The unification of the German Democratic Republic (G.D.R.), or East Germany, with the Federal Republic of Germany (F.R.G.), or West Germany, may eventually unite the rest of Europe, because Europe's division was due in large part to the division of Germany, and vice versa. The fulfillment of German aspirations for unification came not from the West but from the Soviet disengangement, the massive emigration of East Germans, and the breaking of the Berlin wall.

Other European nations and the United States, based on historical experience and the fear of reviving nationalism, are skeptical about German unification. The slogan "*ein Deutschland*" reminds them of the catastrophic results of World War I and World War II. Westerners with historical recall ask: Whom to trust more, the Russians or the Germans? However, advanced technology in communications liquidated the old nationalistic concepts in Europe and prepared the ground for closer cooperation and even unification of neighboring countries.

From an economic standpoint, West Germany and Japan have become the main competitors of the United States. Under the United States defense umbrella, both countries, who were the main United States rivals during the Second World War, managed to develop rapidly and challenge American supremacy in international trade and finance. A unified Germany means a stronger competitor for the United States and other Western countries, but also a larger market for more trade and joint ventures. Germany's current account surpluses, as proportions of GNP, are the highest in the OECD (Organization for Economic Cooperation and Development), which includes Japan and all other advanced Western nations. Germany is not accused of deliberately trying to keep out foreign products, as is Japan. However, in certain areas such as telecommunications, agriculture, and financial services, Germany has a relatively closed economy. Nevertheless, the United States, with a trade deficit of about $120 billion and some $80 billion in interest payments abroad annually, will continue to face problems with Germany and an integrated Europe.

With a European monetary system and a common currency, a united Germany would eventually become the financial center of an integrated Europe and may dominate global finance as well. Moreover, it will be a crucial link with the Soviet Union and other Eastern European countries, sponsoring joint ventures and providing credit and technical training to them.

Therefore, it is more likely that United States firms will be leaning toward linkups with their German and European counterparts, where markets are more open than those of Japan and some other countries. Furthermore, with the Japanese pursuing a Pacific Basin common market and the prevailing bloc mentality, United States firms and policy makers should consider outward-looking policies, notably toward Germany and the EC. For a common response to the developments of Germany and the East Bloc, a consultative partnership between the EC and the United States has been proposed to deal with institutional links, more trade, and investment ventures.

A trans-European partnership extending from Berlin to Washington would include financial matters as well. This will be important as German stocks and bonds are expected to be more attractive, due to the benefits expected from the region's unification and the opening of Eastern Europe. As a result, more American, Japanese, and other money will move to that region and United States markets are bound to suffer. Already, real returns on German bonds are higher than those on United States government bonds.

On January 12, 1990, East Germany permitted joint ventures with foreign ownership up to 49 percent for the first time. However, a few days later majority control was permitted for foreign companies with less than 500 employees. Exceptions, though, can be made for large firms transferring high technology and capital investment important to national interests. As a result of the recent reforms, Volkswagen A.G. of West Germany agreed to set up a venture with VEB IFA-Kombinat Personenkraftwagen, an East German automaker in Karl-Marx-Stadt, which has produced engines for Volkswagen since 1988.

The process of normalization and cooperation between Western and Eastern Europe facilitated the reunification of Germany. West Germany extended $3 billion of credit to Russia to calm opposition to a unified Germany. The EC, by virtue of its economic and sociopolitical strength and powerful influence, was instrumental in accomplishing the unification of Germany and stimulating the concept of a "common European home." Although Washington may be uncomfortable with the challenges in Europe, and in Germany in particular, it can accommodate the growing European independence and accept power as well as burden sharing.

The rush of about 2,000 East Germans a day, or 750,000 a year in a population of 17 million, that moved to West Germany presented economic and sociopolitical problems for both sides. Given that West Germany provided welfare to arriving emigrés (100 marks welcome money and other accommodations) the inflow continued for some time. It was suggested that East Germans should get 200 marks to return home and 300 marks if they took a Pole with them. In a united Germany, low wages in East Germany would stimulate investment and productivity growth.

It is expected that East Bloc countries may first have some arrangements or an associated status with the EC and eventually full EC membership. Assuming that the democratization process continues, similar arrangements or close economic and political relations are to be concluded with the Soviet Union, using the example of East Germany and other East Bloc countries. This trend is bound to lead to a stable, autonomous, and prosperous United States of Europe.

Nevertheless, there are security concerns in the Soviet Union and other neighbors of Germany. The main question is whether a united Germany would become powerful and a threat to the world peace. In any case, things are moving so fast that all economic and political plans proposed are overtaken by events. The idea of integrating East Bloc nations within the EC seems to be ineffective in the short run but the momentum of integration is building up quickly. On the financial front, circulation of a common German currency or a link of the marks of the two Germanys was proposed by both Helmut Kohl, Chancellor of West Germany, and Hans Modrow, Prime Minister of East Germany, and was achieved in July 1990. This was an effective measure of rapid and de facto economic unification of Germany. The two Germanys were officially united on October 3, 1990.

CLOSER COOPERATION AND JOINT VENTURES

A new optimism seems to prevail on the old continent, mainly as a result of the idea of barrier-free EC nations. With the innovative economic restructuring measures in the Soviet Union and the cosmogonic reforms in the other East Bloc nations, a similar optimism is spread in Europe. It would seem that the old concept of "Europessimism" is gradually transformed into "Europtimism."

Recently, Comecon, the Communist trading bloc, signed an agreement to allow its member states to negotiate preferential trade accommodations with EC member countries and accepted that West Berlin was community turf.

Many Western Europeans, including the political leaders of Germany, France, and Italy, think that the EC can reap significant economic and political advantages by supporting the Soviet restructuring program. By enriching the production system of the Soviet Union and other Eastern European countries, mainly through middle- and low-level technology, the West's interests will be enhanced. By offering a new Marshall Plan, in the form of financial, managerial, and technological assistance, the West can enlarge the market all over Europe. In addition to the credit package of $1.6 billion by West Germany, Italy provided the Soviet Union with $775 million of export credits in 1988 and more credit and investment continues to flow into all the Comecon countries from the West.

Thus, a tri-national joint venture of an American-style management school was created in Hungary recently. An American professor (Daniel Fagel) is the dean of the school, which is the result of a joint venture of American, Italian, and Hungarian partners. The establishment of this institute was supported by Abel Aganbegyan, advisor to Mikhail Gorbachev and chairman of the economics section of the Soviet Academy of Sciences, as a sign of active relations between East and West. The students of the school, around 300 in September 1989, including some Russians, would pay tuition of about $12,000 or 600,000 Hungarian forints. Two American professors, two Canadians, one Briton, and five Hungarians constitute the initial faculty.

It becomes more and more acceptable for people from the Eastern European countries to travel and even to emigrate to Western European countries. On the other side, Western Europeans expect to take advantage of cheap labor and a growing East European market in trade and investment, especially if the economic reforms proposed are implemented.

Recently, the EC signed a trade agreement with Hungary, and other East Bloc countries are pursuing similar agreements. It seems that expected economic changes and reforms in these Comecon countries would bring them closer to the EC economies and make stronger ties more attractive between the two groups.

West German concerns are discussing with the Soviet Union and other Eastern European nations the introduction of industrial and development plans which would bring technological changes and organizational know-how. As a result, there is a rush of investment into the East Bloc countries by Western companies. Thus, Berlusconi, an Italian media company, opened up subsidiaries to train people in advertising, public relations, and broadcasting. A number of Western-style pizza shops have been established in Moscow and other places, and Coca-Cola signs can be seen opposite Lenin's tomb. Italian and Japanese companies have joined in a consortium with the Occidental Petroleum Corporation to build a petrochemical plant in the Soviet Union close to the Caspian Sea.

Other United States companies involved in Soviet ventures are Honeywell Inc., providing computerized controls in fertilizer plants, and Combustion Engineering Inc., dealing with renovating oil and petrochemical plants. A number of companies, such as McDonald Restaurants and Pepsico Inc., provide fast food and soft drinks, and others offer audio-video equipment and souvenirs in the hotel shops in Moscow and other cities. Also, American and Canadian firms are opening stores offering copying shops and international electronic transmission printing, with 51 percent Soviet ownership and 49 percent for them, using Apple Computers.

However, a serious problem arises from sales on rubles, which cannot be converted easily into hard currencies. On the other hand, there are complaints that Soviet-West ventures are still small and they do not need high-stakes technology.

Among the Western companies that have entered the Soviet Union are Young and Rubicam, Ogilvy and Mather, and some advertising firms which are trying to help Mercedes-Benz, Allied Lyons, British Airways, ICI, and other companies establish themselves in a Soviet market of some 278 million customers. They follow the example of Pepsi-Cola, which has sold its products there since 1959 and currently manufactures them in the Soviet Union.

The Fiat auto company of Italy, moreover, was involved in establishing a joint venture in the Soviet Union near the Volga River. This is part of the worldwide operations of Fiat that sells around $30 billion worth of cars annually, $1 billion of which are in the United States.

To facilitate Soviet-West transactions and to exploit the opportunities created by *perestroika*, the Deutsche Bank A.G., West Germany's biggest bank, led a consortium and arranged a credit line of $1.6 billion to the Soviet Union. The credit was extended to help Russia to modernize its consumer goods industry and also to benefit the textile and shoe industries of West Germany. About 30 percent of the total $16 billion loans to Moscow since 1984 was from West Germany, 40 percent from Japan, and only 2 percent from American banks.[4] Such West German transactions with the Soviet Union and other Eastern European countries bring closer the economic and political relations of the EC and its Communist-Bloc counterpart, Comecon. Because Comecon was not as effective as the EC, one by one the East European countries started signing agreements with the EC, although they opposed it for years. On the other hand, the Japanese are gradually leapfrogging the walls of both the EC and, to a limited extent as yet, the Comecon by establishing their own operations.

The Soviet Union turned to large Western advertising agencies to place space advertising and to exploit other commercial opportunities. Aeroflot, the Soviet airline, bought five airliners from Airbus Industry, the European consortium, for $300 million, a transaction that paves the way for sales of American jets to Russia as well.

Bloomingdale's Department Store of New York agreed to open stores in Moscow, and Union Carbide sent scientists to the Soviet Union to spread commercial applications of new technologies regarding catalysts and absorbents in oil operations.

Phoenix Group International of Irvine, California, will help set up factories in the Soviet Union to produce and supply personal computers for Soviet, American, and other schools and universities. It is expected that this joint venture will supply about 6 million computers by 1994.

In order to attract foreign investment and modern technology, the Soviet Union allowed in April 1989 joint ventures with up to 99 percent foreign ownership. More than 400 such joint enterprises have been registered and more than thirty of them are in operation. Among the benefits offered are reduction in tariffs for imported production goods, 20 percent tax reduction on exported profits, and freedom in hiring, firing, and personnel appointments. Similar measures in other East Bloc nations would reduce aid and investment in developing countries.[5]

Democratic reforms in the Soviet Union may lead to independent republics which may form a federation, similar to that of the EC. Depending on the success of the EC integration and the democratization of the Soviet Union and the other Comecon countries, a close cooperation between Western and Eastern Europe may eventually create an integrated whole-European economic and political system.

The fact that labor costs are lower in the East Bloc than in the EC, closer cooperation between them creates great opportunities for investment for the EC and other companies. Nevertheless, not to be left behind, American business firms also turned their attention to Eastern Europe.

Thus, U.S. West, Inc., agreed with Hungary to build a mobile cellular telephone system in Budapest, the first such network in the East Bloc that would be expanded eventually to the entire country. This system will be faster and cheaper for the government than to rebuild the entire telephone infrastructure by tearing up the streets and installing miles of cable. U.S. West would own and operate 49 percent of the cellular network and Magyar Post, the Hungarian telephone and postal organization, the rest. Moreover, Citicorp's joint venture bank in Budapest put together a management buyout of Apisz, the largest state-owned stationery supplier. Overall, some sixteen American companies have registered for insurance with the Overseas Private Investment Corporation of the United States, covering $700 million investment in Hungary, and twenty-one companies for a $1.1 billion investment in Poland.

Attracted by the liberalization movement and the new legislation permitting 100 percent ownership, EC and other firms form joint ventures or invest in Hungary. They include the Tengelmann Group of West Germany, which, together with Holland's Philips and Finland's Nokia, acquired, an 18 percent stake in the Skala Co-op, a large Hungarian retailer, for $9.8 million; Telfos, a British engineering firm that acquired a 51 percent stake of the state-owned Ganz Railway Engineering; and a consortium of western banks that bought 49.65 percent of Tungsram, a lightbulb producer. Moreover Novotrade, a software and computer firm, launched a share issue on a western market for further investment in Hungary.

However, Hungary, with a large foreign debt (about $20 billion), needs financial support from the EC, the United States, and Japan to implement reforms and modernize its economy. The United States Congress recently approved $86 million of assistance to Hungary (and $852 million to Poland), and additional assistance is expected from the International Monetary Fund as long as measures are taken to strengthen the economy. In the meantime, better relations of the West with Hungary would increase trade with both the EC and the United States so that Hungarian exports of textiles, steel, auto parts, machinery, wine, foods, and other products would increase.

It should be recognized, though, that it is difficult for the planned economies of the East Bloc, including that of Hungary, to break the chains of centralized controls and to change the policy of subsidized prices and guaranteed sales. Moreover, they have no experience with patents, copyrights, and other protective measures for private investment, and telephone and other infrastructural facilities are backward. On the other hand, about three-fourths of state enterprises are run by Worker's Councils which present problems in the process of privatization.

Hungary was the first East Bloc country to free itself from the ruble in trade settlements with the Soviet Union. Like the other countries under the influence of the Soviet system, Hungary has frequently had a surplus in rubles, which could be spent for Russian goods that might not be wanted. Instead, the Soviets were asked to base trade on dollars, which can be used by Hungary and other Eastern European countries to buy sophisticated industrial and other products from the West. At the same time, efforts were made to make their own currencies convertible into hard Western currencies.

The newly founded Central European Development Corporation (CEDC) announced a $10 million purchase of a 50 percent interest of the General Banking and Trust Company, an important Hungarian Bank. The investment functions of the CEDC, which was established by Americans, would concentrate on tourism, real estate, and communications, not only in Hungary but in Czechoslovakia and other neighboring nations.

There are about sixty American companies doing business in Hungary, but many more from West Germany and Austria. The fact that political and economic changes in Hungary started years ago makes the country more attractive to foreign investment and sophisticated management than other East Bloc countries. Although the country has a large external debt, recent cuts in food, housing and other subsidies, according to the prescriptions of the IMF, are expected to stabilize the Hungarian economy and attract more investment ventures. Moreover, Japan is offering about $2 billion financial aid to Hungary and other East Bloc countries, although such trends are weakening relations with China and other Asian countries.

On November 1989, General Electric Company agreed to buy control of a Hungarian light bulb manufacturer for $150 million. Already it has 40 percent of its total European lighting operations in Eastern Europe, 20 percent in Hungary and 40 percent in Western Europe. Moreover, Coca-Cola Company is negotiating with the East German government to sell its soft drinks in that country. Rapidly growing economic and political reforms, and expectations of Poland, Hungary, East Germany, Czechoslovakia, Rumania, Bulgaria, and Yugoslavia to be associate members of the EC, may attract more United States investment in these countries than in the EC countries. It seems that the labor force in the Eastern Bloc is well educated and trained. Although not very well disciplined or motivated, it is far cheaper (average manufacturing wages are about $2 an hour) than in the West. From that point of view, there are great investment opportunities, especially in hotels and tourism, telecommunications, fast printing and film developing operations, and fast-food services.

Chase Enterprise, a United States communications company, agreed to enter into a joint venture with Poltelkob S.A. of Poland to establish a cable television firm, called Polska Telewizja Kablowa, in Warsaw and other cities. Total investment of Chase Enterprise, which has 70 percent ownership, is estimated at $900 million. The CNN news network and ESPN all-sports channel, among others, would be available to some 1.8 million Polish homes.

The General Motors Corporation plans to form a joint venture with Automobil-Werk Eisenach, the largest car firm in East Germany, worth $600 million. This will be the third G.M. venture in Eastern Europe. Opel A.G., which is G.M.'s West German-based division, will be the majority owner of this venture, which is expected to produce 150,000 cars per year. Other American movers in East Germany include Honeywell, I.B.M., Coca-Cola, Citibank, Philip Morris and Eastman Kodak.

To improve telecommunications between the United States and the Soviet Union, the American Telephone and Telegraph Company (AT&T) proposed to use the Soviet Intersputnik satellite system for a closer connection of the two nations. Also, the Energetics Satellites Corporation of the United States signed a contract with Glavkosmos, the Soviet civilian space agency, to launch eight communication satellites worth $54 million. Furthermore, Rupert Murdoch, who controls Fox Television in the United States and Sky Television in Britain, is eager to use *perestroika* and to enter joint ventures with the Soviet Union on television production, books, and other publications. However, care should be taken to avoid duplication of similar public or private projects that spread rapidly into Eastern Europe.

The Combustion Engineering Company of the United States led a consortium of western firms to sign an agreement with Tobolsk Petrochemical Company of the Soviet Union to build and operate a petrochemical complex in Siberia worth $2 billion. The plant will process oil and gas for use in automobiles and medical items for Soviet and foreign markets.

Fiat S.p.A., Italy's largest auto company based in Turin, which has produced cars in the Soviet Union since 1970, signed a new joint venture to produce 300,000 cars at Velabuga near Moscow. The Soviets will hold 70 percent of the venture. The initial investment is $1.4 billion, but it will increase to accommodate production of up to 900,000 cars. Moreover, Pirelli S.p.A. is considering the establishment of a plant in the Soviet Union to produce about 10 million tires, and the Merloni S.p.A. group would create a plant for electronic goods.

As Western and Eastern Europe come closer to economic collaboration, the movement of Western firms into the East Bloc countries intensifies. Thus, Lufthansa, the West German air carrier, has agreed to buy a 26 percent stake of Interflug, East Germany's state-owned airline, with prospects of an eventual merger of the two carriers. Also, Lufthansa is considering buying the international routes to Berlin of Pan Am Corporation for more than $200 million.

Alcatel, a French-American company formed by CGE of France and ITT of the United States in 1987, agreed with VEB Kombinat Nachrichtenelektronik of East Germany to set up a 50–50 joint venture to improve the poor telephone network in southern East Germany and eventually produce around a million digital telephone lines a year.

The alliance of the Mitsubishi companies of Japan (with about $80 billion sales annually) and Daimler-Benz of West Germany (with around $40 billion sales per year) aims at the exploitation of the EC and East Bloc markets for their automobiles, electronics, and aerospace products. This is a significant business collaboration that brings Japan closer to Europe and intensifies pressures on their American counterparts to become more competitive.

The General Electric Company is negotiating multimillion-dollar contracts to supply jet engines to Aeroflot, the Soviet airline, to power planes it bought from Airbus Industries, the European consortium based in France. Moreover, negotiations between the United States and the Soviet Union are conducted for the expansion of United States airline services to a number of Soviet cities and Aeroflot services to some American cities.

The McDonald Corporation, which serves about 25 million people a day—in 11,000 restaurants in 52 nations—established its first fast-food restaurant in Moscow and serves about 30,000 people daily in spite of forty to fifty minute waiting lines.

Gradually, it became clear that in the name of advancing the working class, the practicians of the communist regimes reduced people into means of production. Through the establishment of the party elites, they turned talented working people into cogs of thudding machines without a clear purpose. As workers under these regimes say: "They pretend they pay us and we pretend we work." The result is inefficiency and low-quality products. This verifies what Aristotle said some twenty-five centuries ago, that "common ownership leads to common neglect."

For a closer cooperation between Western and Eastern European countries, a reorganized and peaceful Europe should have a united Germany as its heart, not as the front line. The security interests of Germany's neighbors should be respected, and United States economic and political institutions should play a decisive role in such a European reorganization. Nevertheless, some Eastern Europeans are skeptical about the rush to restructure their economies. They feel that it may not be proper to get rid of one dictatorship to get another one, that of big business, since it may transform them into poor, unemployed beggars. On the other hand, nationalism and border disputes should be minimized so that a Balkanization of Europe be avoided and a precious alloy of different nationalities be achieved in a fashion similar to that of the United States.

Appendix A   Statistical Correlations of Taxes with Private Consumption, Imports, and Inflation

In this appendix, statistical regressions are used to reveal the relationship between taxes as the dependent variable, and private consumption, imports, and inflation as independent variables for the period 1960–1987.

The simple regression equations are:

$$TT = a + b_1PRC$$

$$TT = a + b_2IMP$$

$$TT = a + b_3INF$$

where TT stands for total taxes, PRC for private consumption, IMP for imports, INF for inflation, a is a constant, and b_1, b_2, b_3, the regression coefficients, respectively.

For the multiple regressions the equations are:

$$TT = a + b_1PRC + b_3INF$$

$$TT = a + b_2IMP + b_3INF$$

$$TT = a + b_1PRC + b_2IMP + b_3INF$$

Mutatis mutadis, the same equations were used for the correlations of direct and indirect taxes with private consumption, imports, and inflation.

As Table A.1 shows, for both the United States and the EC group of countries, inflation is a better explanatory variable of changes in total taxes compared to private consumption and imports. Thus, a 1 percent increase in inflation is associated with an almost 9 percent increase in total taxes for the United States and a 5 percent increase in the EC taxes. Comparatively speaking, the United States tax system is primarily based on progressive income taxes and less on consumption-proportional taxes, and large amounts of tax revenue are collected with increases in inflation and nominal incomes. Next to inflation are the variable "imports" with regression coefficients, in the simple correlation of total taxes on imports, 3.74 for the United States and 1.47 for the EC. Tariffs or custom duties are the main source of tax revenue from imports, and sales taxes are the main source of tax revenue from private consumption.

For the United States, the multiple regression coefficient of total taxes on inflation was 2.36, for private consumption 0.79, and for imports 0.24. For the EC, they were 1.68 for inflation, 0.25 for private consumption, and 0.47 for imports, respectively. This means that, *ceteris paribus*, a unit change in inflation is associated with a change of 2.36 units in total taxes in the United States and 1.68 in the EC, and so on.

Also, in the simple and multiple regressions of direct taxes on private consumption, imports, and inflation, it was found that inflation is the most influential variable for changes in direct or income taxes, compared to consumption and imports. Inflation pushes taxpayers into higher income tax brackets where, under the progressive tax system, tax rates are higher, thereby transferring proportionally more and more income from the private to the public sector. Thus, inflation, the vicious hidden tax, helps the government increase revenue without introducing new tax legislation.

A regression analysis of indirect taxes on private consumption for the period 1960–1987 was also used to determine the slope and its reliability. Similar simple regressions of indirect taxes on imports, as well as on inflation, were calculated. Thus, the slope of the regression line for private consumption was 0.14 for the United States. This means that, on the average, an increase in private consumption by $100 is related to an increase in government revenue from indirect taxes by $14. However, imports were more important in explaining indirect taxes and inflation even more important.

In all cases considered, the fit for the regression lines was very good. The corrected coefficient of determination, $\overline{R}^2$, was more than 0.900 in all regressions, for both the United States and the EC countries as a whole. However, the Durbin-Watson (D-W) statistic for most cases was not high enough (above 1.10 at a 5 percent level of significance) to indicate the absence of serial correlation and the results should be interpreted with caution.

The regression coefficients for the EC were different from those for the United States. For the United States "inflation" was a more important variable than "private consumption" and "imports," whereas for the EC the variable "imports" were more important in explaining indirect taxes. The fact that a large part of indirect taxes in the United States comes from state and local sales taxes, which are proportional to prices, may be responsible for the difference. Com-

Table A.1

Simple and Multiple Regressions of Total (General Government) Taxes (TT) on Private Consumption (PRC), Imports (IMP), and Inflation (INF), 1960–1986

	CONSTANT a	COEFFICIENTS b1	b2	b3	$\overline{R^2}$	D-W
UNITED STATES	-40.99	0.59 PRC (102.97)			0.997	1.62
	72.42		3.74 IMP (21.57)		0.945	0.638
	3.32			8.95 INF (50.80)	0.990	0.89
	52.02	0.79 PRC (10.11)		2.93 INF (2.49)	0.998	1.949
	-349.62		0.26 IMP (0.68)	9.56 INF (10.50)	0.989	0.945
	27.35	0.79 PRC (10.29)	0.24 IMP (1.41)	2.36 INF (1.92)	0.998	1.809
THE EC	2.56	0.71 PRC (56.54)			0.991	0.786
	35.66		1.47 IMP (48.82)		0.988	0.630
	-248.34			5.01 INF (40.55)	0.988	0.742
	85.30	0.47 PRC (7.12)		1.73 INF (3.71)	0.994	0.935
	-87.25		0.85 IMP (7.20)	2.14 INF (5.29)	0.994	1.109
	-72.60	0.25 PRC (2.18)	0.47 IMP (2.29)	1.68 INF (3.88)	0.995	0.887

Note: Figures in parenthesis are t values.

Source: Calculations were based on Organization of Economic Cooperations and Development (OECD), *National Accounts*, various issues.

paratively speaking, the regression coefficient of indirect taxes on private consumption was lower for the United States (0.14) than for the EC (0.22) and that on inflation was higher (2.12).

With the usual caveats regarding causation, the above regressions imply that imports and inflation are the dominant determinants of indirect taxes for the United States and imports and private consumption for the EC. A change of 1 percent in imports associates with 0.4 percent change in indirect taxes for the United States and 0.9 percent for the EC, and 1 percent change in the cost of living associates with 0.2 percent change in indirect taxes for both the United States and the EC, after other factors are considered to be constant.

For both, the United States and the EC, the fit for the multiple regressions was very good. The corrected coefficient of determination, $\overline{R}^2$, was more than 0.920 in both cases. However, the Durbin-Watson (D-W) statistic for the United States was not high enough (as was for the EC) to signify the absence of serial correlation and the results should be interpreted with caution.

As multiple regressions indicated, the inflation coefficient (0.20) was higher for the United States than for the EC (0.16), but the United States import coefficient (0.40) was lower than that of the EC (0.81); and the private consumption coefficient (0.19) was the same in both cases. This means that, *ceteris paribus*, policy makers on matters of public finance may expect a close relationship between indirect taxes and inflation in the United States; and indirect taxes and imports in the EC. More or less, the same results were found for similar regressions in a logarithmic form.

Similar high correlations ($\overline{R}^2 > 0.900$) can be observed for Canada and Japan. Simple correlations of indirect taxes on inflation resulted in a 2.15 regression coefficient for Canada and 1.48 for Japan. The regression coefficients of indirect taxes on private consumption were 0.23 for Canada and 0.11 for Japan. This means that as for the United States, inflation is a more influential variable on indirect taxes than imports and private consumption for both countries, although to a lesser degree for Japan than for Canada. Imports had about the same importance for revenue collection from indirect taxes for both countries, whereas private consumption was more important for Canada than Japan.

Appendix B   Statistical Correlations of Trade Deficits with Budget Deficits, Gross Domestic Product, and Interest Rates

A correlation analysis of trade deficits on budget deficits shows a close relationship of the two variables in the United States. Although correlation does not establish causality, this statistical result shows that when budget deficits in the United States increase by a certain percentage, trade deficits increase by about half of that percentage. Therefore, reductions in budget deficits are expected to bring about reductions in foreign trade deficits. The regression coefficient of trade deficits (TD) on budget deficits (BD) is 0.46, that is:

$$TD = 21.4 + 0.46BD \qquad \overline{R}^2 = 0.937$$

$$D\text{-}W = 1.63$$

On the contrary, the regression results for the EC indicate a very weak or no correlation between trade deficits and budget deficits for the period 1960–1987. However, in multiple regressions the GDP coefficient (b_2) of the EC was higher than that of the United States, while the interest rate coefficient (b_3) was higher for the United States than for the EC, as Table B.1 shows.

The fit of regression was very good for the United States and poor for the EC. The adjusted coefficient of determination, $\overline{R}^2$, was 0.937 for the United States and 0.263 for the EC. However, the Durbin-Watson (D-W) statistic, at a 5 percent level of significance, was high enough in both cases to signify non-existence of serial correlation and the result should be interpreted with confidence.

Table B.1

Multiple Regression Analysis of Trade Deficits (TD) on Budget Deficits (BD), Gross Domestic Product (GDP), and Interest Rates (IR), 1960–1986

	CONSTANT	REGRESSION COEFFICIENTS				
	a	b_1	b_2	b_3	$\overline{R}_2$	D-W
For the USA	-23.37	0.41BD (3.72)	0.12GDP (1.47)	0.75IR (4.55)	0.937	1.63
For the EC	-25.10	0.18BD (1.04)	0.29GDP (2.76)	0.68IR (0.56)	0.263	1.87

Note: Figures in parentheses are t values. For interest rates, long-term government bond yields were used.

Source: Calculations were based on data provided by the Organization for Economic Cooperation and Development (OECD), *National Accounts*; and International Monetary Fund (IMF), *International Financial Statistics*, various issues.

These results indicate that, for the United States, "budget deficits" and "interest rates" are more significant variables in explaining changes in "trade deficits," compared to the EC. This difference may be justified because of the more uniform budgetary and monetary policies in the United States than in the EC countries.

Notes

CHAPTER 1

1. For the fears of some Europeans that the reunification of Germany may create a "Fourth Reich," see "One Germany? First, One Europe," *New York Times*, November 25, 1989, A22.

2. For such evaluations, see Jane Kramer, *Europeans* (New York: Farrar, Straus and Giroux, 1988).

3. For such pessimistic predictions, see Harry Browne, *The Economic Time Bomb: How You Can Profit from the Emerging Crises* (New York: St. Martin's Press, 1989). Also, Paul Kennedy, *The Rise and Fall of the Great Powers: Economic Change and Military Conflict from 1500 to 2000* (New York: Vintage, 1988).

4. Nicholas Gianaris, *Contemporary Public Finance* (New York: Praeger, 1989), chap. 9.

CHAPTER 2

1. More details in Terrot Glover, *The Challenge of the Greeks and Other Essays* (New York: Macmillan, 1942), chaps. 1–3; C. Stanley, *Roots of the Tree* (London: Oxford University Press, 1936), chap. 1; and S. Todd Lowry, "Recent Literature on Ancient Greek Economic Thought," *Journal of Economic Literature*, vol. 17, March 1979, 65–86.

2. Further valuable information is provided in Frank Tenny, *An Economic History of Ancient Rome* (Baltimore: Johns Hopkins University Press, 1933), chaps. 1–2; and Paul Louis, *Ancient Rome at Work* (New York: Alfred A. Knopf, 1927), chaps. 1–3.

3. Roman merchants used the Aegean islands for the transport and exchange of commodities and slaves from east to west. Some 10,000 slaves were sold in a single day on the island of Delos alone. Jules Toutain, *The Economic Life of the Ancient World* (New York: Alfred A. Knopf, 1930), 232.

4. J. Carey and A. Carey, *The Web of Modern Greek Politics* (New York: Columbia University Press, 1968), 35. Also, Barbara Ward, *The Interplay of East and West* (London: Allen and Unwin, 1957), 22.

5. Paul Taylor, *The Limits of European Integration* (New York: Columbia University Press, 1983), chap. 2; and Frances Nicholson and Roger East, *From the Six to the Twelve: The Enlargement of the European Community* (London: St. James Press, 1987), chaps. 8, 10, 11.

6. For problems of integration, see the valuable papers in Bella Balassa, ed., *European Economic Integration* (Amsterdam: North Holland, 1975); and Michael Emerson, ed., *Europe's Stagflation* (Oxford: Clarendon Press, 1984).

CHAPTER 3

1. Peter Jones, *An Economic History of the United States Since 1783* (London: Routledge and Kegan Paul, 1969), chap. I. For economic conditions during colonial times, see Susan Lee and Peter Passell, *A New Economic View of American History* (New York: W. W. Norton, 1979), chap. 1. For the Treaty of Peace with Great Britain, see Henry Commager, ed., *Documents of American History* (New York: Crafts and Co., 1938), 117–119.

2. Edward Humphrey, *An Economic History of the United States* (New York: The Century Co., 1931), chap. XIV. More details in Chester Wright, *Economic History of the United States*, 2d edition (New York: McGraw-Hill, 1949).

3. Elizabeth Gilboy and Edgar Hoover, "Population and Immigration," in Seymour E. Harris, *American Economic History* (New York: McGraw-Hill, 1961), 247–280.

4. Related information in George Soule and Vincent Carosso, *American Economic History* (New York: Dryden Press, 1957), chap. 19; and Merton Peck, "Transportation in the American Economy," in Seymour E. Harris, ed., *American Economic History*, chap. 12.

5. Frank Tuttle and Joseph Perry, *An Economic History of the United States* (Cincinnati, Ohio: South-Western Publishing Co., 1970), 117–118.

6. Peter Jones, *An Economic History of the United States Since 1783*, chap. XI.

7. United States Government, *Historical Statistics of the United States, 1789–1945* (Washington, D.C.: U.S. Bureau of Census, 1949), 246.

8. Gary Walton and Ross Robertson, *History of the American Economy*, 5th edition (New York: Harcourt, 1983), 474–478; and Susan Lee and Peter Passel, *A New Economic View of American History* (New York: Norton 1979), 146–152.

9. More details in Norman Angell, *The Story of Money* (New York: Frederick A. Stokes Co., 1929), chaps. IV and IX; and Walter Haines, *Money, Prices and Policy* (New York: McGraw-Hill, 1961), chaps. 5, 6.

10. More details in Robert C. Puth, *American Economic History* (Chicago: Dryden Press, 1981), 342–348; and Peter Jones, *An Economic History of the United States Since 1783*, chap. XIII.

11. A useful statistical presentation in John M. Keynes, *Economic Consequences of the Peace* (London: 1919); and U.S. Department of Commerce, *The United States in World Economy* (Washington, D.C.: 1943).

12. United States Government, *Historical Statistics of the United States, 1789–1945* (Washington, D.C.: U.S. Bureau of Census, 1949), 65 (Series D 52–76) and 216 (Series

K 158–167); and Garry Walton and Ross Robertson, *History of the American Economy* (New York: Harcourt, 1983), chap. 24.

13. American businesses and farm groups initially supported the program but, with the recession of 1949, many firms demanded discouragement of imports from Europe. More details in William F. Sanford, Jr., *The American Business Community and the European Recovery Program, 1947–1952* (New York: Garland Publishing Co., 1952).

14. Walter Lippmann in the *Herald Tribune*, April 1, 1967, reprinted in Stephen Rousseas, *The Death of a Democracy: Greece and the American Conscience* (New York: Grove Press, 1967), 84; and Nicholas Gianaris, *Greece and Turkey: Economic and Geopolitical Perspectives* (New York: Praeger, 1988), chaps. 3, 10.

15. For such a suggestion, see Leonard Silk, "Looking Ahead in World Trade," *New York Times*, August 26, 1988, D2.

16. More details in David McKee, ed., *Canadian-American Economic Relations: Conflict and Cooperation on a Continental Scale* (New York: Praeger, 1988); and Clyde H. Farnsworth, "Canadian Trade Pact Accelerated," *New York Times*, March 14, 1989, D1, D9. Also, Richard Pomfret, *Unequal Trade: The Economics of Discriminatory International Trade Policies* (New York: Blackwell, 1988).

17. Clyde H. Farnsworth, "A Panel on Trade Urges Better U.S.-Mexico Ties," *New York Times*, November 16, 1988, D2. See also the valuable articles in Khosrow Fatemi, ed., *U.S.-Mexican Economic Relations: Prospects and Problems* (New York: Praeger, 1988).

CHAPTER 4

1. J. A. Kay and D. J. Thompson, "Privatization: A Policy in Search of a Rationale," *The Economic Journal*, vol. 96, March 1986, 18–32.

2. It is estimated that federal regulations in the United States are responsible for 12 to 21 percent of the slowdown in the growth of labor productivity in manufacturing. Gregory Christainsen and Robert Haveman, "Public Regulations and the Slowdown in Productivity Growth," *American Economic Review, Proceedings*, vol. 71, no. 2, May 1981, 320–325.

3. For pro and con arguments, see Robert Reich, "Leveraged Buyouts: America Pays the Price," *New York Times Magazine*, January 29, 1989, 32, 36, 40; and Carl Icahn, "The Case for Takeovers," 34.

4. "Insider Trading in West Germany," *Economist*, vol. 310, no. 7593, 1989, 78, 83.

5. Adam Smith, *An Inquiry into the Nature and Causes of the Wealth of Nations*, Edwin Cannan, ed. (New York: Modern Library, 1937), 284.

6. John Stuart Mill, *Considerations and Representative Government* (London: Routledge, 1905), 114; Jean Jacques Rousseau, *Social Contract*, Book One, chap. 9; C. Lindblom, *Politics and Markets* (New York: Basic Books, 1977), chap. 24.

7. Joseph Schumpeter, *Capitalism, Socialism and Democracy*, 3rd edition (New York: Harper Colophon Books, 1975), 205. For some review lessons in Europe, see J. Carby-Hall, *Worker Participation in Europe* (London: C. Helm Ltd., 1977), chap. 3; G. Garson, ed., *Worker Self-Management in Industry: The West European Experience* (New York: Praeger, 1977), chaps. 1–5.

8. Nicholas Gianaris, *Greece and Yugoslavia: An Economic Comparison* (New York:

Praeger, 1984), chap. 3; and his *The Economies of the Balkan Countries: Albania, Bulgaria, Greece, Rumania, Turkey, Yugoslavia* (New York: Praeger, 1982), chap. 4.

9. Corey M. Rosen, Katherine J. Klein and Karen M. Young, *Employee Ownership in America: The Equity Solution* (Lexington, Mass.: Lexington Books, 1986), chap. 2; and Robert D. Hershey, Jr., "Employee Stock Ownership Plans: Including Labor in the Division of Capital," *New York Times*, April 24, 1988, E5. Also, Frederick Ungeheuer, "They Own the Place," *Time*, February 6, 1989, 50–51; and Joseph Blasi, *Employee Ownership: Revolution or Ripoff?* (New York: Ballinger, 1988), chaps. 1–3.

10. "Sprucing Up Savings," *Economist*, vol. 310, no. 7594, March 18, 1989, 60.

11. Irini Hrysolora, "Measures of People's Capitalism," in Greek, *E Kathimerini*, Athens, October 25, 1987, 7; and Nicholas Gianaris and Constantine Papoulias, "Participation of Employees in Enterprises," *Oikonomikos Tahydromos*, January 2, 1986, 73–74.

12. For such pioneering proposals, see Martin L. Weitzman, *The Share Economy: Conquering Stagflation* (Cambridge: Harvard University Press, 1984), 73–74; and his "The Simple Macroeconomics of Profit Sharing," *American Economic Review*, vol. 75, December 1985, 937–953.

13. World Bank, *World Bank Report* (New York: Oxford University Press, 1989), 225. For comparative analysis, see Robert Lawrence and Charles Shultze, eds., *Barriers to European Growth* (Washington, D.C.: Brookings Institution, 1987). Also, Europa Publications, *Western Europe 1989: A Political and Economic Survey*, 1st edition (London: Europa Publications Ltd., 1989).

14. OECD, *Employment Outlook, 1988* (Paris: OECD, 1989); and United Nations, *Yearbook of Labor Statistics*, 1988, Tables 3, 9. Unit labor costs in 1987 were lower in the United States (60) and France (72) than in Japan (83), Italy (93), and West Germany (113). Bela Balassa and Marcus Noland, *Japan in the World Economy* (Washington, D.C.: Institute for International Economics, 1988), 44. For short-run advantages but long-run problems of the Japanese economy, because of parochialism, protectionism and narrow nationalism, see Naohiro Amaya, "The Japanese Economy in Transition," *Japan and the World Economy*, vol. 1, no. 1, 1988/1989, 101–111. Also, Tom Kemp, *Industrialization in the Non-Western World*, 2d ed. (New York: Longmans, 1989), chap. 2.

15. For the relationship between investment and economic growth, see Nicholas Gianaris, *Economic Development: Thought and Problems* (West Hanover, Mass.: Christopher Publishing House, 1978), chap. 8; and "International Differences in Capital Output Ratios," *American Economic Review*, vol. 67, June 1970, 465–477. For country surveys, see OECD, *OECD Economic Surveys* (Paris: OECD, 1989).

16. Plato, *Laws*, 765e.

17. Roger C. Altman, "America Needs an Investment Boom," *New York Times*, July 2, 1989, F3.

18. For valuable comments, see Lester C. Thurow, "The Post-Industrial Era Is Over," *New York Times*, September 4, 1989, 27.

19. For regional and demographic policies in Western Europe, see Allan Williams, *The Western Europe Economy: A Geography of Post-War Development* (Savage, Maryland: Rowman and Littlefield, Barnes and Noble Books, 1988); and Norbert Vanhove and Leo Klaassen, *Regional Policy: A European Approach* (Savage, Maryland: Rowman and Littlefield, Barnes and Noble Books, 1987).

20. For the differences of the European cities and countries, see Flora Lewis, *Europe: A Tapestry of Nations* (New York: Simon and Schuster, 1988). For problems of decen-

tralization, see Raffaella Nanetti, *Growth and Territorial Policies: The Italian Model of Social Capitalism* (New York: Printing, Distribution by Columbia University, 1988).

CHAPTER 5

1. Adam Smith, *An Inquiry into the Nature and Causes of the Wealth of Nations*, Edwin Cannon, ed. (New York: Modern Library 1937), 689.

2. Adolph Wagner, *Financzwissenschaft*, 3rd edition (Leipzig: 1890). For empirical findings, see Warren Nutter, *Growth of Government in the West* (Washington, D.C.: American Enterprise Institute, 1978).

3. A valuable analysis in Felix Rohatyn, "America's Economic Dependence," *Foreign Affairs*, vol. 68, no. 1, 1989, 53–65.

4. For statistical regressions of total (general government) taxes (TT) on private consumption (PRC), imports (IMP) and inflation (INF), see Appendix A.

5. Nicholas Gianaris, *Contemporary Public Finance* (New York: Praeger, 1989), chap. 6. On other fiscal matters, see Donald Puchala, *Fiscal Harmonization in the European Community: National Politics and International Cooperation* (Washington, D.C.: Q. M. Dabney and Co., 1984).

6. Michel Glautier and Frederick Bassinger, *A Reference Guide to International Taxation* (Lexington, Mass.: Lexington Books, 1987), 96, 117, 125, 136.

7. A statistical regression of direct and indirect taxes on private consumption for the period 1950–1986 was used to determine the relative slopes and their reliability. Similar regressions of direct and indirect taxes on imports, as well as on inflation, were also used during the same period. More details appear in Appendix A.

8. More on VAT in Alan A. Tait, *Value Added Tax: International Practice and Problems* (Washington, D.C.: International Monetary Fund, 1988); and Charles E. McLare, Jr., *The Value Added Tax: Key to Deficit Reduction* (Washington, D.C.: The American Enterprise Institute, 1987).

9. International Monetary Fund (IMF), *World Economic Outlook* (Washington, D.C.: IMF, 1986), 78–79.

10. Geoffrey Fitchew, "1992: The Community and the Creation of an Internal Market in Financial Services," *European Access*, November 1988, 7–10.

11. "The Loan Arranger Rides Again," *Economist*, vol. 311, no. 7602, May 13, 1989, 83.

12. Robert Brusca, "Nuking European Currencies," *Financial World*, May 30, 1989, 52.

13. Michael Melvin, *International Money and Finance*, 2d edition (New York: Harper and Row, 1989), 202–205.

14. A deeper survey in Thomas L. Ilgen, *Autonomy and Interdependence: U.S.-Western European Monetary and Trade Relations, 1958–1984* (Savage, Maryland: Rowman and Littlefield, Barnes and Noble Books, 1988).

15. "Serious Money," *Global Investor*, Euromoney Publications, no. 19, February 1989, 31–40. For useful insights and analysis, see the valuable articles in Samuel Katz, ed., *U.S.-European Monetary Relations* (Washington, D.C.: American Enterprise Institute, 1979).

16. For empirical results and doubts on the short-run usefulness of the equation of exchange, see L. Douglas Lee, " 'P-Star' Can Spot Inflationary Trends," *New York Times*, Section 3, October 22, 1989, F2.

CHAPTER 6

1. In 1820 and 1840–1860, about 90 percent of government revenue came from tariffs. Grant Gardner and Kent Kimbrough, "The Behavior of U.S. Tariff Rates," *American Economic Review*, vol. 79, no. 1, March 1989, 211–218.

2. More details in Jagdish Bhagwati, *Protectionism* (Cambridge, Mass.: The MIT Press, 1989), chap. 3; and Rudiger Dornbusch and Jeffrey Frankel, "Macroeconomics and Protection," in Robert Stern, ed., *U.S. Trade Policies in a Changing World Economy* (Cambridge, Mass.: The MIT Press, 1989), 107–109; and OECD, *Economic Outlook*, December 1984, 131.

3. "U.S. Rules on Japanese 'Dumping,' " *New York Times*, January 30, 1989, D9.

4. Jonathan P. Hicks, "Big Cast of Characters in Steel Quotas Debate," *New York Times*, May 29, 1989, 32.

5. "Trade: Mote and Beam," *Economist*, vol. 311, no. 7601, May 6, 1989, 22–23.

6. Edmund L. Andrews, "A Foreign Push for U.S. Patents," *New York Times*, June 4, 1989, F7.

7. More on trade problems, in Robert Baldwin, Carl Hamilton, and Andre Sapir, eds., *Issues in U.S.-EC Trade Relations* (Chicago: University of Chicago Press, 1988); and "European Plan on Farm Aid," *New York Times*, June 13, 1988, D6. Also, "A Tale of Eleven Myths," *Europe*, no. 265, April 1987, 16–18.

8. For a quantification and analysis of protectionism, see related articles in Andrews Stoeckel, David Vincent, and Sandy Cuthbertson, eds., *Macroeconomic Consequences of Farm Support Policies* (Durham, North Carolina: Duke University Press, 1989). See also the valuable articles in Robert Baldwin et al., eds., *Issues in U.S.-EC Trade Relations* (Chicago: University of Chicago Press, 1988).

9. Jagdish N. Bhagwati, "Hormones and Trade Wars," *New York Times*, January 9, 1989, A27; and Paul L. Montgomery, "Europe Fires a New Shot in Trade War," *New York Times*, January 6, 1989, D1. For farm policy, see Harrison W. Glenn, et al., "The Economic Impact of the European Community," *American Economic Review, Proceedings*, vol. 79, no. 2, May 1989, 288–294; and International Monetary Fund (IMF), *The Common Agricultural Policy of the European Community* (Washington, D.C.: IMF, 1988).

10. U.S. Government Bureau of Labor Statistics, various issues. More details in David G. Tarr, "The Steel Crisis in the United States and the European Community: Causes and Adjustments," in Robert E. Baldwin, et al., eds., *Issues in U.S.-EC Trade Relations* (Chicago: University of Chicago Press, 1988), 173–198.

11. Ibid., 185.

12. More details in "American Steel: Plea Bargaining," *Economist*, vol. 311, no. 7603, March 20, 1989, 79; Loukas Tsoukalis and Robert Strauss, "Crisis and Adjustment in European Steel: Beyond Laissez-faire," *Journal of Common Market Studies*, vol. 23, 1985, 207–225; and Robert Lawrence, "Protectionism: Is There a Better Way?" *American Economic Review, Proceedings*, vol. 79, no. 2, May 1989, 118–122.

13. Paula Stern, "Should Steel Quotas Be Extended?" *New York Times*, March 18, 1989, A27. Arguments in favor of steel quotas are offered by Senator John Heinz and Congressman John Murtha of Pennsylvania in this article. Close to 25 percent of United States imports are under special protection, mainly through the trade policy or, more politely, the policy of managed trade during the 1980s. "America's Trade Policy: Perestroika in Reverse," *Economist*, February 25, 1989, 59–60.

CHAPTER 7

1. More details in Rudiger W. Dornbusch, "Flexible Exchange Rates and Capital Mobility," *Brookings Papers on Economic Activity*, 1, 1986, 209–226.

2. For previous developments, see Francesco Giavazzi, et al. eds., *The European Monetary System* (Cambridge: Cambridge University Press, 1988).

3. Regarding trade deficits with Europe, see Michael M. Knetter, "Price Discrimination by U.S. and German Exports," *American Economic Review*, Vol. 79, No. 1, March 1989, 198–210. Also, Stephen Marris, *Deficits and the Dollar: The World Economy at Risk* (Washington, D.C.: Institute for International Economics, 1987), chap. 5.

4. The relationship between interest rates (i_s in the United States and i_f in France) and exchange rates, forward (F) and spot (S), is determined by the equation: $F = S + (i_s - i_f)S$. Assuming $i_s = 0.15$, $i_f = 0.10$ and $S = 6$ French francs per dollar, the forward exchange rate for a year would be: $F = 6 + (0.15 - 0.10)6 = 6.30$ francs per dollar and the forward premium would be equal to 0.05 (interest differential).

5. Martin Feldstein, "U.S. Budget Deficits and the European Economies: Resolving the Political Economy Puzzle," *American Economic Review*, Vol. 76, No. 2, May 1986, 342–346. Also, John Cuddington and José Vinals, "Budget Deficits and the Current Account in the Presence of Classical Unemployment," *Economic Journal*, 96, March 1986, 101–119.

6. For the relationship between trade deficits and the value of the dollar, see Ralph C. Bryant, Gerald Holtham and Peter Hooper, eds., *External Deficits and the Dollar* (Washington, D.C.: The Brookings Institution, 1988).

7. For a proposal of borrowing dollars from the Eurodollar market and other foreign central banks by the United States Treasury to offset balance of payments disequilibria, see Xenophon Zolotas, *The Dollar Crisis and Other Papers* (Athens: Bank of Greece, 1979), 9–16.

8. Lester Thurow, *Should America Adopt an Industrial Policy?*, Burkett Miller Distinguished Lecture (Chattanooga, Tenn.: Center for Economic Education, University of Tennessee, 1984), 9. Further related comments in Gottfried Haberler, *Government and International Trade, Essays in International Finance*, No. 129 (Princeton, N.J.: Princeton University Press, 1982); and Martin Bailey and George Tavlas, "Dollar Appreciation, Deficit Stimulation and the New Protectionism," *Journal of Policy Modeling*, February 1985.

9. Similar to the EC relationships between budget deficits and trade deficits or surpluses can be observed in Canada. In all cases, the huge American trade deficits are primarily responsible for trade surpluses in the EC and Canada, in spite of the large budget deficits in all countries considered.

10. Charles Morris, "Deficit Figuring Doesn't Add Up," *New York Times Magazine*, February 11, 1989, 36–40.

CHAPTER 8

1. Jonathan P. Hicks, "Foreign Owners Are Shaking Up Competition," *New York Times*, May 28, 1989, F9.

2. More discussion in Felix Rohatyn, "America's Economic Dependence," *Foreign*

Affairs, Vol. 68, No. 1, 1989, 60–65; and "Foreign Investment in America," *Economist*, Vol. 313, No. 7625, October 21, 1989, 76.

3. Such arguments in John K. Galbraith, *Balancing Acts: Technology, Finance and the American Future* (New York: Basic Books, 1989). Moreover John K. Galbraith thinks that managers congratulate themselves for moving large sums of money in acquisitions instead of investing in real capital. James Srodes, "Curmudgeon in Winter," *Financial World*, November 28, 1989, 82–83.

4. Francis M. Bator, "Must We Retrench?" *Foreign Affairs*, Vol. 68, No. 2, Spring 1989, 92–116.

5. A United States affiliate is a United States company in which a single foreign person owns or controls, directly or indirectly, 10 percent or more of the voting interest. Ned Howenstine, "U.S. Affiliates of Foreign Companies: 1987 Benchmark Survey Results," *Survey of Current Business*, July 1989, 116.

6. John Whitelegg, *Transport Policy in the EEC* (London: Routledge, 1989).

7. More details in Kevin Done, "Ford to Expand Electronics Side," *Financial Times*, July 11, 1989, 28.

8. Compaq's European sales jumped from $20 million in 1984 to $733 million in 1988. Steve Lohr, "Compaq's Conquests in Europe," *New York Times*, July 9, 1989, F4.

9. Steven Greenhouse, "5 RJR Units Sold for $2.5 Billion," *New York Times*, June 7, 1989, D1, D13.

10. More comments in Norman J. Glickman and Douglas P. Woodward, *The New Competitors: How Foreign Investors Are Changing the U.S. Economy* (New York: Basic Books, 1989).

11. "Hanson's Future: The Conglomerate as Antique Dealer," *Economist*, vol. 310, no. 7593, 71–73.

12. Nikki Tait, "Harrisons and Crosfield Expands in U.S. with $85m Deal," *Financial Times*, July 7, 1989, 25.

13. "Unilever to Buy Fabergè and Arden," *International Herald Tribune*, July 14, 1989, 13.

14. More details in Steve Lohr, "Is Europe Ready for Big Takeovers?" *New York Times*, January 26, 1989, D1, D2; John Drew, *Doing Business in the European Community*, 2d edition (London: Butterworths, 1983); and Joseph Decker and Matthew Powers, "DOJ International Antitrust Guidelines," *Barrister*, vol. 16, no. 3, Fall 1989, 47–49.

CHAPTER 9

1. Thomas A. Wolf, "Reform, Inflation, and Adjustment in Planned Economies," *Finance and Development*, Vol. 27. No. 1, March 1990, 2–5; and Nicholas V. Gianaris, "Helping Eastern Europe Helps the West," *New York Times*, February 6, 1990, A28.

2. Jim Hoagland, "Europe's Destiny," *Foreign Affairs*, Vol. 69, No. 1, 1989/90, 38, 45.

3. Ed A. Hewett, "Economic Reforms in the U.S.S.R., Eastern Europe and China: The Politics of Economics," *American Economic Review, Proceedings*, Vol. 79, No. 2, May 1989, 16–20. Also, Hubert Gabrisch, ed., *Economic Reforms in Eastern Europe and the Soviet Union* (New York: Westview, 1988).

4. Michael Farr, "Bonn Sets Credit Line For Soviets," *New York Times*, October 12,

1988, D1, D9. See also review articles in Ronald Liebowitz, ed., *Gorbachev's New Thinking: Prospects for Joint Ventures* (New York: Ballinger, 1988).

5. More information in Majorie Lister, *The European Community and the Developing Countries* (Brookfield, Vermont: Gower Publishing Co., 1989); and Loukas Tsoukalis, ed., *Europe, America and the World Economy* (New York: Basil Blackwell, 1986).

Bibliography

Altman, Roger C. "America Needs an Investment Boom." *New York Times* (July 2, 1989): F3.

Amaya, Naohiro. "The Japanese Economy in Transition." *Japan and The World Economy*, vol. 1, no. 1 (1988/1989).

Andrews, Edmund L. "A Foreign Push for U.S. Patents." *New York Times* (June 4, 1989): F7.

Angell, Norman. *The Story of Money*. New York: Frederick A. Stokes Co., 1929.

Bailey, Martin, and George Tavlas. "Dollar Appreciation, Deficit Stimulation and the New Protectionism." *Journal of Policy Modeling* (February 1985).

Balassa, Bela, ed. *European Economic Integration*. Amsterdam: North Holland, 1975.

————, and Marcus Noland. *Japan in the World Economy*. Washington, D.C.: Institute for International Economics, 1988.

Baldwin, Robert, Carl Hamilton and Andre Sapir, eds. *Issues in U.S.-EC Trade Relations*. Chicago: University of Chicago Press, 1988.

Bator, Francis M. "Must We Retrench?" *Foreign Affairs*, vol. 68, no. 2 (Spring 1989): 92–116.

Bhagwati, Jagdish N. "Hormones and Trade Wars." *New York Times* (January 9, 1989): A27.

————. *Protectionism*. Cambridge, Mass.: The MIT Press, 1989.

Blasi, Joseph. *Employee Ownership: Revolution or Ripoff?* New York: Ballinger, 1988.

Browne, Harry. *The Economic Time Bomb: How You Can Profit from the Emerging Crises*. New York: St. Martin's Press, 1989.

Brusca, Robert. "Nuking European Currencies." *Financial World* (May 30, 1989).

Bryant, Ralph C., Gerald Holtham and Peter Hooper, eds. *External Deficits and the Dollar*. Washington, D.C.: The Brookings Institution, 1988.

Carby-Hall, J. *Worker Participation in Europe*. London: C. Helm Ltd., 1977.

Carey, J., and A. Carey. *The Web of Modern Greek Politics*. New York: Columbia University Press, 1968.

Christainsen, Gregory, and Robert Haveman. "Public Regulations and the Slowdown in Productivity Growth." *American Economic Review, Proceedings*, vol. 71, no. 2 (May 1981).

Commager, Henry, ed. *Documents of American History*. New York: Crafts and Co., 1938.

Cuddington, John, and José Vinals. "Budget Deficits and the Current Account in the Presence of Classical Unemployment." *Economic Journal*, 96 (March 1986): 101–119.

Decker, Joseph, and Matthew Powers. "DOJ International Antitrust Guidelines." *Barrister*, vol. 16, no. 3: 47–49.

Done, Kevin. "Ford to Expand Electronics Side." *Financial Times* (July 11, 1989): 28.

Dornbusch, Rudiger W. "Flexible Exchange Rates and Capital Mobility." *Brookings Papers on Economic Activity*, 1 (1986).

———, and Jeffrey Frankel. "Macroeconomics and Protection," in Robert Stern, ed., *U.S. Trade Policies in a Changing World Economy* Cambridge, Mass.: The MIT Press, 1989.

Drew, John. *Doing Business in the European Community*, 2d edition. London: Butterworths, 1983.

Emerson, Michael, ed. *Europe's Stagflation*. Oxford: Clarendon Press, 1984.

Farnsworth, Clyde H. "A Panel on Trade Urges Better U.S.-Mexico Ties." *New York Times* (November 16, 1988): D2.

———. "Canadian Trade Pact Accelerated." *New York Times* (March 14, 1989): D1, D9.

Farr, Michael. "Bonn Sets Credit Line for Soviets." *New York Times* (October 12, 1988): D1, D9.

Fatemi, Khosrow, ed. *U.S.-Mexican Economic Relations: Prospects and Problems*. New York: Praeger, 1988.

Feldstein, Martin. "U.S. Budget Deficits and the European Economies: Resolving the Political Economy Puzzle." *American Economic Review*, vol. 76, no. 2 (May 1986): 342–46.

Fitchew, Geoffrey. "1992: The Community and the Creation of an Internal Market in Financial Services." *European Access* (November 1988).

Frankel, Jeffrey. "Macroeconomics and Protection." In Robert Stern, ed., *U.S. Trade Policies in a Changing World Economy*. Cambridge, Mass.: The MIT Press, 1989.

Gabrisch, Hubert, ed. *Economic Reforms in Eastern Europe and the Soviet Union*. New York: Westview, 1988.

Galbraith, James, K. *Balanced Acts: Technology, Finance and the American Future*. New York: Basic Books, 1989.

Gardner, Grant, and Kent Kimbrough. "The Behavior of U.S. Tariff Rates." *American Economic Review*, vol. 79, no. 1 (March 1989).

Garson, G., ed. *Worker Self-Management in Industry: The West European Experience*. New York: Praeger, 1977.

Gianaris, Nicholas V. "International Differences in Capital Output Ratios," *American Economic Review*, vol. 67 (June 1970): 465–477.

———. *Economic Development: Thought and Problems*. West Hanover, Mass.: Christopher Publishing House, 1978.

————. *The Economies of the Balkan Countries: Albania, Bulgaria, Greece, Rumania, Turkey, Yugoslavia*. New York: Praeger, 1982.

————. *Greece and Yugoslavia: An Economic Comparison*. New York: Praeger, 1984.

————. *Greece and Turkey: Economic and Geopolitical Perspectives*. New York: Praeger, 1988.

————. *Contemporary Public Finance*. New York: Praeger, 1989.

————. "Helping Eastern Europe Helps the West." *New York Times* (February 6, 1990): A28.

————, and Constantine Papoulias. "Participation of Employees in Enterprises." *Oikonomikos Tahydromos* (January 2, 1986).

Giavazzi, Francesco, et al., eds. *The European Monetary System*. Cambridge: Cambridge University Press, 1988.

Gilboy, Elizabeth, and J. Edgar Hoover. "Population and Immigration." In Seymour E. Harris, *American Economic History*. New York: McGraw-Hill, 1961.

Glautier, Michel, and Frederick Bassinger. *A Reference Guide to International Taxation*. Lexington, Mass.: Lexington Books, 1987.

Glenn, Harrison W., et al. "The Economic Impact of the European Community." *American Economic Review, Proceedings*, vol. 79, no. 2 (May 1989).

Glickman, Norman J., and Douglas P. Woodward. *The New Competitors: How Foreign Investors Are Changing the U.S. Economy*. New York: Basic Books, 1989.

Glover, Terrot. *The Challenge of the Greeks and Other Essays*. New York: Macmillan, 1942.

Greenhouse, Steven. "5 RJR Units Sold for $2.5 Billion." *New York Times* (June 7, 1989): D1, D13.

Haberler, Gottfried. *Government and International Trade, Essays in International Finance*, no. 129. Princeton, N.J.: Princeton University Press, 1982.

Haines, Walter. *Money, Prices and Policy*. New York: McGraw-Hill, 1961.

Hershey, Robert D., Jr. "Employee Stock Ownership Plans: Including Labor in the Division of Capital." *New York Times* (April 24, 1988): E5.

Hewett, Ed A. "Economic Reforms in the U.S.S.R., Eastern Europe and China: The Politics of Economics." *American Economic Review, Proceedings*, vol. 79, no. 2 (May 1989): 16–20.

Hicks, Jonathan P. "Foreign Owners Are Shaking Up Competition." *New York Times* (May 28, 1989): F9.

————. "Big Cast of Characters in Steel Quotas Debate." *New York Times* (May 29, 1989): 32.

Hoagland, Jim. "Europe's Destiny," *Foreign Affairs*, Vol. 69, No. 1 (1989/90): 38, 45.

Howenstine, Ned. "U.S. Affiliates of Foreign Companies: 1987 Benchmark Survey Results." *Survey of Current Business* (July 1989): 116.

Hrysolora, Irini. "Measures of People's Capitalism." In Greek, *E Kathimerini*. Athens (October 25, 1987).

Humphrey, Edward. *An Economic History of the United States*. New York: The Century Co., 1931.

Icahn, Carl. "The Case for Takeovers." *New York Times Magazine* (January 29, 1989): 34.

Ilgen, Thomas L. *Autonomy and Interdependence: U.S.-Western European Monetary and Trade Relations, 1958–1984*. Savage, Maryland: Rowman and Littlefield, Barnes and Noble Books, 1988.

International Monetary Fund. *The Common Agricultural Policy of the European Community*. Washington, D.C.: IMF, 1988.

————. *World Economic Outlook*. Washington, D.C.: IMF, 1986.

Jones, Peter. *An Economic History of the United States Since 1783*. London: Routledge and Kegan Paul, 1969.

Katz, Samuel, ed. *U.S.-European Monetary Relations*. Washington, D.C.: American Enterprise Institute, 1979.

Kay, J. A., and D. J. Thompson. "Privatization: A Policy in Search of a Rationale." *The Economic Journal*, vol. 96 (March 1986).

Kemp, Tom. *Industrialization in the Non-Western World*, 2d edition. New York: Longmans, 1989.

Kennedy, Paul. *The Rise and Fall of the Great Powers: Economic Change and Military Conflict from 1500 to 2000*. New York: Vintage, 1988.

Keynes, John M. *Economic Consequences of the Peace*. London: Macmillan, 1919.

Knetter, Michael M. "Price Discrimination by U.S. and German Exports." *American Economic Review*, vol. 79, no. 1 (March 1989): 198–210.

Kramer, Jane. *Europeans*. New York: Farrar, Straus and Giroux, 1988.

Lawrence, Robert. "Protectionism: Is There a Better Way?" *American Economic Review, Proceedings*, vol. 79, no. 2 (May 1989): 118–122.

————, and Charles Shultze, ed. *Barriers to European Growth*. Washington, D.C.: Brookings Institution, 1987.

Lee, L. Douglas. " 'P-Star' Can Spot Inflationary Trends." *New York Times*, Section 3 (October 22, 1989): F2.

Lee, Susan, and Peter Passel. *A New Economic View of American History*. New York: W. W. Norton, 1979.

Lewis, Flora. *Europe: A Tapestry of Nations*. New York: Simon and Schuster, 1988.

Liebowitz, Ronald, ed. *Gorbachev's New Thinking: Prospects for Joint Ventures*. New York: Ballinger, 1988.

Lindblom, C. *Politics and Markets*. New York: Basic Books, 1977.

Lister, Majorie. *The European Community and the Developing Countries*. Brookfield, Vermont: Gower Publishing Co., 1989.

Lohr, Steve. "Is Europe Ready for Big Takeovers?" *New York Times* (January 26, 1989): D1, D2.

————. "Compaq's Conquests in Europe." *New York Times* (July 9, 1989): F4.

Louis, Paul. *Ancient Rome at Work*. New York: Alfred A. Knopf, 1927.

Lowry, S. Todd. "Recent Literature on Ancient Greek Economic Thought." *Journal of Economic Literature*. vol. 17 (March 1979).

Marris, Stephen. *Deficits and the Dollar: The World Economy at Risk*. Washington, D.C.: Institute for International Economics, 1987.

McKee, David, ed. *Canadian-American Economic Relations: Conflict and Cooperation on a Continental Scale*. New York: Praeger, 1988.

McLare, Charles E., Jr. *The Value Added Tax: Key to Deficit Reduction*. Washington, D.C.: The American Enterprise Institute, 1987.

Melvin, Michael. *International Money and Finance*, 2d edition. New York: Harper and Row, 1989.

Mill, John Stuart. *Considerations and Representative Government*. London: Routledge, 1905.

Montgomery, Paul L. "Europe Fires a New Shot in Trade War." *New York Times* (January 6, 1989): D1.

Morris, Charles. "Deficit Figuring Doesn't Add Up." *New York Times Magazine* (February 11, 1989): 36–40.

Nanetti, Raffaella. *Growth and Territorial Policies: The Italian Model of Social Capitalism*. New York: Printing, Distribution by Columbia University, 1988.

Nicholson, Frances, and Roger East. *From the Six to the Twelve: The Enlargement of the European Community*. London: St.James Press, 1987.

Nutter, Warren. *Growth of Government in the West*. Washington, D.C.: American Enterprise Institute, 1978.

Organization for Economic Cooperation and Development (OECD). *Economic Outlook* (December 1984).

———. *Employment Outlook, 1988*. Paris: OECD, 1989.

———. *OECD Economic Surveys*. Paris: OECD, 1989.

Peck, Merton. "Transportation in the American Economy." In Seymour E. Harris, ed., *American Economic History*. New York: McGraw-Hill, 1961.

Plato. *Laws*.

Pomfret, Richard. *Unequal Trade: The Economics of Discriminatory International Trade Policies*. New York: Blackwell, 1988.

Puchala, Donald. *Fiscal Harmonization in the European Community: National Politics and International Cooperation*. Washington, D.C.: Q. M. Dabney and Co., 1984.

Puth, Robert C. *American Economic History*. Chicago: Dryden Press, 1981.

Reich, Robert. "Leveraged Buyouts: America Pays the Price." *New York Times Magazine* (January 29, 1989): 32, 36, 40.

Rohatyn, Felix. "America's Economic Dependence." *Foreign Affairs*, vol. 68, no. 1 (1989): 60–65.

Rosen, Corey M., Katherine J. Klein and Karen M. Young. *Employee Ownership in America: The Equity Solution*. Lexington, Mass.: Lexington Books, 1986.

Rousseau, Jean Jacques. *Social Contract*.

Russeas, Stephen. *The Death of a Democracy: Greece and the American Conscience*. New York: Grove Press, 1967.

Sanford, William F., Jr. *The American Business Community and the European Recovery Program, 1947–1952*. New York: Garland Publishing Co., 1952.

Schumpeter, Joseph. *Capitalism, Socialism and Democracy*, 3d edition. New York: Harper Colophon Books, 1975.

Silk, Leonard. "Looking Ahead in World Trade." *New York Times* (August 26, 1988): D2.

Smith, Adam. *An Inquiry into the Nature and Causes of the Wealth of Nations*, Edwin Cannan, ed. New York: Modern Library, 1937.

Soule, George, and Vincent Carosso. *American Economic History*. New York: Dryden Press, 1957.

Srodes, James. "Curmudgeon in Winter." *Financial World* (November 28, 1989): 82–83.

Stanley, C. *Roots of the Tree*. London: Oxford University Press, 1936.

Stern, Paula. "Should Steel Quotas Be Extended?" *New York Times* (March 18, 1989): A27.

Stoeckel, Andrews, David Vincent and Sandy Cuthbertson, eds. *Macroeconomic Con-

sequences of Farm Support Policies. Durham, North Carolina: Duke University Press, 1989.

Tait, Alan A. *Value Added Tax: International Practice and Problems*. Washington, D.C.: International Monetary Fund, 1988.

Tait, Nikki. "Harrisons and Crosfield Expands in U.S. with $85m Deal." *Financial Times* (July 7, 1989): 25.

Tarr, David G. "The Steel Crisis in the United States and the European Community: Causes and Adjustments." In Robert E. Baldwin, et al., eds., *Issues in U.S.-EC Trade Relations*. Chicago: The University of Chicago Press, 1988.

Taylor, Paul. *The Limits of European Integration*. New York: Columbia University Press, 1983.

Tenny, Frank. *An Economic History of Ancient Rome*. Baltimore, Maryland: Johns Hopkins University Press, 1933.

Thurow, Lester C. *Should America Adopt an Industrial Policy?* Burkett Miller Distinguished Lecture. Chattanooga, Tenn.: Center for Economic Education, University of Tennessee, 1984.

———. "The Post-Industrial Era Is Over." *New York Times* (September 4, 1989): 27.

Toutain, Jules. *The Economic Life of the Ancient World*. New York: Alfred A. Knopf, 1930.

Tsoukalis, Loukas, and Robert Strauss. "Crisis and Adjustment in European Steel: Beyond Laissez-faire." *Journal of Common Market Studies*, vol. 23 (1985).

———, ed. *Europe, America and the World Economy*. New York: Basil Blackwell, 1986.

Tuttle, Frank, and Joseph Perry. *An Economic History of the United States*. Cincinnati, Ohio: South-Western Publishing Co., 1970.

Ungeheuer, Frederick. "They Own the Place." *Time* (February 6, 1989).

United Nations. *Yearbook of Labor Statistics, 1988*.

United States Government. *Bureau of Labor Statistics*, various issues.

———. Department of Commerce. *The United States in World Economy*. Washington, D.C.: 1943.

———. *Historical Statistics of the United States, 1789–1945*. Washington, D.C.: U.S. Bureau of Census, 1949.

Vanhove, Norbert, and Leo Klaassen. *Regional Policy: A European Approach*. Savage, Maryland: Rowman and Littlefield, Barnes and Noble Books, 1987.

Wagner, Adolph. *Financzwissenschaft*, 3d edition. Leipzig: 1890.

Walton, Garry, and Ross Robertson. *History of the American Economy*. New York: Harcourt, 1983.

Ward, Barbara. *The Interplay of East and West*. London: Allen and Unwin, 1957.

Weitzman, Martin L. *The Share Economy: Conquering Stagflation*. Cambridge: Harvard University Press, 1984.

———. "The Simple Macroeconomics of Profit Sharing." *American Economic Review*, vol. 75 (December 1985).

Whitelegg, John. *Transport Policy in the EEC*. London: Routledge, 1989.

Williams, Allan. *The Western Europe Economy: A Geography of Post-War Development*. Savage, Maryland: Rowman and Littlefield, Barnes and Noble Books, 1988.

Wolf, Thomas. "Reform, Inflation, and Adjustment in Planned Economies," *Finance and Development*, Vol. 27, No. 1 (March 1990): 2–5.

World Bank. *World Bank Report*. New York: Oxford University Press, 1989.

Wright, Chester. *Economic History of the United States*, 2d edition. New York: McGraw-
    Hill, 1949.
Zolotas, Xenophon. *The Dollar Crisis and Other Papers*. Athens: Bank of Greece, 1979.

Index